Missio Dei in a Digital Age

Missio Dei in a Digital Age

Edited by

Jonas Kurlberg
and
Peter M. Phillips

scm press

© Editors and Contributors 2020

Published in 2020 by SCM Press
Editorial office
3rd Floor, Invicta House,
108–114 Golden Lane,
London EC1Y 0TG, UK
www.scmpress.co.uk

SCM Press is an imprint of Hymns Ancient & Modern Ltd
(a registered charity)

Hymns Ancient & Modern® is a registered trademark of
Hymns Ancient & Modern Ltd
13A Hellesdon Park Road, Norwich,
Norfolk NR6 5DR, UK

British Library Cataloguing in Publication data

A catalogue record for this book is available
from the British Library

978-0-334-05911-0

Typeset by Regent Typesetting
Printed and bound by
CPI Group (UK) Ltd

Contents

List of Contributors

Jonny Baker is Director of Mission Education at the Church Mission Society, where he founded and leads the pioneer ministry leadership training. He is also a speaker, writer, photographer, musician, and lay pioneer, and loves all things creative. He blogs at jonnybaker.blogs.com.

Alexander Chow is Senior Lecturer in Theology and World Christianity at the School of Divinity, University of Edinburgh, and is co-director of the Centre for the Study of World Christianity. He is the author of two books, most recently *Chinese Public Theology: Generational Shifts and Confucian Imagination in Chinese Christianity* (Oxford University Press, 2018).

Anthony-Paul Cooper is Co-director of the Centre for Church Growth Research at Cranmer Hall, Durham University. He has a background in social research, with previous research topics including new church use of 'secular' and 'sacred' space, and the use of social media data to better understand church attendance and church growth.

Rei Lemuel Crizaldo is the theological education network co-ordinator for East and South East Asia of Tearfund UK. In the Philippines, he serves in the faculty of the Asian Seminary of Christian Ministries and as the advocacy coordinator for Integral Mission of Micah Philippines. He is also a local author, with several books in the vernacular published by OMF Literature, including *Boring Ba Ang Bible Mo?* (Is Your Bible Boring?), which won the Filipino Reader's Choice Award.

Tim J. Davy is Lecturer and Head of Research and Consultancy at All Nations Christian College. His teaching and research focus on two main areas: the missional interpretation of the Bible, and vulnerable children. He has been on the Council of Reference for Home for Good, and is working on a book about vulnerable children in the Old Testament. His volume *The Book of Job and the Mission of God* was published by Pickwick Publications in 2020.

Maggi Dawn is Professor of Theology, Principal of St Mary's College, and Assistant Director of the Centre for Poetry and Poetics at Durham University. After a first career in music, she studied theology and literature at Cambridge, since when she has taught at Cambridge, Yale and Durham Universities. She is the author of five books, and numerous hymns and songs for the church.

John Drane has spent much of his adult life wrestling with the challenge of being a Christian in a rapidly changing culture, and has written extensively on missional topics as well as three best-selling books on the Bible, which have been translated into more than 90 languages. He has taught in the universities of Stirling and Aberdeen in Scotland, and at Fuller Seminary in the US. He is currently Co-chair of the Mission Theology Advisory Group (a joint venture of the Church of England and Churches Together in Britain and Ireland).

Olive Fleming Drane studied at the Graduate Theological Union in Berkeley and the University of Aberdeen, and has had a lifelong interest in research into the spiritual practices of ordinary people, including their online expressions. She has been teaching at Fuller Seminary, California, for more than 20 years, and was one of the earliest faculty members to offer online courses on a regular basis. She lives in Glasgow, and until recently was chaplain to theology students at the University of the West of Scotland. She is also a visiting fellow at St John's College, Durham.

Christian Grund Sørensen is a postdoctoral researcher at The Kaj Munk Research Center in the Department of Communication and Psychology, Aalborg University, Denmark. He is the author of articles about theology, persuasive technologies, homiletics and communication. He is also a priest in the Danish Lutheran Church.

Steve Hollinghurst is Evangelism Enabler with an Environmental Focus for Lichfield Diocese and a freelance trainer, consultant and researcher in contemporary culture and evangelism. He has a background in social science and theology, particularly looking at culture and spirituality in today's world and Christian responses to that as well as many years working and teaching in mission and evangelism. His publications include *Mission-Shaped Evangelism* (Canterbury Press, 2010) and *Starting, Assessing and Sustaining Pioneer Mission* (Grove, 2013).

Jonas Kurlberg is Deputy Director of the Centre for Digital Theology at Durham University and the Convenor of the Global Network for Digital Theology. He is the author of *Christian Modernism in an Age of Totalitarianism: T. S. Eliot, Karl Mannheim and the Moot* (Bloomsbury, 2019).

Frida Mannerfelt is a priest in the Swedish Lutheran Church and a doctoral student in practical theology and church history at Stockholm School of Theology. The working title of her dissertation project is 'Preaching in the Age of Digitalization'. She also lectures at Lund University.

Peter M. Phillips is Director of the Centre for Digital Theology at Durham University, where he serves as a Research Fellow in the Department of Theology and Religion. He is also Head of Digital Theology at Premier Christian Media. He has recently been working on biblical literacy in digital culture and on exploring digital theology in all its forms.

Katherine G. Schmidt is Assistant Professor of Theology at Molloy College, New York. She writes on the intersection of theology and digital culture. She is the author of *Virtual Communion* (Fortress Academic/Lexington Press, 2020).

Erkki Sutinen is Professor of Computer Science (Interaction Design), leading the plug-in campus (ftlab.utu.fi) of the University of Turku, Finland, in Windhoek, Namibia. He has been researching educational technology, computing education, ICT4D and co-design, and has supervised about 30 PhDs and co-authored around 300 papers. An ordained Lutheran priest, his current interests include digital theology.

I

Introduction:
Missio Dei in a Digital Age

JONAS KURLBERG

In 1974 the Japanese missionary Kosuke Koyama wrote *Water Buffalo Theology* based on his experience of working among Thai farmers. The image of the animal in his 'theology from below' served to remind him that 'the people to whom I am to bring the gospel of Christ spend most of their time with these water buffaloes in the rice field' (1999, p. xv). The book still features on many missiology curricula around the world, but in the almost half-century that has passed since Koyama grappled with making Christianity comprehensible to the farmers in the paddy fields the world has radically changed. Thai farmers are today more likely to spend time gazing upon the screens of their smartphones than upon their cattle. It is suggestive that as of 2019 Thailand had 92.22 million mobile subscriptions within a total population of 69.24 million (Kemp 2019). If Koyama were alive today would he have written an *iPhone Theology*? 'The animals [iPhones] tell me that I must preach to these farmers [millennials] in simple sentence structure and thought development' (1999, p. xv).[1]

This book offers reflections on the impact of the digital revolution on missions, and can be located within the emerging field of digital theology. A central contention of digital theology is that encounters with digitality compel a re-examination of faith and practice (Phillips et al. 2019). Hence, considering missions in a digital age demands appraisal of past and present missional theology. It was for this purpose that this volume was written. The chapters that follow reflect on how digital tools change missional practices, discuss the implications of such digitally mediated practices and explore how the new conditions of digitality force reassessment of missiological truisms. In many ways the book is a continuation of conversations that have been held since the day of Pentecost, but in other ways it marks a new chapter in missiological reflection. The hope is that this process will be life-giving to the Church as it seeks to faithfully participate in the activities of a missionary God.

Digital Tools for Missions

At a basic level, digital artefacts are tools. In this sense digital technology provides the Church with the means to further its commission to be God's eschatological community communicating and manifesting the gospel in the world. All over the world Christians are already using digital tools in both basic and imaginative ways: from church websites that provide visitors with information, to blogposts, online churches, podcasts, videos that communicate Christian messages, apps and video games created for spiritual formation purposes, individual Christians sharing stories, images, memes and Bible verses on social media platforms, and initiatives that use technology for poverty alleviation or social needs. All these can be seen as part of the spirituality of dialogue that Stephen Bevans and Roger Schroeder speak of, in which the life of the Church is a manifestation of missions (2011, pp. 21–4).

Today, many churches view the internet as a powerful communication tool for evangelism. The Catholic Church, in its 2002 document 'The Church and the Internet' by the Pontifical Council for Social Communications, suggests that the internet can aid the Church in its commission to 'both re-evangelization and new evangelization and the traditional missionary work *ad gentes*', but offers little suggestion as to what such usage might entail. In 2016 the Church of England created its Digital Team primarily for missional purposes (Church of England). Some of its more successful evangelistic outputs have been videos posted online around Christmas and Easter, such as the

#GodWithUs campaign in 2017 which attracted 6.8 million views alone. Some churches have appointed 'digital evangelists', such as the Methodist Church in the UK that has an employee dedicated to running courses at theological institutions and producing online evangelistic content. With the sudden shift to online services in the wake of the Covid-19 pandemic many churches have been further exposed to the evangelistic potentials of digital communications technology. Online services have hugely outstripped average church attendance, attracting many who would normally not attend a church service (Chow and Kurlberg 2020).

Beyond the work of institutional churches there are a number of para-church organizations making considered use of the possibilities that this technology affords. This is evident in the work of many evangelical mission agencies that have taken to online platforms to proselytize. For example, the Billy Graham Evangelistic Association's interactive site PeaceWithGod.net leads any willing visitors through a process whereby they are first introduced to the Christian message via four animated videos, then asked to pray a prayer of repentance, and following this, given the opportunity to engage with a 'chat coach', either to talk about their 'decision' or to ask further questions. In a snappy sketch video, the viewer is told that this 'entire process is an exciting online crusade (searchforjesus.net)'. The organization claims that the number of people 'indicating decisions for Christ' through its work has exponentially increased since its migration to online spaces (www.billygraham.ca). Indigitous, founded by Cru International, is another such organization. It has a created a global network of people (mostly evangelicals) engaging in 'strategies that are effective and projects that are on the cutting edge of missional innovation (indigitous.org)'. An interesting initiative of Indigitous brings together Christians who work in the tech industry for hackathons to create digital tools for missions whether in aid, social action or evangelism. Given the emphasis placed on conversionism within evangelicalism, it comes as little surprise that evangelical groups have been innovative in their use of digital tools for evangelism. Nevertheless, they are not the only Christian tradition to have used such tools. A prominent Catholic organization, Catholic Answer, identifies itself as a 'media ministry' that explains and defends the Catholic faith to bring renewal to Catholics and 'lead non-Catholics into the fullness of the truth'. Its website hosts an online radio programme, podcasts and videos, as well as a search engine that serves as a gateway to 'the world's largest database of answers about the beliefs and practices of the Catholic faith' (Catholic Answer). Their approach appears to chime with Pope Francis' appeal to Catholics in *Evangelii Gaudium* to evangelize 'by attraction' and not proselytism (2013, p. 15).

The internet has also given rise to new mission agencies. A large site for online evangelism is jesus.net which is supported by 85 different organizations from around the world. The website acts as a library of short articles and videos inviting visitors to explore aspects of Christian faith and life. Another example is Christian Vision, which focuses on creating high-quality content that individuals are encouraged to share after they have undergone in-app confidence boosting evangelism training. Some of these organizations are developing more advanced uses of technology chatbots, AI, virtual reality and apps for evangelism, raising a number of ethical and theological questions. There are also organizations that focus on specific subcultures within digital environments. Game Church is just one example of the many Christian organizations operating in the world of gaming. The organization offers podcasts, reviews and YouTube videos in order 'to tell gamers about the love of Jesus' (Game Church).

Beyond this organized instrumentalization of digital communications tools, millions of Christians deliberately or unwittingly bear witness to their faith by sharing stories, prayers, memes, or Bible verses on their social media accounts. A survey conducted by Barna Group in 2018 suggests that 28% of self-professing Christians in the US share their faith on social media (Barna Group). Arguably, the nature of web 2.0 is particularly suitable for this sort of evangelism as it functions best on a peer-to-peer basis. There is here a convergence between the suspicion of hierarchy within digital culture and the downplaying of institutionalism implied within the concept of *missio Dei*. It also seems more in tune with the relational evangelism propagated by many churches today.

Mission, especially when understood through the lens of *missio Dei*, is not limited to explicitly evangelistic efforts but includes all that brings God's redemptive purposes for the world to fruition. As such, digital tools that are used for charity, aid and development, the common good and social justice work can also be defined as missional. There are a limited but growing number of such faith-based initiatives. For many who are housebound or have disabilities digital communications tools have been socially redemptive, bringing a sense of belonging. A great example of this is the initiative Disability and Jesus, which has sought to educate the Church and build bridges between churches and disability communities largely through digital channels (disabilityandjesus.org.uk). In the area of education Fr Benigno Beltran, through his organization Sandiwaan Center for Learning, has used digital technology to provide educational opportunities for out of school youth in the garbage heaps of Manila. Recognizing that even the poor have access to mobile phones, Sandiwaan has used online learning platforms to engage young people who for various reasons will not attain formal education (Handley Macmath 2016).

However, developing digital tools requires resources and knowhow, and there is a case to be made for Christians to join forces with existing secular initiatives. While technology is being deployed to a greater extent by faith-based organizations, the *missio Dei* perspective invites the Church to ask how it can join, support and promote any work that bears marks of God's work beyond its institutions. There are numerous such examples of tech for the common good. In India e-Choupal, an initiative by ICT Limited, offers small farmers the possibility of access to real-time market prices of crops, advice on best practice and the option of buying quality seeds through computers set up in thousands of villages. This simple service not only enables poor farmers to obtain better pay for their produce but also improves its quality (ICT Limited). TraffickCam is an app created by Exchange Initiative to combat sex-trafficking.

It encourages individuals to upload photos of hotel rooms they stay in. Pimps and traffickers often use hotel rooms for photo shoots. By developing a catalogue of hotel rooms, Exchange Initiative can use algorithms to identify the locations of victims (Exchange Initiative). Other examples include more ethically minded digital initiatives. The search engine Ecosia uses its profits to combat climate change, and does not sell users' data, thereby providing an alternative to Google.

Digitally Mediated Missions

Given this flurry of activity there is a need for sustained reflection, education and knowledge so that the Church can use the opportunities afforded to it to faithfully communicate and embody the gospel. Several chapters in this volume explore further not only how digital technology can aid participation in the *missio Dei*, but also some of the challenges associated with this.

However, the use of digital technology in missional practices also provokes interesting questions concerning mediation. Missions have always been closely linked with communication technologies whether through texts, symbols, images, or printed tracts, and in the modern era through mass communication via radio, television and photography. In this sense, as a cost-effective communications tool with the promise of an instantaneous reach to global audiences, digital communication technology merely offers acceleration of the same. Yet as media theorists have argued for decades, media technologies are not mere conduits or channels for uninterrupted communication between sender and receiver. Conversely, the very form and design of media technology conditions how the message is communicated, interpreted and received.

Marshall McLuhan's thesis 'the medium is the message' has become somewhat of a tired cliché, but its sentiment still captures some of the dynamics involved (2001 (1964), p. 8). The communicator adjusts their message to the logic of the medium and the audience interprets the message according to the conduits through which it is channelled. Thus, in a world where influence is determined by numbers of followers on Twitter, even the pope has to learn to communicate in Twitter-friendly sentences. On platforms where millions are competing for attention, preachers are compelled to TED-talk timed sermons. Under the interactivity of web 2.0, the Church has to be attentively listening rather than blasting its message to passive media consumers of a bygone age.

Nevertheless, the fact that there is user agency suggests that digital artefacts can be designed and adapted in different ways. Among social theorists the politics of the technological artefact has long been a topic for discussion. Views range from Jacques Ellul's bleak fatalism in which increased mechanization through modern technology leads to the domination of humanity (1964, p. 428f.), to those that veer towards the neutrality of technology as tools that can be used to different ends. A more convincing stance is that expressed in a theory labelled the Social Shaping of Technology. This perspective sees technological innovations as the outcome of multiple social, political and cultural processes (Williams and Edge 1996, pp. 865–99). In effect, technological artefacts are imbued with the cultural biases of the designer that in turn shape their users. At the same time, agency applies not only to the producer but also to the user. The smartphone is a prime example. When Apple announced the iPhone in 2007 it came with a full operating system pre-installed with 13 apps. Commentators could only speculate on what could be done with this device and the executives at Apple have since admitted that they could not have dreamt of the ways in which the smartphone would come to be used. These continuous negotiations between artefacts, designers and users suggest that there is a demand for sustained reflection on digital missional practices. Mission agencies, churches and individuals have to adjust to the medium of digital communications technology to make their communications comprehensible, but while they have to reckon with the limitations and possibilities of the technology, they can also be part of the design process of websites, platforms and apps, and thereby effect the technology itself.

JONAS KURLBERG

Digital as the New Condition for Missions

A further premise of this volume is that beyond the promise of
new utilities, digitalization is radically changing the conditions
in which missions are carried out. In the 1990s and early
2000s 'cyberspace' was commonly used to denote the internet
as a separate sphere consisting of bits and bytes that could be
visited and inhabited. According to this logic the internet is a
'foreign land' to which missionaries should be sent (Campbell
2010, pp. 138–9). Tim Hutchings argues, for example, that the
missionary impulse to reach the unreached in cyberspace was a
prevalent motivation in early attempts to populate the internet
with cyber-churches (2017, pp. 28–9).

While some churches continue to send digital evangelists
into 'cyberspace', our conception of the internet has undergone a shift. As digital technology is becoming more embedded
in the everyday life of contemporary society, the idea of the
internet as a parallel and alternative space increasingly appears
outdated (Campbell 2013; Floridi 2014; Hine 2015). Today
everything is being digitalized, changing the ways that we
communicate and interact, how and where we work, manage
our finances and use our leisure time, how we conceive of the
human and non-human body, engage with the Bible, and so
forth. As the distinction between offline and online is blurred
and as the digital is becoming embedded in all spheres of life
it has radical implications for human cultures. Digitality is the
new condition in which mission is carried out.

The idea that the gospel needs translation, or to be contextualized or enculturated into different cultures and contexts has
become an axiom in missiological discourse over the last half
century or so (Bosch 1991, pp. 420–32, 447–57). This task of
translation remains with us in the digital context we now find
ourselves in. Returning to Koyama, his writings in the 1970s
now appear to have remarkable foresight. As the old world of
the 'oxcart' clashed with the age of the 'supersonic aircraft', he
was acutely aware of the colossal challenges facing the Church
in 'the coming of the technological civilization'. For Koyama,
the symbol of the technological global civilization was the

8

supersonic jet rather than the iPhone, nevertheless he recognized the importance of re-interpreting the gospel afresh in this new condition: 'If we can do this, then the universal technological civilization becomes an occasion to point out the glory of Christ at this crucial period in the history of humankind' (Koyama 1999, p. 45). Koyama's juxtaposition of the oxcart and the supersonic jet is in some sense false as both are technological artefacts. Nevertheless, they do symbolize clashes between different cultural paradigms; namely, the traditional local versus the emerging technological global order. These tensions can even today be seen all over the world between local and global, conservative and progressive, poor and rich, between the 'somewheres' and the 'anywheres' (Goodhart 2017), and are manifest not least in the anti-cosmopolitan surge of right-wing populism and extremism (Norris and Inglehart 2019). Sociologist Manuel Castells argues that such tensions are the outcome of a hyper-connective 'network society' created in the wake of the digital revolution. Under these conditions, identity comes to the fore as individuals at once recognize an interdependence which undermines their individuality and the demand to negotiate new (often particularistic) identities in a pluralistic networked society leading to a surge in nationalism or religious fundamentalism (2010, pp. 21–5).

The smartphone epitomizes this tension between global and local. The smartphone is globalizing for we have to recognize that technological artefacts are value-laden agents that shape our communications, identities and the very condition we find ourselves in. It does this in a number of ways. The hyper-connectivity it affords plays a central role in the aforementioned 'networked society' and the identity-shaping and meaning-making that this implies. People's constant engagement on social media plays an important factor in this. Think about the increasing emphasis on the cameras on our devices. They invite us to project images of ourselves, turning us into mediated personalities. There is some merit in Pete Ward's claim that social media celebritizes us by making us more aware of how we represent ourselves and what image we project to the world (2020, pp. 8–9). Social media compels us to identity management.

In the wake of the digital tidal wave across the planet, these shifts even have a bearing upon conceptions of the divine. In *A Theology for a Mediated God* Dennis Ford suggests that the dominant media technology of any given age gives rise to epistemes which influence our very conceptions of God. In oral cultures, argues Ford, the divine is conceived of as concrete, unpredictable and pluralistic, whereas in literate cultures the static nature of the written text invites more authoritarian, transcendent and unchanging conceptions of God. Conversely, the multisensory 'digital God' is experiential, accessible and 'customizable' (2017, pp. 94–8). What are the implications for missions in a context of such individualized theologizing?

One can, as such, point towards what appear to be general cultural trends, that are, if not caused by digitality, at least fuelled by it. Nevertheless, because of user agency we cannot speak of a global digital *culture* but of digital *cultures*. As we have seen, how technology is created, adopted and adapted is preconditioned by political, cultural and religious contexts. How technology is used is to a degree culturally conditioned, and this can in turn reinforce and create geographically local digital cultures. The internet also gives rise to myriad non-geographical sub-cultures that emerge around shared interests, hobbies or ideologies and so forth, connecting like-minded people across the world. Filter-bubbles on social media illustrate how powerfully such environments can be in reinforcing and shaping held worldviews (Sunstein 2018). Further, micro-cultures also emerge on different digital platforms. By way of illustration, the world of TikTok – the new kid on the block of social media platforms – has its own norms and prac-tices, as well as 'in-house jokes' that are bewildering for the uninitiated. And finally, as evident in the wake of the Covid-19 pandemic and how churches have digitally adjusted to social isolating, digital innovation and adaptation is rapidly progressing, shifting and changing, resulting in new liturgical practices. Digital cultures are not static.

In the symbol of the smartphone, then, the global and the local converge, collide and negotiate. It is a symbol of digital globalization yet its adaption can be localized. What is needed is a water buffalo theology *and* iPhone theology, or perhaps the amalgamation of both. In a world that is increasingly defined by globalization and its processes of the fragmentation, fusion and evolution of cultures, the missiological tasks of inculturation and contextualization are daunting. If the gospel demands imaginative translation into every culture, this work is endless. How does one live and interact incarnationally in this bewildering network of digital cultures? The digital age will then no doubt see a continuation of missional thought and practice, but the disruptiveness of digitality might also lead to reassessment.

Inculturation and contextualization are founded upon the assumption that God in the incarnation marks his desire to communicate with humanity. Nevertheless, the assumption of contextualization, that the missional church follows the example of the incarnation, is somewhat deficient. That God-became-flesh, the divine manifested in a human body in a specific socio-political context, can be taken as a validation of human culture is something the Church needs to embrace. However, we are not outside of history stepping in, we are already deeply embedded in cultures in ways that are obscured even to ourselves. Christian use of language is a good case in point. As Kathryn Tanner suggests, Christian identity has always depended upon the borrowing and adapting of language and metaphors from 'other ways of life' (1997, p. 113). The boundaries between gospel and culture, or 'Christ and Culture' cannot easily be maintained. We are all conditioned by digital media, have negotiated the identity shaping force of technology, and are hooked in its eco-systems. Digital culture is not 'out there' in a foreign land, it is in the midst of us all. We are already digitally enculturated. Although generational differences persist, rather than visitors to exotic lands we are already digital natives. The concept of contextualization in this context invites us to self-reflect on our own digital embeddedness.

Missio Dei in a Digital Age

While digitality gives reason to pause and reflect on dominant missiological concepts, there is no virtue in discarding held conventions for novelty's sake. This book is framed by the *missio Dei* theology prevalent in the post-WWII era. This arguably remains a fruitful framework for missiological engagement with digitality, not least since there are resonances with digital cultures.

While Maggi Dawn and other contributors to this volume provide competent overviews of the *missio Dei* framework, some comments are in place here. With his turn to transcendence, Karl Barth has been credited for placing the idea that mission is the activity of God onto the agenda of modern missiology (Bosch 1991, p. 389). It gained currency in ecumenical circles in the wake of the breakdown of colonial empires after WWII and as a critique of the cultural imperialist assumptions undergirding much of the nineteenth-century missionary movement. While definitions vary, *missio Dei* signifies a shift away from the conception of mission as the enterprise of the Church, and towards the proposition that mission is the activity of God or even an attribute of God. With mission firmly rooted in the doctrine of God, the Church becomes a participant or instrument in God's redemptive work in creation. Further, *missio Dei* suggests a broadening of mission as it insinuates all of God's redemptive activities wherever they can be found in the world. While *missio Dei* has its limitations – it is not always easy to determine where God is at work and missions can become so broadly defined that the word loses its descriptive property – it is nevertheless a useful corrective to past emphases in mission's history. Here it will be used heuristically. As a critical lens it constantly forces self-reflection on missional practices and serves as a reminder that missiological engagement in a digital age must shun the temptation of ecclesial and cultural imperialism.

Further, there are arguably affinities between *missio Dei* and digital cultures that make it particularly fertile for the task at hand. *Missio Dei* compels us to an attentive listening that correlates with the interactivity of Web 2.0. To determine where God is active in the world, and the Church's role within this, not only requires a discernment that is sensitive to the whisperings of the Spirit, but a training of the eye and ear to understand the cultural currents of our digitalized societies. The interactivity of social media suggests that we have moved past the logic of a unidirectional broadcasting of modern mass-media in which the Church as a communicative institution proclaimed its message to the world. On social media the Church not only speaks but will be spoken back at. Further, *missio Dei* places emphasis on participation in God's activities which implies a diminished interest in ecclesial institutionalism. Such notions of moving away from institutional forms of religion resonate with a digital culture defined by interconnectivity and networks. In short, *missio Dei* bids us to search for the One who is already omnipotently present and active in online spaces and cultures.

Outline of the Book

This volume brings together a number of perspectives on missions in a digital age. Most of the chapters were originally presented as papers at the *Missio Dei in a Digital Age* symposium, organized by CODEC Research Centre (now the Centre for Digital Theology) at St John's College, Durham University in April 2019. Some of its contributors work at academic institutions within disciplines such as theology, digital humanities and computer science, while others are practitioners working in ecclesial and para-church contexts. The authors also represent a number of church traditions from different parts of the world. This diversity is reflected in the variety of approaches, methodologies and, at times, divergent perspectives.

The chapters are grouped into three parts. Part 1 consists of more general explorations of missiology and digitality.

In Chapter 2 Katherine Schmidt argues that as the Church engages with digital culture, it is best served to do so through the lens of 'inculturation', as advocated by Pope John Paul II. She develops her argument on the premise that digital technology should be understood as a culture, rather than instruments or tools. She suggests that being digital from an ecclesial perspective must consider digital culture as a complex entity, irreducible to a passing trend or optional tool for ministry.

Jonny Baker then proposes in Chapter 3 that reflecting on mission in a digital age requires imagination rather than technique. He maintains that while it is tempting to use new technologies to reproduce the old world or to communicate the old message in a new way, it is more interesting to imagine what possibilities are emerging in and afforded by the new environment. As such, he contends that missiological reflection in a digital age requires presence, attention, imagination and then translation, including consideration of digital technologies' use in actual lived practice.

Rey Lemuel Crizaldo subsequently outlines in Chapter 4 the implications of digital communications technology for constructing contextual theologies. He discusses the possibilities that digitality affords as theologians in the Global South seek to further decolonialize and localize theology.

While the following chapters in many ways continue these important missiological reflections, the focus in Part 2 is turned to enquiries into more specific aspects of missional practices in a digital age.

In Chapter 5 Steve Hollinghurst approaches digital evangelism from the perspective of mediation. He draws upon perspectives from media theorists to suggest that digital media are not just a means of communication; rather, the nature of digital media changes how we communicate and who we communicate with. This, in turn, has important consequences for fulfilment of 'the Great Commission'. He argues that missions in a digital era require a digital missiology not just digital action.

In Chapter 6 Christian Grund Sørensen focuses more on the technology itself, in examining the implications of the algorithms of search engines for missions. Referencing the Pauline idiom 'faith comes from hearing' (Rom. 10.17a), he postulates that information and knowledge are prerequisites for faith. For this reason, free and unbiased dissemination and reception of knowledge of faith is a vital concern for the *missio Dei* in a digital age. However, the algorithms of search engines such as Google tend to create biases in search results limiting the possibility of encountering material advocating for positions which are not yet a part of the user's conceptual framework. In effect the non-religious user is less likely to be exposed to meaningful spiritual content. This chapter, then, aims to identify the problem and suggest possible pathways for the Church to surpass the search engine Cherubim.

Erkki Sutinen and Anthony Cooper's Chapter 7 outlines how design processes can afford tools for a renewed grassroots engagement in the *missio Dei*. They argue that this requires a design process that shuns the drive towards automation solutions often seen in hierarchical organizations, towards distributed digital designs that are implemented in comprehensive co-design schemes with groups that consist of stakeholders from diverse actors. Through such designs the digitalization of the mission of the Body of Christ can offer services in which all members of the church universal can participate in mission, drawing upon each and everyone's unique strengths, talents and resources.

John Drane and Olive Fleming Drane take their cue from Neil Postman's contention that through our media consumption we are 'amusing ourselves to death' and in the process being anaesthetized from facing the realities of the world. Challenging this assessment in Chapter 8, they explore whether, rather than this anaesthetizing effect, our engagement on digital environments can instead be life-giving and redemptive. As such, they propose that missions in a digital age must begin by searching for echoes of the gospel in digital spaces.

Maggi Dawn traces the influence of the *missio Dei* discourse on recent ecclesial movements which blur the distinctions between worship and mission. In these movements mission becomes less about conversion and more about creating environments in which the divine can be encountered. Within this context she explores in Chapter 9 the challenges and opportunities of worship as mission in a digital world. She suggests that since God is at work in all cultures yet no culture realizes the gospel fully, adaptations of digital technology in worship must be creative, contextual and judicious.

In Chapter 10 Frida Mannerfelt offers a homological perspective on the shift towards orality seen in digital culture. She points out that preaching has been a vital and central part of church mission since the days of the apostles. While today's digitalization offers new possibilities for such missional practices of preaching, her contention is that aspects of digital culture resonate with the oral cultures of the early church. In what ways, she asks, is preaching in digital culture a going back to the roots, and in what ways is it growing new branches? And what might this imply for the practice of preaching in the digital era?

The final chapters of the volume speak to the socio-political task of the Church. Clearly, the internet presents new challenges to which the Church needs to respond. The following chapters exemplify some of the opportunities and challenges that face the Church in a digital age. In Chapter 11, Tim Davy highlights some of the darker applications of digital technology. With reference to perspectives offered by practitioners in the field, he discusses ways in which digital environments can be harmful for vulnerable children. Adopting the Lausanne Movement's resolution of 'mission to, for and with' vulnerable children as a framework, he draws out the implications of these for the Church's participation in the *missio Dei*.

Finally, in the context of the first phase of China's Social Credit System (SCS) and its ability to extend state control over religious communities, Alexander Chow discusses the implications of digitality on the public faith of Chinese churches. In Chapter 12 he argues that culturally, digital advances are used to assess long-standing Chinese collectivist notions of shame and honour. Theologically, this is at odds with Chinese public theology, informed in part by Western individualism and Western political liberalism. The chapter argues that the rise of digital technologies like SCS complicate the course of Chinese public theology, which seeks to be public in certain ways while attempting to preserve a level of privacy in other ways. Chow suggests that these technological changes raise new questions for theological notions of human nature and the doctrine of sin.

Peter Phillips concludes the volume in Chapter 13 by returning to the fundamental affirmation of *missio Dei*: that mission is God's activity. Despite the near-universal acceptance of this assertion today, Phillips notes that it is all too easy to lapse into past notions of mission as the Church's activity. This temptation persists in missiological reflection on missions in a digital era where our attention is readily distracted by dazzling technologies. As an antidote, Phillips turns to Jean-Luc Marion's emphasis on the icon in visual cultures. The icon becomes a symbol that beckons the Church to resist the temptation of idolizing technology by using it iconically. In this way technology can point beyond itself, becoming a window into the mysteries of God.

Note

1 This suggestion is not as far-fetched as one would think. The Finnish Bible Society is doing exactly this by working on a digitally friendly Bible translation which uses shorter sentences that can be more readily consumed and shared on digital devices.

References

Barna Group, 2018, 'Evangelism in a Digital Age: An Infographic', www.barna.com/research/evangelism-in-a-digital-age-an-infographic/, accessed 10 May 2020.

Billy Graham Evangelistic Association of Canada, n.d., 'How It Works', https://searchforjesus.net/how-it-works/, accessed 2 April 2020.

Billy Graham Evangelistic Association of Canada, n.d., 'Eternal Results', www.billygraham.ca/about/eternal-results/, accessed 6 April 2020.

Bevans, Stephen B. and Schroeder, Roger P., 2011, *Prophetic Dialogue: Reflections on Christian Mission Today*, Maryknoll: Orbis.

Bosch, David J., 1991, *Transforming Mission – Paradigm Shifts in Theology of Mission*, Maryknoll: Orbis.

Campbell, Heidi, 2010, *When Religion Meets New Media*, Abingdon: Routledge.

Campbell, Heidi, 2012, 'Introduction: The Rise in the Study of Digital Religion', in Heidi Campbell (ed.), *Digital Religion: Understanding Religious Practices in New Media Worlds*, Abingdon: Routledge, pp. 1–21.

Catholic Answers, n.d., www.catholic.com, accessed 6 April 2020.

Castells, Manuel, 2010, *The Rise of the Network Society*, Chichester: Blackwell.

Chow, Alexander and Kurlberg, Jonas, 2020, 'Two or Three Gathered Online: Asian and European Responses to Covid-19 and the Digital Church', *Studies in World Christianity*, 26:4.

Christian Vision, n.d., www.cvglobal.co, accessed 2 April 2020.

Church of England, n.d., 'Digital Team', www.churchofengland.org/about/renewal-reform/digital-team, accessed 10 June 2020.

Disability and Jesus n.d., http://disabilityandjesus.org.uk, accessed 10 May 2020.

Ellul, Jacques, 1964, *The Technological Society*, New York: Vintage Books.

Exchange Initiative, n.d., 'Ending Sex Trafficking? There's an App for That', www.exchangeinitiative.com/ending-sex-trafficking-theres-an-app-for-that/, accessed 11 May 2020.

Floridi, Luciano, 2014, *The Fourth Revolution: How the Infosphere is Reshaping Human Reality*, Oxford: Oxford University Press.

Ford, Dennis, 2016, *A Theology for a Mediated God: How New Media Shapes Our Notions About Divinity*, New York: Routledge.

Game Church, n.d., https://gamechurch.com, accessed 7 April 2020.

Goodhart, David, 2017, *The Road to Somewhere: The Populist Revolt and the Future of Politics*, London: C. Hurst & Co.

Handley Macmath, Terence, 2016, 'Interview: Fr Benigno Beltran SVD, "asset-based developer", author', in *Church Times*, www.churchtimes.co.uk/articles/2016/19-august/features/interviews/interview-fr-benigno-beltran-svd-asset-based-developer-author, accessed 11 May 2020.

Hine, Christine, 2015, *Ethnography for the Internet: Embedded, Embodied and Everyday*, London: Bloomsbury.

Hjarvard, Stig, 2008, 'The Mediatization of Religion: A Theory of the Media as Agents of Religious Change', *Nothern Lights*, 6, pp. 1–21.

Hutchings, Tim, 2017, *Creating Church Online: Ritual, Community and New Media*, Abingdon: Routledge.

ICT Limited, n.d., 'E-Choupal', www.itcportal.com/businesses/agri-business/e-choupal.aspx, accessed 11 May 2020.

Indigitous, n.d., https://indigitous.org, accessed 17 January 2020.

Jesus.net, n.d. 'About Jesus.net', https://jesus.net/who-we-are/story-sheet/, accessed 2 April 2020.

Kemp, Simon, 2019, 'Digital 2019: Global Digital Yearbook', https://

datareportal.com/reports/digital-2019-global-digital-yearbook, accessed 14 January 2020.

Koyama, Kosuke, 1999 [1974], *Water Buffalo Theology*, Maryknoll: Orbis Books.

Norris, Pippa and Inglehart, Roland, 2019, *Cultural Backlash: Trump, Brexit and Authoritarian Populism*, Cambridge: Cambridge University Press.

McLuhan, Marshall, 2001 [1964], *Understanding Media: The Extension of Man*, Abingdon: Routledge.

Phillips, Peter M., Schiefelbein-Guerrero, Kyle and Kurlberg, Jonas, 2019, 'Defining Digital Theology: Digital Humanities, Digital Religion and the Particular Work of the CODEC Research Centre and Network', *Open Theology*, 5.

The Pontifical Council for Social Communications, 2002, 'The Church and Internet', www.vatican.va/roman_curia/pontifical_councils/pccs/documents/rc_pc_pccs_doc_20020228_church-internet_en.html#_ftn55, accessed 6 April 2020.

Pope Francis, 2013, *Evangelii Gaudium*, Vatican Press.

Sunstein, Cass R., 2018, *#Republic – Divided Democracy in the Age of Social Media*, Princeton; Oxford: Princeton University Press.

Tanner, Kathryn, 1997, *Theories of Culture: A New Agenda for Theology*, Minneapolis: Augsburg Fortress.

Ward, Pete, 2020, *Celebrity Worship*, London: Routledge.

Williams, Robi & Edge, David, 1996, 'The Social Shaping of Technology', *Research Policy*, 25, pp. 865–99.

PART I

Missiological Perspectives

2

Digital Inculturation

KATHERINE G. SCHMIDT

In 1990, Pope John Paul II closed his message for World Communications Day with a prayer 'that the "computer age" potentialities are used in the service of the human and transcendent vocation of man [sic], so as to glorify the Father from whom all good things originate'. This message was one of the most positive statements on digital technology from John Paul II, indeed from all three pontiffs who have led the Church during the 'computer age'. The most positive ecclesial perspectives in the Catholic Church have come from the (now defunct) Pontifical Council for Social Communications (PCSC). The Council rightly understood all social communications in light of Christ as the Perfect Communicator, thus establishing a continuum between the mediation of God in Christ and the multimodal mediations of the digital context (PCSC, *Communio et Progressio*, para. 11).

As optimistic as some ecclesial statements have been within the Catholic tradition, there persists a temptation that afflicts all Christian traditions with regard to digital technology. The missional impulse at the heart of Christianity may lead, and often does lead, to an instrumentalizing of technology that may actually prove counter-productive to that same impulse. The more Christians use the language of instrument or tool with regard to digital technology, the more they will struggle to imagine effectively the relationship between the gospel and the modern world.

It is admittedly very difficult to remove an instrumentalist framework from our discussions of technology entirely. Digital platforms and devices so easily present themselves as tools at our disposal. In the context of ministry, it becomes even more tempting to see them as an array of tools for conveying the content of the gospel to various audiences, both internal and external. The temptation is both practical and historical. Christians (and other religious communities, to be fair) have long used the media of their time to spread their message. The disciples left the upper room and used their words; Paul used his letters; the evangelists used manuscripts. Perhaps the clearest example is the Reformers' wielding of the printing press for their efforts in the sixteenth century and beyond. At the heart of Christianity is the use of media, and there is a particular affinity for its use within Protestant Christianity because of its infancy in the nursery of print culture. In American Protestant Christianity, one can follow this thread from the printing press to Christian radio and televangelism.

Thus it seems a bit strange if not unfaithful to church history to insist that various media should not be primarily understood as instruments or tools. In truth, media do often function simply as tools. But this should not be the primary framework for our theological understanding of media, especially when it comes to digital technology. The impulse to imagine digital technology as tools comes largely from the legacy of mass media, in which a dichotomy between producer and consumer is more evident and appropriate.

Mass media are characterized by relatively few producers creating content for mass audiences. Benedict Anderson and John B. Thompson have both demonstrated that the printing press marks a turning point in the development of modern society precisely because of its ability to draw individuals into a unified whole: 'individuals gradually became aware of the fact that they belonged to a virtual community of fellow readers with whom they would never directly interact, but to whom they were connected via the medium of print' (Thompson 1995, p. 62). And so it was for all the remediations after print: the listeners of radio, the viewers of film and television.

At this point, we are tempted to add 'users of the internet' to this history of media, and there is a sense in which the multimodal medium of the internet does inherit some of the mass media logic of its predecessors. But applying the framework of mass media to digital technology is ultimately unhelpful for at least two reasons. First, the producer/consumer dichotomy is unsustainable if not unintelligible within digital culture, especially after the advent of social media. As a Twitter user, am I a producer or a consumer? Clearly, I am both (even the most silent of lurkers often interact with the platform in some way). Or perhaps I am neither; I am not 'producing' in any way that is truly like the production of book publishers or filmmakers, and I am not 'consuming' in the same way as a television viewer.

Second, while the internet does inherit much from mass media, it fundamentally alters the effects of mass media in a way that complicates our understanding of it as a simple continuation of that trajectory. According to Benedict Anderson, print culture in particular created 'mass ceremonies' such as the twice-daily reading and disposing the newspaper. Although very individual, 'the communicant is well aware that the ceremony he performs is being replicated simultaneously by thousands (or millions) of others of whose existence he is confident, yet of whose identity he has not the slightest notion' (1991, p. 35). Thus mass media, beginning with print-capitalism, effects an 'imagined community', namely, the modern nation-state. Print standardizes language, creating the basis for shared cultural imaginations that eventually replace Christendom. Anderson's narrative is important for understanding the cultural power of mass media. It is also important for highlighting important differences in the logics of digital media.

Anderson's example of the twice-daily paper – the morning and evening editions – is illustrative of his thesis about the role of print-capitalism in establishing a shared imagination that is the necessary basis for national identity. In the digital context, however, these 'mass ceremonies' are few and far between, for they need to be both massive and identical. They 'work' in the creation of an imagined community because they are both individual and communal; I come to know my identity as a Frenchwoman because I read *Le Monde* along with all other French people, the vast majority of whom I will never know directly. One could say the same about habitual practices regarding the radio or the television. But what of digital media? The internet, and all of the platforms and spaces that people occupy therein, is surely massive, but it is only communal on very rare occasions. And even then, the community formed by shared habits online trend in the direction of consumerism. To be clear, this is not to say that there aren't true communities online. Indeed there are symbolic forms shared by communities all over the internet. But very rarely does a particular symbolic form – a phrase, an image, a video, an image – penetrate all of the boundaries of these communities to be considered truly communal in the sense of the artifacts of mass media. Perhaps the closest analogy in internet culture is when something 'goes viral'. But these are exceptional, and usually banal or sentimental in ways that do not have the staying power of the consistent and habitual ceremony of mass media.

These two distinctive features of digital technology – the complication of the producer/consumer dichotomy and the disruption of mediatization toward a shared imagination – are important for any analysis of the internet. These two features complicate any attempts to apply the same understanding to digital culture as we have to mass media. One of the primary attempts has been to understand digital technology as another tool for producing content for mass consumption. Without acknowledging its differences, many in the Church continue to understand digital technology primarily in these terms. This has surely been the case in the Catholic tradition, as can be seen in some of the aforementioned ecclesial statements. When the Church has been optimistic or positive in its evaluation of digital media, it is often because of its potential for spreading the gospel. Continuing with this framework for understanding digital media, however, fails to account for the nature of that media itself as well as its relationship to modern culture, especially with regard to the place of religion therein.

Digital media should thus be understood not as tools for our use but as a culture unto itself with which other cultures contend, conflict, overlap and mix. Therefore, going forward, I will refer to what I have been calling 'digital technology' or 'digital media' only as 'digital culture'. I take digital culture to include both the hardware and software of digital platforms, as well as all of the symbolic forms, languages and history that one could apply to the internet particularly. I am thinking here primarily of 'Web 2.0', or the internet after social media, although much what I argue about digital culture can be found in the earliest iterations of the 'Web'.

Understanding the internet not as a tool but as a culture is more fruitful in general, but it has particular advantages in the ecclesial context. Remaining in the paradigm of instrumentalism fails to account for the complexities of both individual and communal interactions with and within digital culture. If the Church remains focused on a producer/consumer mentality, it will fail in its mission in the modern world. It cannot remain convinced that the production of content in an online context can operate in the same way as television or radio; this production simply cannot create the kind of shared imagination necessary for the Church.

The aforementioned Pontifical Council made many recommendations to the Church over the years. In 1992, the Council produced the pastoral instruction *Aetatis Novae*, and in 2002, *The Church and Internet*. In both documents, the Council strongly advises the Church – all of its members, lay and clerical alike – on matters related to digital culture. Although it could not predict the influence of social media in these documents, it does acknowledge that digital literacy is required of the Church, especially for those in leadership, again lay and clerical alike. Unfortunately, these recommendations (which get very specific in *Aetatis Novae*) were mostly overshadowed by more pressing concerns in the pontificate of John Paul II. They became even less important in the pontificate of Benedict XVI, who spent more energy lamenting the waning influence of the Church in Europe than on the means by which the Church needs to adapt to cultural shifts.

Yet there are in the pontificates of John Paul II and Benedict XVI two themes that are of particular note for digital culture: inculturation and new evangelization, respectively. In 1990, the same year that he reflected on the possibilities of the 'computer age', John Paul II published *Redemptoris Missio*. In the document, he details the notion of 'inculturation', which had been around in spirit since at least the Second Vatican Council (1962–65) and in the pontificates of Paul VI and John XXIII. But *Redemptoris Missio* has meant a firm association between John Paul II and the term. He quotes a 1985 report to offer a definition for inculturation: 'the intimate transformation of authentic cultural values through their integration in Christianity and the insertion of Christianity in the various human cultures' (John Paul II, *Redemptoris Missio*, para. 52). It is not simply a tactic for evangelization; inculturation brings together the missionary activity of the Church with its incarnational logic. 'Through inculturation,' writes John Paul II, 'the Church makes the Gospel incarnate in different cultures and at the same time introduces peoples, together with their cultures, into her own community' (para. 52). He goes on to explain what this actually means in the missionary context, focusing specifically on the cultural identities of individual missionaries:

Missionaries, who come from other churches and countries, must immerse themselves in the cultural milieu of those to whom they are sent, moving beyond their own cultural limitations. Hence they must learn the language of the place in which they work, become familiar with the most important expressions of the local culture, and discover its values through direct experience. Only if they have this kind of awareness will they be able to bring to people the knowledge of the hidden mystery (cf. Rom. 16.25–27; Eph. 3.5) in a credible and fruitful way. It is not of course a matter of missionaries renouncing their own cultural identity, but of understanding, appreciating, fostering and evangelizing the culture of the environment in which they are working, and therefore of equipping themselves to communicate effectively with it, adopting a manner of living which is a sign of gospel witness and of solidarity with the people. (Para. 53)

This section is worth quoting in full because it provides a rich explanation of the willingness of Christian witnesses to open themselves to cultures with which they may be unfamiliar. John Paul II mostly has in mind here missionaries who leave their home nations to bring the gospel to people of foreign nations. But given that Christians are called to be first members of the Kingdom of God, all interactions with cultures of this world, even one's home culture, are subject to inculturation.

John Paul II's theme of inculturation sets the stage for Benedict XVI's insistence on a 'new evangelization'. Like inculturation, this theme pre-dates Benedict but comes to be associated with him because of his repeated emphasis on it. In 2010, Benedict established a new Pontifical Council directly addressed to the 'Promotion of the New Evangelization'. Although there is a natural relationship between inculturation and new evangelization, Benedict's emphasis was not as dialectic as John Paul II; his efforts were based in a defensive posture, as can be seen in the apostolic letter that established the Council: 'In our own time, it has been particularly challenged by an abandonment of the faith – a phenomenon progressively more manifest in societies and cultures which for centuries seemed to be permeated by the Gospel' (Benedict XVI, *Ubicumque et semper*). What Benedict has in mind, then, are people in countries where Christianity long dominated as the cultural paradigm until recently. This means western Europe primarily, but one could also argue that the United States could fall into this category especially considering younger generations of Americans' attitudes toward religious traditions.

The initially defensive impetus of the new evangelization efforts under Benedict and beyond reflects a dichotomy in which the Church has the truth to which these post-Christian cultures are, for many reasons, unwilling to assent. That is, they are simply abandoning their responsibility to consume that which the Church produces. At the first plenary gathering of the Council for the Promotion of the New Evangelization, Pope Benedict described the situation thus: 'that same message needs renewed vigour to convince contemporary man, who is often distracted and insensitive. For this reason, the new evangelization must try to find ways of making the proclamation of salvation more effective' (Benedict XVI, Address, May 2011). The problem, according to Benedict, is that evangelization must be more 'effective'. It's an uphill battle, with the Church facing a 'distracted and insensitive' subject before it.

Francis brings together John Paul II's theme of inculturation with Benedict's emphasis on new evangelization, despite many in the Church wanting to distinguish their projects sharply. Francis is admittedly very different in style from his predecessor, and seems more focused on issues of economic and ecological justice. Francis' pontificate thus far, however, has had an evangelical tenor. He speaks repeatedly about two themes: encounter and accompaniment. Admittedly, these themes have a different tone from Benedict's account of evangelization in western Europe, but they are evangelical nonetheless. Francis advocates for a culture of encounter that privileges the needs of the poor and vulnerable as the way of bringing Christ to the world. Encountering others with compassion and justice is how we spread the good news of Christ.

One of the clearest expressions of Francis' pastoral concerns regarding evangelization came in February 2020 in the form of *Querida Amazonia*, his apostolic exhortation that followed a synod addressed to the issues in the Amazon. Progressive Catholics were largely frustrated by the document, because they wanted and expected the pope to allow for a relaxation *in extremis* regarding priesthood regulations because of priest shortages in the region. The document delivered no such relaxation, but it did reflect Francis' indebtedness to John Paul II in thinking about the role of the Church in mission territories. Moreover, Francis demonstrates what inculturation might mean when the Church centres encounter in the process. In short, it involves a more careful encounter with cultures foreign to those from which the Church arose. When the Church encounters such a culture, 'she constantly reshapes her identity through listening and dialogue with the people, the realities and the history of the lands in which she finds herself' (Francis, *Querida Amazonia*, para. 66). Echoing John Paul II, Francis writes that the Church must pay close attention to what is good and beautiful in the cultures it encounters, and 'she needs to listen to its ancestral wisdom, listen once more to the voice of its elders, recognize the values present in the way of life of the original communities, and recover the rich stories of its peoples' (para. 66).

The process of evangelization, then, is just that: a process. First and foremost, it requires an awareness and appreciation of the culture in which the Church is working, be it in lands far from the European context of the Church's coming of age, or in cultures that have abandoned the Christian imagination of their medieval ancestors. It is hard to argue that Christianity should not keep evangelism of some kind or other at its core. The Church is missional by nature; good news that remains unshared makes little sense to the Christian imagination. The mission territories of an abandoned Christianity, however, put new challenges in front of the Church, challenges which have arisen due in no small part to her own failings.

Pope Benedict insists on a new evangelization of 'an increasing number of people [who], although they have received the Gospel proclamation, have forgotten or abandoned it and no longer recognize that they belong to the Church' (Benedict XVI, January 2011). He sees moral relativism and individualism at the core of the problem and offers more of a critique of the role of capitalism therein than he is often credited with. Any process of 'new' evangelization, however, must contend with the wounds caused by the Church itself. Francis seems aware of this reality, and his powerful image of the Church as a field hospital, first and foremost concerned with witnessing to God's mercy, is an important step forward on this count.

In the 1960s, Cistercian monk Thomas Merton offered a compelling reflection on the wounds caused by the Church. 'So I am apologizing to you', he writes to the unbeliever, 'for the inadequacy and impertinence of so much that has been inflicted on you in the name of religion' (1969, p. 205). He goes on to question the reality of a 'religious renewal', and although his words cannot chronologically refer to the new evangelization, they are nonetheless applicable: 'Are the Believers trying to convince themselves of their singular importance by selling a new image of themselves? ... I think too many churchmen are still toying with the vain hope that their various institutions are going to continue to play dominant roles in society. I very much doubt it!' (p. 206).

Here Merton provides an important reminder about the world in which the Church seeks to do its evangelical work, especially in the post-Christian context that Benedict had in mind when he established the Council for the Promotion of New Evangelization. For evangelization to truly be new, the Church must delve deeper into the wisdom of inculturation, especially in its encounter-centred form à la Francis. In his exploration of New Testament models for new evangelization, Marcel Dumais offers Emmaus as a model that reminds the Church that 'the process of evangelization remains profoundly and entirely human' (2014, p. 74). Dumais' reflections are helpful in that they foreground relationality in the new evangelization. This is the only way forward for new evangelization in the twenty-first century, especially when we consider the media landscape we inhabit.

The Church must navigate this media landscape. It must do so as not just another set of tools but as a complex system of symbolic forms, embedded values, networks of relationships and languages. In short, it must navigate a culture. Luckily, according to the three pontiffs in the past few decades, the Church does its evangelical work with quite an awareness that what is truly happening is an encounter between cultures. For Francis, this encounter must be marked by mercy, compassion for the poor, and a willingness to accompany people in their darkest moments.

I propose here an approach to evangelization in the twenty-first century that follows Francis' theme of encounter and couples it with an understanding of digitality as culture. When one comes to understand digital platforms as part of a larger digital culture, one can then begin to analyse and critique the values and meanings being negotiated within it, as one would in any other culture. If Christians privilege encounter, they are able to recognize two things: 1) to live in the context of the global north is to live within digital culture (albeit in varying degrees); and 2) digitality is not just a tool for encounter but the very social matrix in which it takes place and therefore adopts its symbolic economy. That is, we encounter people as much online as we do offline, and we live with them in a digital culture.

In practical terms, I propose three things. First, all ministers and leaders in the Church, lay and clerical alike, should be intentionally trained in digital literacy. This means courses or modules in seminaries, universities, parishes, congregations – wherever people are being trained and formed for ministry. Ideally, digital literacy training would then be extended on local levels to all people involved in the work of ministry, like volunteers. However, digital literacy should be implemented more formally in pastoral training first.

Second, equipped with the critical tools of digital literacy, the Church should prioritize active listening on individual and communal levels in online contexts. That is, Christians should first seek spaces in which to listen to the concerns and values within social networks online. This includes communities or spaces that seem superfluous or unrelated to 'churchy' concerns. I propose this as a step in the process of inculturation, whereby any efforts to evangelize approach with openness and charity the culture in which the Church seeks to embed itself. It may mean adopting the online practice of 'lurking', which refers to users who simply read/watch the activities of a community but do not often or ever participate. Strange as it may seem, I propose that anyone who is interested in evangelization in digital culture spend a significant amount of time learning its language(s), its symbols, its tones – even the absurd – before taking any active steps toward evangelization.

Third, any efforts of evangelization in an online context should focus not on content-delivery (what we can produce) but on relationality (whom we can accompany). Many efforts on the part of Christians to participate in digital culture are focused on what they produce instead of whom they may encounter. Although she did not live long enough to see the digital revolution, the life's work of Dorothy Day can help contemporary Christians bring together the complexity of digital culture and the call to evangelization-by-encounter. Day advocated for personalism, a philosophy she learned from Peter Maurin, in her work with the poor of New York City. A Catholic anarchist, Day argued that Christians should enact the corporal works of mercy on an individual or family level, insisting that whenever one encounters the poor, one does not guide them elsewhere but bears the responsibility for them on a personal level.

There is certainly a place for online-content production from the Church, but most ministers and most Christians should focus less on developing sleek videos or running abstract social media accounts. Instead, most Christians should be in digital spaces as themselves, witnessing to the mercy of God through relationships. Indeed, this would require an intentional reflection of spiritual practices as they relate to online habits, and perhaps this reflection should be coupled with the digital literacy training mentioned above at the level of formation.

Engaging in evangelization in digital culture in these three steps recognizes that digital spaces are a culture, that personal relationships are central to any Christian witness, and most importantly, that the Church cannot proceed with evangelization under the assumption that they know the hearts and minds of those they seek to engage. As Merton puts it when speaking to the unbeliever, believers 'not only claim to know all about you, they take it upon themselves to expose the hidden sins which (according to them) explain your unbelief' (1969, p. 204). Such is the temptation of Christians in the realm of evangelization particularly, and this temptation has a certain power when it comes to the digital. Claiming to have true embodiment, we criticize the digital for being disembodied. Claiming to have true contemplation, we accuse the digital of being a distraction. Claiming to have true community, we accuse the digital of being a simulacrum at best and an anti-community at worst. By spending time becoming digitally literate and listening first, the hope is that we might pause to reflect on whether our claims about the Church itself are actually true. We might also consider the ways in which our assumptions about digital culture are founded or not. All of this takes a careful process of charitable engagement with culture, or the hard work of inculturation.

New as the digital context seems to us sometimes, its challenges are nothing new for the Church. Ever tasked with bringing the gospel to the world, the Church has always had to navigate and negotiate culture. The mission field has always been a paradoxical combination of the familiar and the alien. We would do well to draw on our rich tradition and history of evangelization as inculturation, keeping humility and a willingness for self-criticism at the centre of our work.

References

Anderson, Benedict, 1991, *Imagined Communities: Reflections on the Origin and Spread of Nationalism*, New York: Verso.

Benedict XVI, 2011, 'Address of His Holiness Benedict XVI to Participants in the Plenary Assembly of the Pontifical Council for Promoting the New Evangelization', 30 May.

Benedict XVI, 2011, 'Message for the World Mission Sunday', 6 January.

Dumais, Marcel, 2014, *After Emmaus: Biblical Models for the New Evangelization*, Collegeville: Liturgical Press.

Francis, 2016, 'For a Culture of Encounter', *L'Osservatore Romano*, 23 September, Weekly ed. in English, n. 38.

Francis, 2020, *Querida Amazonia*, 2 February.

John Paul II, 1990, 'World Communications Day Speech'.

Merton, Thomas, 1969, 'Apologies to an Unbeliever', *Faith and Violence: Christian Teaching and Christian Practice*, South Bend, IN: University of Notre Dame Press, pp. 205–6.

Pontifical Council for Social Communications, 1971, *Communio et Progressio*.

Thompson, John B., 1995, *The Media and Modernity: A Social Theory of the Media*, Stanford, CA: Stanford University Press.

3

Mission: An Adventure of the (Digital) Imagination

JONNY BAKER

Introduction

Reflecting on mission in a digital age requires imagination rather than technique. While it is tempting to use new technologies to reproduce the old world or to communicate the old message in a new way, what is more interesting with regard to mission is to imagine what possibilities are emerging in and afforded by the new environment. Missiology has lots of nous in relation to the issues that arise in relation to discerning and communicating the gospel within and across cultures. At its best that is done from the inside through patient presence and listening, which leads to working towards expressions of theology and church in the vernacular, with local theology, leadership and imagination. A digital age simply requires this same kind of presence, attention, imagination and then translation. An ethnographic approach would enable this kind of attention to digital technologies use in actual lived practice which can then be reflected upon theologically and missiologically.

The Currency of Translation

When it comes to the translation of the gospel, the currency of mission is imagination. For example, John Taylor in reflecting on the challenge of translating the gospel for primal cultures in

Africa describes this process as an adventure of the imagination and wonders if we took it seriously whether the results would be recognizable to the rest of the Church universal (1963, p. 24). In missiology there are a range of terms for the process of translation – for example, inculturation, contextualization, prophetic dialogue, incarnational mission and hybridity. Any study of mission across cultures will doubtless show up that, whatever name you choose for it, what sounds straightforward is actually far from it. It is an art that requires simultaneously a deep immersion in the gospel, its stories and traditions out of which improvisation can take place. And at the same time a letting-go of the forms of language and culture with which that gospel has been framed. Bevans and Schroeder elucidate this dual process and suggest that it requires a letting-go of the gospel for the sake of the gospel (Bevans and Schroeder 2011, p. 93). It requires an undoing for genuine newness to have a chance to emerge from the soil of the local context/culture. It is made all the more tricky because it works best when insiders to that culture become the carriers of the message and the builders of new communities who follow Christ. This presumably is fairly obvious as they are the ones of course who know how to speak their own vernacular best – so you might say there is also a second letting-go for the sake of the gospel.

We're all painfully aware, in the West at least, as we look back at the history of missions that far too often the process of translation has not been done as well as it might. Put simply the main reason for this is that the imagination is colonized. In the name of Christ it ends up imposing its own cultural clothes on others rather than enabling the gospel to be culturally robed in the clothes of local culture. This is partly blindness. By that I mean that the intentions are usually good but without due self-awareness of cross-cultural issues the translator cannot see that what they call 'the gospel' turns out to be a lot more than sharing Jesus Christ. It includes architecture of church buildings, songs, theology in Western categories, ways to pray, ways to run discipleship groups, ways of doing pretty much everything that is done in church. It also unwittingly fails to see that local ritual and ceremony may be a key component of the vernacular and calls people away from their own cultural forms. Translation is often then reduced to the words only and not paying attention to the wider anthropological issues. As well as blindness, there is, second, a failure of control, by which I mean a failure to let go of control and trust local leaders. A very simple example of this lack of imagination is music – translators simply translate the words of their own songs and before you know it the local worship is effectively foreign. It seems like translation has taken place but it hasn't at any depth. Missionaries should be banned from translating their own songbooks for this very reason. This is why I say the currency of translation is imagination. In this example there is very little currency. There are of course layers of complexity to this. For example, it may be that Western culture is aspirational which is what I found in India when I was involved in a discussion about music in churches, so there are negotiations to be had and it is to do with the imagination of both missionaries and local people who both have agency and need to journey together. The history of missions is also full of fantastic examples of translation done well. There is a whole range of examples of what Shaw and Burrows (2018) term hybridity in cultures across the world. The current debate in missiology on insider movements also foregrounds the challenge and exciting opportunities of translation with multiple examples. Again, to give a simple example, there is a case study of contextualization among Muslims which uses confession of faith, prayer, giving, fasting and pilgrimage as a framework for discipleship (Talman and Travis 2015, p. 407). These are of course the five pillars of Islam. Another wonderful example is *The Way of The Sevenfold Secret*, which was published by Lilias Trotter in 1926 in Arabic to reach Muslim mystics or Sufis in North Africa.

Translating at Home

This issue of translation has classically been discussed concerning 'overseas' mission because it is clear then that you are crossing cultural boundaries. In recent times it has been seen to be equally important in our own culture(s) which changes over time and in which the gospel needs translating afresh. For example, in the UK the movement of fresh expressions of church made a specific connection with issues of translation in mission on two counts: first by drawing on the Church of England declaration of assent that the gospel be proclaimed afresh in every generation; second by recommending that the training of leaders of fresh expressions of church should be done through the lens of cross-cultural mission (Cray 2004, p. 147). Translation in this case is to do with societal changes over time. Since we have seen huge cultural shifts in the UK over the last few decades alone, so this remains a pressing concern. And it is to do with reaching people outside of the Church, whose way of doing things is very different to the way church is constructed. To be clear this is not solely a concern for those who have migrated from other countries but equally to do with young people, estate cultures, postmodern urban cultures, people at home in popular culture, rural life and so on.

It is not only when translating overseas that problems can arise. The same issues are at play closer to home. In some ways I wonder if the problems are greater because in travelling overseas there is at least the recognition that culture is an issue and you get some critical distance from the way things are done. The blindness and control referred to above are real concerns. There are various powerful forces in the Church in the UK that it seems to me work against this translation across culture – forces of homogeneity for the sake of growth so that we can sell the gospel to more people, of defended theologies and ecclesiologies, of church taste cultures, of particular religious sweet teeth that have become absolutized and stuck rather than remembered as simply something we made up or constructed once upon a time to translate the gospel – I don't just mean musical styles, I mean bishops and parishes as well which were once something people constructed as a local way of doing things. These forces do not trade in the currency of imagination. As a result they can be experienced as alienating or simply irrelevant as a result of their foreignness. Indeed I have come to think that they must fear what might happen if people really started to imagine and dream and theologize for themselves. I recently had an exchange with Stephen Bevans on the issue of imagination in relation to contextualization. He has taught me so much and is seen to be one of the leading theologians in this area. He was remarking how often when he was asked questions about contextual theology and mission they were defensive or cautious. People worry about how you know that what is being done is 'sound' or avoids 'dangerous syncretism'. He finds it much rarer to be asked questions that want to explore what is possible, to imagine what might be, in translation. When did we get so anxious, defensive and fearful I wonder?

There is an irony to this in the Church of England at least. Cathy Ross did some research where she looked at all of the Lambeth conference resolutions since 1867. She distilled out of that what the concerns and foci have been of the Anglican Communion. This is one way of getting at what is at the heart of Anglican identity. Those themes are contextualization and culture, world Christianity, creativity and the importance of addressing contemporary issues (Avis and Guyer 2017, p. 297). These are all really issues of the currency of imagination in relation to translation! In a similar vein, in recognition of the issues faced internationally around translation the focus of the 1989 International Anglican Liturgical Consultation was on liturgical inculturation and produced an incredibly inspiring and freeing statement 'Down to earth worship' which stressed the need for openness to innovation and experimentation, local creativity and continual reflection (Holeton 1990, p. 10). This was a response to international questions and the navigation of a post-colonial world. But the logic of these international themes is that they are the same issues in our own context. We just haven't paid as much attention to them. It is probably easier to say to the Church in Kenya that of course they should translate in a deep imaginative way than it is to think we might need to change the way we do things. One of the classic mission texts on translation is Lamin Sanneh's *Translating the Message*. In that he argues that the Church is always tempted to resist translation because it much prefers to absolutize its own expression of faith. If the gospel and ways of doing things are fixed she feels a lot safer. Yet the Church must continue to translate if it is not to get stuck in the past or in a single ethnic identity (Ward 2017, p. 84).

A Gift of Sight

Perhaps another way of coming at this issue of imagination is to think of it as seeing, a gift of sight, of vision. Through attention and presence and listening to God and the culture, translators (by which I am thinking of pioneers) notice stuff. They notice what is happening in the flows of language and culture (through identity, representation, meaning making and so on) – i.e. what's happening around them, attention to the lived as ethnographers would say. They notice in their spirit a sense of what God might be nudging them towards. They notice that what they have known before makes no sense in this new world and that they have to let it go and risk openness. They notice stuff about themselves. They notice things in the scriptures pop out that they hadn't seen before. They notice that the Kingdom is already present. They notice that where others have seen paganism or whatever other ways otherness has been negatively labelled there are possibilities and connections. They notice people who they are drawn towards or who are drawn towards them. They notice God is here and at work before their arrival. They notice the presence of God and seek to follow it. And if this imagination really begins to flow there is often an inventiveness, a creativity with and alongside new friends with whom they have connected and they do stuff together. And as the Spirit who is ahead and alongside co-missions with them, the gospel takes root and grows and lives are transformed. This process we discerned in a research project called Beautiful Witness. The noticing or seeing is a skill or takes effort or practice and can be nurtured through practices of mission spirituality. It is also entirely possible for the things that one person sees to be totally invisible to someone else especially if they come with a colonized imagination. This is what I meant above by blindness. This is a very real issue for pioneers. On multiple occasions I have had conversations with pioneers who are baffled by the inability of their sponsoring diocese or circuit or board to understand what they are doing or in fact even to see it – it is somehow invisible to them. It is all the more baffling because what they see is obvious to them. The powers that be can generally see something new if it looks like what they think of as church – a building, Sunday services, a priest in charge and so on. But they struggle if it is something deeper by way of translation.

The purpose of this collection of essays is to reflect on mission in relation to digital technologies which are now a huge part of (real) life. The concept of *missio Dei* has been explored in other chapters so I won't rehearse that in detail here. But the key insight behind it is that mission is something God both initiates and remains involved in – redeeming, renewing, healing all things. The challenge for us who wish to participate in mission is to see what God is doing and join in. This is the kind of process I outline above in relation to noticing. The particular aspect of mission I am focusing on is translation.

I was fascinated to see that there is a Radio 4 programme series on digital technology just started called 'New Ways of Seeing' inspired by John Berger's brilliant book of the same name. James Bridle, the programme producer, says in the *Guardian* newspaper article about the series: 'It's one of the ironies of the present age that while we feel that everything has changed, our view seems to be unaltered. If you walk down the street, the buildings, vehicles and people all look much the same as in Berger's heyday. The digital revolution is largely an invisible one – until you start to look closer.

Beneath the surface of the street, and behind the screens of our computers, hide powerful forces that shape all of our lives. To reckon with them requires a new way of seeing: an understanding of the connections between infrastructure and code, state surveillance and corporate power, social prejudice and algorithmic bias, and the environment and computation. It is a form of seeing vital to understanding the times we live in, and as at every previous time in history, it is artists who are helping us to forge it. (Bridle 2019)

I love the insight that things are not clear (even though there has been radical change) until you start to look closer. And we may need artists to help us see. Equally pioneers who are translators are those who need to look closer and may help us to see.

John Taylor calls mission 'an adventure of the imagination' and I have stolen his phrase for the title of this chapter – Mission: An Adventure of the (Digital) Imagination (Taylor 1963, p. 24). He recognizes that imagination is the currency we need in translation. In his case he was reflecting on the question of translation in relation to the primal religions of Africa. But it seems to me that it is exactly what we need to reflect on mission in relation to digital technologies and communication and the way they have shaped our culture almost beyond recognition in a very short space of time while seemingly everything looks the same on the surface.

Imagination, Seeing and Inventiveness

Let me share a couple of examples of imagination, seeing and inventiveness in our digital age. Nomad podcast explores Christian faith in today's world. Their strapline is 'stumbling through the post-christendom wilderness, looking for signs of hope'. It is honest, searching, and on a genuine quest. Each episode carries an in-depth conversation with someone for about an hour and is topped and tailed by the hosts chatting about it. Typically, the people interviewed have published a book though not always. Because they are not bound by the constraints of pleasing a political church environment or denomination there is a great freedom in exploring issues fearlessly and honestly – the interview with Vicky Beeching was a very good example of that (Nomad issue 175). Tim Nash, who has been funded as a pioneer by the Methodist Church as a translator, says in their tenth anniversary marathon issue that Nomad is 'just a podcast' (Nomad issue 190). I had a wry smile on my face when he said that. At one level it is just a podcast and because the content is consistently good it is growing followers. But at another level it is part of a changing environment in which people are working out how to follow Christ and connect with others. There are huge numbers of people who follow Christ but do not engage with traditional patterns of church attendance but they do meet with friends to discuss faith over coffee or the meal table, they listen to podcasts, they attend festivals and read books and chat online. The Nomad podcast interview with Steve Aisthorpe, the author of *The Invisible Church*, really lifts the lid off this new kind of practising of Christian faith (Nomad issue 179). He has done a few pieces of research and has found that there are a lot more followers of Christ not in church on a Sunday, not because they have given up but they are making faith in other ways and often because church as they have known it is not working for them any more perhaps due to the imagination failure I was touching on earlier. For some of those people Nomad and things like it are so helpful – people in that space identify with it and feel they are not alone or mad. Part of Nomad's inventiveness has been to develop a listener map so that you can add your postcode and then be connected with other listeners. There have been meet ups and gatherings of listeners. There is also now a listener lounge and a book club online and the beginnings of a model of money exchange. So there is community, communication (of the word), devotions, and a core membership with a very large fringe. In the Church of England, 'resource church' is a new way to describe a large church in a city centre usually attracting young adults. It is currently flavour of the month with various bishops and funders. Looking at the numbers on Nomad I cannot help wondering whether it could be conceived of as something akin to a resource church! I am noticing something wonderful as Christ is present and communicated afresh, a liquid ecclesiology if you will. But there is a newness, a remaking that could well be unrecognizable to the guardians of the old world. In fact I suspect they may not even see it – it is invisible. Digital technology affords discipleship and Christian community in a very different way in the new environment. I am a fan of Marshall McLuhan's thinking and writing. He was extraordinarily ahead of his time seeing the impact of new technologies and media. He focused very much on the significance of environment – in other words the kind of world and space opened by and through technologies. Heidi Campbell and Stephen Garner explore the notion of technology as environment or ecology, suggesting it is a good starting point for theologizing about technology in a digital media age (Campbell and Garner 2016, p. 35). One of McLuhan's often quoted insights is that people use new media to remake the old world, rather than open up the imaginative possibilities the new media afford, which you can see in so many places in the Church. But he also suggests that if you change the technology you get a whole lot more change than you bargained for (McLuhan and Carson 2011, p. 499). Nomad is an example of this sort of change. The shift in technology has enabled very different ways of being church, learning, discipleship. It has not simply carried the old ways of being church into the new environment.

Anj and Ash Barker are amazing translators – they have lived in multiple cultures for a dozen years at a time. Following their time in a slum in Bangkok, they moved to Winson Green where the mission they are involved in is really inspiring – I take groups of pioneers there to sit at their feet and learn. They have spent time noticing and imagining and being inventive. One group that Anj noticed and connected with were women from multiple cultures many of whom either could not work or were out of work. They co-created a social enterprise called Flavours of Winson Green where these women cook dishes from their cultures at events in and around Birmingham. They cooked for us. The digital part is that Anj asked some teenagers they knew in South Africa to design an app. On this app

the women sign up and when they do a job whoever is oversee-
ing it writes them a reference/review of their work which goes
with their profile on the app. There is also a system of points
for jobs they do which they can accumulate. Various stores
or other providers have signed up to an exchange scheme
whereby these points can be traded for goods and services such
as a driving lesson or bag of rice. This alternative economy
is particularly significant because many of the women cannot
work while seeking asylum. The references are also very helpful because typically for a job an employer wants six months'
worth of references but if you can't work how do you get references? But through the app as soon as asylum is granted there
is a collection of references for jobs done. The local council has
approved this app and system. It is a fine example of hacking.
It is brilliant, it is good news and I had no doubt that Christ
is present in the midst of the mix of relationships – I am sure
some of the women would have been among the 200 people
who passed through their house on Easter Sunday. This is an
example where mission is definitely trading in the currency of
imagination.

A third example is the Disability and Jesus network. When I
was presenting on the need for imagination in translation at the
2019 *Missio Dei* in a Digital Age conference in Durham, several
people were slow to catch on to what I was talking about. This
was partly because I was unsure what level I needed to pitch
the missiology – I was unsure what people were familiar with.
But the person who was the most enthusiastic both during and
afterwards was Dave Lucas, who has a visual impairment. On
speaking with him afterwards I realized why. The future has
already arrived for disabled people when it comes to digital
technology. Depending on their disability, navigating the old
world and ways of doing things is a huge challenge and has
been for many years. It is a world that requires mobility, sight,
attendance and access. And it is also a world where those leading it do not see the issues for those with disability. But through
digital technologies this community has already engaged with
community, discipleship, teaching, friendship, prayer, church
online (and offline though often in different ways). In the book

Pilgrims in the Dark Lucas describes those Christians with disabilities as being church at the margins. Of necessity they have had to imagine and embody different ways of being church but in doing so they may be prophets and forerunners of the future. They too find themselves inhabiting a liquid ecclesiology.

Digital Technology in Pioneering Practice

I did some research through an online questionnaire with CMS pioneers to find out in what ways digital technologies are part of their pioneering practice. I asked two simple questions: How do you use digital technologies in your own life and discipleship? How do you use digital technologies in your pioneering?

The first thing that struck me is what I have called extension. Digital culture is not a different thing or world. It is an extension of life that is just assumed to be normal. It is real life. No one is imagining crossing a culture to digital culture – it is more a means of mediating and communication and (self) representation and connection. What pioneers use is quite ordinary – Facebook, WhatsApp, Twitter, apps and so on. To give an example: an extension of prayer and spirituality might be through the use of the Bible on a phone, of practising the examen using the examine app. Teaching and indeed sharing with others might come through podcasts or TED talks or shared links on Facebook. Community is extended through texting and WhatsApp both with fellow Christians for prayer and support and with those in the wider community they are pioneering among.

Then, second, digital technology is used inventively to amplify something – communication, connection, participation, community. It is most times used really simply to do this. So in a new housing area a pioneer amplifies the community through a Facebook group. One pioneer suggested that people with little experience of being community might be helped through social media.

Third, there is something really interesting about the public visibility of digital technology. The blurring of what parts of life are visible to whom is a good thing when it comes to mission. It used to be much easier to compartmentalize church conversation with Christians at church events. But online, assuming people don't connect with just church people, their friends see their faith posts as well as their music interests and so on. There is a visibility that will shine if it is good news and authentic and it will lead to connections.

I don't know what I was expecting but at first I was disappointed that the research did not come up with some new revelations. It all seemed quite ordinary but then gradually I realized that that is the point. It is simply part of the flow of life. I also began to reflect on imagination. If there is the kind of imagination that I am suggesting is the currency of mission translation (which there ought to be for CMS pioneers) then digital technologies are naturally part of that flow enabling seeing, research, connection, relationships, inventiveness, amplification and a space where pioneers can be present in the world sharing the crazy love of God. But the converse is also true – if a disciple of Christ lives in a church bubble the amplification will be of their anti-missional practice and lack of imagination and digital technology will support that rather than change it. If the habit of a disciple of Christ is to be fearful and problematize the wider culture while living in a subculture then that will be amplified. So the things that work against mission are probably also perpetuated in the new environment. That is why I suggest that the most important issue if we are concerned with this aspect of the *missio Dei* – the translation of the gospel into cultures – is imagination. We need spaces and communities that will help nurture and spark such imagination and vision. Sadly I find it is not a common currency in today's Church which is why I have chosen to hang out with pioneers at the Church Mission Society (who, I am glad to say, see its value).

I have said very little about the negative side of digital technologies whether our own use and its effects or the powerful media companies and their levels of control and influence over our lives, abuse, trolling, echo chambers, the immediacy of unhelpful content and so on. I also found I had questions about the performance of gender and the digital environment. But I am here influenced by John Taylor, who suggests that in situations of translation judgement is unhelpful. Yes of course there is sin but usually sin is the last truth to be told (Taylor 1963, p. 172). In my experience the Church does plenty of this already and the pendulum usually needs swinging to celebrate and see what is good.

I have twice used the term 'liquid ecclesiology' without explanation. This term comes from Pete Ward's work on liquid church (Ward 2002) and liquid ecclesiology (Ward 2017). In my preparation for this chapter his second book was my conversation partner and I found it to be an extremely helpful text on these issues as he pays attention to cultural dynamics and the presence of Christ in the world, drawing on a number of missiologists. Essentially, liquid church is a 'way of thinking about Christian community that takes the fluid nature of culture seriously' (Ward 2017, p. 9). Rather than directly elaborate on his work in the flow of the text I have tried to absorb it and use it in a more improvizational way. I am sure this will be clear to Pete if he reads this but it may not be to others. But I wanted to close by acknowledging that I have been inspired and helped by Pete's work and I really commend it to you. I have also tried to gently nudge his work into discernment in the world and not just the body, or maybe it is the body in the world, and into more liquid forms than the case study in the book.

References

Aisthorpe, Steve, 2016, *The Invisible Church*, Edinburgh: Saint Andrew Press.

Avis, Paul and Guyer, Benjamin M., 2017, *The Lambeth Conference*, London: Bloomsbury.

Berger, John, 1972, *Ways of Seeing*, London: Penguin.

Bevans, Stephen and Schroeder, Roger P., 2011, *Prophetic Dialogue: Reflections on Christian Mission Today*, Maryknoll: Orbis.

Bridle, James, 2019, 'New Ways of Seeing', *The Guardian*, www.theguardian.com/tv-and-radio/2019/apr/16/new-ways-of-seeing-john-berger-digital-age-decode-radio-4, accessed 9 September 2020.

Campbell, Heidi and Garner, Stephen, 2016, *Networked Theology: Negotiating Faith in a Digital Culture*, Grand Rapids: Baker Academic.

Cray, Graham (ed.), 2004, *Mission Shaped Church*, London: Church House Publishing.

Holeton, David R. (ed.), 1990, *Liturgical Inculturation in the Anglican Communion*, Nottingham: Grove Books Ltd.

McLuhan, Marshall and Carson, David, 2011, *The Book of Probes*, Berkeley, CA: Gingko Press.

McLuhan, Marshall and Fiore, Quentin, 1967, *The Medium is the Message*, New York: Bantam Books.

Nomad Podcast, www.nomadpodcast.co.uk, accessed 10 September 2020.

Sanneh, Lamin, 1989, *Translating the Message: The Missionary Impact on Culture*, Maryknoll, NY: Orbis.

Shaw, R. Daniel and Burrows, William R. (eds), 2018, *Traditional Ritual as Christian Worship*, Maryknoll: Orbis.

Talman, Harley and Travis, John Jay, 2015, *Understanding Insider Movements*, William Carey Library.

Taylor, John, 1963, *The Primal Vision: Christian Presence amid African Religion*, London: SCM Press.

Trotter, Lilias, 1926, *The Way of The Sevenfold Secret*, Tunbridge Wells: Nile Mission Press.

Tupling, Katie, Lucas, Dave and Braviner, Bill, 2018, *Pilgrims in the Dark*, Disability and Jesus.

Ward, Pete, 2002, *Liquid Church*, Milton Keynes: Paternoster.

Ward, Pete, 2017, *Liquid Ecclesiology*, Leiden: Brill.

4

Digital Theology: Practising Local Theology in an Age of Global Technology

REI LEMUEL CRIZALDO

Google ... is a little bit like God. God is wireless,
God is everywhere and God sees everything ...
for many questions in the world, you ask Google.
(Alan Cohen, VP of AireSpace)

Contextual Theology and Communication Technology

In the twentieth century, liberation theologians raised our awareness about the need to practise theology in light of socio-economic realities. In the twenty-first century, we must reflect on how to practise local theology in light of the changing landscape of media and communications technology. While Karl Marx and his disciples were conscious of the need to seize and control the 'mode of production' in order to gain rightful freedom and identity, power is now in the hands of whoever wields the 'mode of communication'.

As countries continue to be shaped by the forces of globalization, the rapid changes in global communication prove to be one of the most daunting. Some would even say that media technology is globalization's significant other, because globalization would not have occurred without the rapid changes in communications brought about by media (Lule 2012, p. 5).

Manuel Castells, in a masterful trilogy about the Information Society, refused to engage in any sort of 'futurology' but still arrived at a conclusion way back in 1998 that is no less than prophetic of where we are today. He wrote:

> The information technology revolution will accentuate its transformative potential. The twenty-first century will be marked by the completion of a global information super-highway, and by mobile telecommunication and computing power, thus decentralizing and diffusing the power of information, delivering the promise of multi-media, and enhancing the joy of interactive communication. Electronic communication networks will constitute the backbone of our lives. (2010c, p. 389)

The prescient part of Castell's work is his analysis of the trends in the realm of communication technology and its impact in radically altering the way our societies are ordered. In particular, he notes the critical role of 'digital networking technologies' for 'ushering in the new form of globalization characteristic of our time' which he described as 'the network society' (2010a, xvii–xviii).

Today, societies in every corner of the world continue to move in this direction. The 2020 figures released by the global agency *We Are Social* reveal the massive digitalization happening all over the globe with nearly 60% of the world's population now connected online and more than half doing it via social media (Kemp 2020, para. 2). Its definitive report, *Digital 2020*, features in-depth data for every country in the world, showing how digital media has 'become an indispensable part of everyday life for people all over the world' (para. 1).

Along with the complex forces of globalization, the emergence of social media and other social networking platforms has largely democratized the way people communicate. People now inhabit an environment where someone can be connected instantaneously to someone else on the other side of the globe. Through communication technology, our world is being drawn continuously into a 'global village', as originally described by the Canadian media guru Marshall McLuhan (1989, p. 31). Cultural studies of communication tell us that 'all forms of intellectual activities, like thought and expression, social organization and culture, are decisively influenced by the predominant communication medium and language of the period. This has far-reaching consequences for all sciences, including philosophy and theology' (Palakeel 2011, p. 1). Fortunately, noted historians of early Christianity, such as Andrew Walls (2002) and Philip Jenkins (2009), remind us that Christianity has always been a global religion and is familiar with the impulses of globalization which will include technological development and its utilization in the spread of the faith.

In his book, *The New Catholicity: Theology Between the Global and the Local*, Robert Schreiter (2004) took note of the critical role communication technologies have played in shaping the interaction between the homogenizing forces of globalization and the resisting impulse within local contexts including the impact of such 'interaction' to theologizing. Acknowledged as the pioneer of the approach 'doing local theology' in the field of contextualization, or the indigenization of theology, Schreiter has come to recognize how 'emerging communication technologies represent a new opportunity to be dialogical and theological within local cultures' (Plude 2011, p. 4). More recently, the Asia Theological Association (ATA) published the textbook *Asian Christian Theology*, the first of its kind on systematic theology for use of seminaries in Asia, wherein Timoteo Gener identified 'rapid technological change' as a 'continuing theological concern being addressed' among evangelical theologians in Asia desiring to make the gospel come alive in the region (2019, p. 32). This chapter explores this concern including the dialogical dynamic that is at work in the interplay of digital media and the contextualization of theology.

The Philippines will be an interesting case study for this endeavour considering that Filipinos have always been hailed as among the most active people in social media and regarded as acknowledged 'global leaders' in pioneering its adoption (Hjorth and Arnold 2013, p. 69). Cited for having the highest penetration of social networking among internet users (Universal McCann 2008, p. 36), the Philippines have earned the title 'The Social Networking Capital of the World' (Russel 2013, p. 19). In 2020, 'Filipinos are still the world's most "social" people, with the average internet user aged 16 to 64 spending almost four hours per day on social platforms' (Kemp 2020). The country continues to beat the rest of the world in terms of the longest hours spent online with an average of nine hours and 45 minutes per day (2020, p. 43). As to what Filipinos do in social media, a pioneer piece of qualitative research done at the University of the Philippines Diliman identified a good range of behaviours that still rings true today:

> view their Facebook account as extensions of their personalities, a way for them to keep updated on current events, both here and around the world, through links provided by their Facebook friends, and an avenue for the Filipino spirit of '*Bayanihan*' in times of devastating typhoons, with the site becoming an information hub for people who wanted to help. (Media Center of the College of Mass Communication 2010)

These figures and findings simply highlight how the social connectivity that is deeply embedded in the local culture made social networking a most perfect fit in the everyday lives of Filipinos. Furthermore, considering that 11 million Filipinos, roughly a tenth of the entire population, live outside the Philippines either as migrants or contract workers, social media has become a cost-efficient way to keep families together and communicate with each other (Crizaldo 2019, p. 11).

Unfortunately, with regard to how digital technology has been influencing and shaping the religiosity and the theological thinking in the Philippines, much work still needs to be done. This chapter hopes to highlight several concepts in digital communication that have critical implications for those engaging in local theology amidst the developing terrain of the Philippine cyberspace and its importance to shaping the ministry of the Church.

Social Media's Trinitarian Identity

In terms of social networking, there are at least three things to keep in mind as one engages with digital technology: 1) using social media as a new tool in communication; 2) recognizing social media as the very environment wherein such communication takes place; and 3) realizing that social media is an 'entity' in itself that participates in the communication process.

Serving as a *tool* for communication will be the most familiar to local theologians. Susan George notes:

> One of the main thrusts of Christianity that make the Internet a most appropriate partner is the 'evangelistic' nature of the religion. There is a definite thrust towards 'spreading the message' and evangelism. Just as Christians were charged to 'go out into all the world' at the inception of the religion in the first-century Roman Empire, so the Internet is considered by many to be a 'Roman Road' in which Christians are charged to venture in the twenty-first century. (2006, p. 103)

While acknowledging the need 'to help people develop a more critical awareness of the messages they receive, and of the worldview behind them', the Lausanne Movement (2011, p. 36) speaks of the Church's relationship to media and technology in the same utilitarian spirit identified by Susan George. In the landmark document, *The Cape Town Commitment*, the global movement lends itself to 'a renewed critical and creative engagement with media and technology, as part of making the case for the truth of Christ in our media cultures' (p. 36). Lars Dahle, Lausanne catalyst for media engagement, explains further what this means for the movement:

> The printing press was the first modern media revolution; the second revolution was the mass media. In both eras, evangelicals were innovative and creative in their media engagement. Today, we live in the era of digital transformation and social media, which may be described as the third media revolution. We need courage, wisdom, and an entrepreneurial spirit 'to

bear witness to Jesus Christ and all his teaching' (as quoted in the Lausanne Cape Town Commitment) in such an age as this! (2017, para. 5)

But social media is no longer just a communication tool for Christianity to spread its message. Reflecting on how the Church ought to conduct itself in a Google-shaped world, Philip Clayton remarked, 'Mastering the new communication technologies is not enough, though it's essential; it's also crucial to understand what it means to be religious and Christian, in a technology-dominated age' (2010, p. 11). In a globalized world that is continuously saturated and shaped by communication technology, social media has already become the *environment* in which Christianity shall 'move and have its being'. As the next generation of worshippers relentlessly Tweet even inside the sacred halls of God's sanctuary, social media is now the stage upon which we forge our spirituality and theology. The stage features a global character transcending geographic national boundaries and summoning the whole wide world to itself. What was tweeted in New York reverberates in the slums of Manila and gets preached the next Sunday morning.

But at the same time, there is also the emergence of *reverse colonization*. As described by Anthony Giddens of the London School of Economics, reverse colonization is a curious situation in which non-Western countries extend their influence in the West (2004, p. 16). Contrary to the expectation that globalization will promote a sort of universal cultural norm for free-floating cosmopolitan citizens of the world, the reversal can also be starkly dramatic. Giddens notes, 'a more profound effect of globalization is to produce greater local cultural diversity, not homogeneity' and that 'globalization tends to promote a renewal of local cultural identities' (p. xxiv). This is evident with the worldwide popularity of Japanese animation and Korean drama and pop music. The Philippines have their own share of this phenomenon by exporting films of local actor Piolo Pascual and syndicating novelty shows such as the popular noon-time show *Eat Bulaga*. Social media makes this environment of cultural exchange possible for those in the underside of the world.

Lastly, attention has to be paid to how social media shapes the content of the messages it transmits and how a medium also changes the messengers that send and receive the messages. As Marshall McLuhan says, 'The medium is the message' (1964, p. 7). Though there is the aphorism, 'methods must change but the message stays the same', this is not a realistic portrayal of communication. Reflecting on his long experience in the advertising industry, Shane Hipps affirms the hidden power of technology, 'whenever methods or media change, the message automatically changes with them' (2005, p. 30). Raul Pertierra's analysis of the dynamics of being empowered by technology is worth heeding especially with regard to the capacity of transforming the agency of its users. He writes:

> Technology is not only a new way of relating to the forces of nature but also a subjective transformation of our sense of self. It not only affects how we deal with the material world but enters into our relationships with ourselves and with others. (2007, p. ix)

In other words, social networking applications assume a life of their own as each platform grows and renews its lease on life in every updated version. It is an *entity* that, in one way or another, engages its user. Every time people ponder upon the screen and behold the glory of an app's latest interface, social media interacts with them and communicates a message as well.

These facets of social media's identity as a form of digital technology have three profound implications for doing local theology.

Social Media as a New Communication Tool

First, social media is an available tool for accessing and spreading a message. The world is now 'flat' as Thomas Friedman would say (2005, p. 7). YouTube has placed a camera before anyone in the world. Blogging has freed up the world of publishing. Anyone now can have their own fifteen minutes of fame. Incidentally, the theological stage is no longer dominated by long-established creeds, such as Reformed theology or Dispensational theology, among others. Today, people flock around 'thought leaders' such as John Piper, Timothy Keller, John MacArthur and N. T. Wright, to name a few. But thanks to social media, these theological superstars in the West need not have the monopoly of the discourse. Not any more, since anyone from the global South can trade theological ideas with and even issue a necessary critique on their personal Facebook timeline and Twitter account. Filipino social anthropologist Melba Maggay has observed that 'one gift of globalization is the increasing awareness ... that there is a plurality of theologies' (2016, p. 185).

Voices of non-Western theologians need not be muted and left unnoticed in an obscure corner of the world. They can actually steer the global theological discourse towards the reality of diversity in terms of theological reflections. But this calls for an active digital engagement – which is critical because, as Maggay has also observed, the 'monocultural forces of globalization' are at work. In a 'technologically mediated social environment', if people are not mindful enough, the gospel will simply come across 'pre-packaged and mass-marketed to many cultures which does not quite fit the Bible's own concern for culture specificity' (2017, p. 124). This concern will have theologians from Asia, Africa and Latin America master and leverage the power that social media offers as a tool of global communication so that they can become effective witnesses to the Jerusalems, Judeas and Samarias of our day, which have now come to include the secularized soil of North America and Europe.

It is important, though, for local theologians to temper one's technological confidence. Communication scholar Quentin Schultze put it well when he warns of falling into a form of 'media idolatry' that so easily generates false hopes of what media technologies can deliver (2000, p. 118). In a global discourse that remains tilted to voices that have become familiar and popular, the quality of one's theologizing is what will count at the end of the day. As Schultze would say, 'technology can be no more effective than the people who use it' (p. 119). This is a challenge for theologians from the global South to root deeply their theologizing in specific contexts, engage well the pressing issues of the day, and readily make their voices accessible and available in various digital platforms. It is this commitment towards a sustained wave of local voices that will make way for 'decolonized' and therefore fresh and alternative ways of reading Scriptures contributing to the enrichment of the ongoing global discourse.

But if churches in the global South desire to rise and take the lead in 'theology-making today', Wonsuk Ma rightfully recognized the need for this cacophony of voices to be in 'concerted effort to collaborate in theological construction' as it fills in the gap of where 'Western-imported theology would ultimately be handicapped in properly responding to Asian contextual issues' (2019, pp. 135–6). Surely, the optimal utilization of digital connectivity as a means of continuous exchange will greatly help facilitate the collaborative work in the region. Initial signs of this regional effort among evangelicals can be seen in a recent initiative by the Asia Theological Association (ATA) called A.CROSS or Asian Christian Reflections on Society and Spirituality, an online forum that brings together Bible scholars and theologians from more than 300 theological institutions all over Asia with the aim of providing a digital space for 'ongoing dialogue on key issues in Asian societies and how the Church through theological education can address them' (ATA 2020).

Social Media and the New Theological Environment

Second, the marketplace of ideas has been liberalized by social media, which has changed the theological environment. Access to what was once expensive theological literature is just a download or a 'torrent' away. The logical and legal framework of piracy has become increasingly outdated. To be digitally accurate, piracy is now simply an archaic term for what we know now as peer-to-peer file-sharing (Schwarz 2014). More than ever, local theologians have access to the resources needed either to build or deconstruct a theological edifice, all of which are available free of charge or at a very cheap price. In many ways, the World Wide Web is one big black market of theological freebies operating out of interlinked communities of online storage via Google Drive, Dropbox and iCloud.

Again, this opportunity poses a challenge for local theologians to go beyond being consumers of whatever digital resources are available on the internet. But it won't happen until we lose the appetite for devouring round after round of imported foreign theological goodies and instead crave theologies that are locally made. With the bulk of Christians coming from and being born in the global South, local theologians have the responsibility to speak to their own people. This they can do by joining the ranks of digital producers. The time has come to stop being the white man's burden. Speaking of the evangelical community in Asia, Gener and Pardue remarked in what could be the first evangelical theology textbook published in Asia:

so much work remains in supporting the flourishing of evangelical theology in the Asian church. Although Christians in Asia now outnumber their counterparts in North America, evangelical theological resources still reflect an exclusively North American outlook. Very few theological resources that reflect classically evangelical commitments are deeply engaged with the issues that are of distinctive significance for the Asian church. (2019, pp. 1–2)

But the relentless flow of theological goods from the West will continue until the non-West no longer become a too enthusiastic market. Now, more than ever, the opportunity opens up to stop being outsourced theological technicians, translators and marketers of Western theology(ies). There is great need for 'app developers' (i.e., local theologians) who will innovate and produce theological resources for the local church. As Federico Villanueva forcefully put it, 'there ought to be a shift in the way biblical interpretation and theology are done. Those in the

Majority World ought to be the ones doing biblical interpretation for their own contexts' (2014, p. 6).

Perhaps it will help local theologians to develop the conviction that the frontier of theological exploration no longer needs to go around the Western shore. There are already good reasons to believe that should churches from the global South chart a different trail from that of Western Christianity, it will not necessarily fall off the edge of the world. Korean and African theologians, for example, have dared to sail on their own by putting a moratorium on foreign resources and developing their own local theologies including the hermeneutical tools needed to construct it (Kwon 2018; Mburu 2019). If well-intentioned efforts like these continue, the global village of worldwide Christianity will see the tables of theological economy overturned. That is, if fewer and fewer in the global South procure the products of Western theological enterprises, Western theologians will have to find their place within the body of Christ. An apt illustration of this realization is Kevin Vanhoozer's plea to still include Western theologians (such as himself) in the current global theological discourse. He writes in a compendium on global theologizing:

I am a mid-Western theologian who seeks to do theology amid the detritus of Western civilization. My passion for the gospel disposes me to be critical of my own culture, most of all for how it has strayed from its biblical moorings. At the same time, with African and Asian theologians, I have to believe that God's Word has been and still can be translated in *my* culture too. (2006, p. 108)

If the turning of the tables continues, Western Christianity, as exemplified by Vanhoozer's plea, will find how best to reposition itself with the rest of the global church which consists primarily of people from diverse ethnic backgrounds. Perhaps, the West will have to learn to trade by exchanging goods rather than extracting money from their cash-strapped brothers and sisters in the global South under the guise of theological publication. For in the world of social media, buying information is no longer the order of the day. People merely exchange social goods. From an old economy of purchasing theological resources, members of global Christianity rooted in the digital sphere will have to learn the ancient art of bartering. This moves toward a theology that has nothing to claim from the other but has much to offer from itself.

Social Media and A New Theological Discourse

Third, for those who would engage in developing local theology, social media presents an indispensable content for theological articulation. While indigenous theology seeks to utilize local cultural resources as categories for articulating the faith, social media expands the semantic range and vocabulary from which contextual theology can draw. Though local language provides a window to peek into the deepest chamber of a country's parochial soul, the cosmopolitan language of social media opens the door to meet the world at large. For example, the Filipino cultural concept of *kalooban* (selfhood/being) gets a 'selfie' in Instagram. *Kamag-anak* Inc. (extended family) gets a Facebook group. *Pakitang-tao*, a carefully managed version of one's public self, gets a moment in Snapchat.

Social media has its own 'language game' that mashes up with the vernacular language in a true 'glo-cal' fashion. It is not enough therefore for Filipino theologians who are contextualizing the faith to go beyond standard theological terminologies and concepts from the Council of Chalcedon to the sixteenth-century Reformation, such as the hypostatic union, justification by faith alone, etc. They will now have to take in concepts such as 'virtual', 'network' and 'augmented reality' alongside local indispensables such as *ginhawa* (well-being), *loob* (self) and *mukha* (face). Most recently, a collaborative project of local theologians in the Philippines has produced what is regarded as the maiden offering that exhibits a genuinely Filipino theology anchored on the indigenous aesthetic concept of *ganda* or beauty (De Mesa et al, 2017). It would be great to see a succeeding volume that explores the remarkable preoccupation with visual aesthetics among Filipinos merrily curating boards in Pinterest and videos in TikTok.

Furthermore, the global but diverse character of social media as a digital platform shows an entity in which local theology can learn a thing or two regarding the nature of ontology and 'being' as applied to theological formulations. For instance, Kevin Vanhoozer faults 'theological ethnification' for spawning a variety of local theologies: Aboriginal, African-American, African, American Indian, Asian, Dalit, MinJung, etc. He argues that 'location should never become the essential characteristic of Christian theology' (2006, pp. 104, 106). But his proposal for a method that might serve as a unifying cord to tie together all the theological strands enumerated in the *Dictionary of Third World Theologies* (Fabella and Sugirtharajah, 2000) appears to spring from a nostalgia for systematics. Vanhoozer's sentiments rehash echoes of the old Western colonial tendency for command and control.

The kind of centripetal impulse towards theologizing proposed by Vanhoozer is a stark contrast to how the world of social networking operates in a more centrifugal virtue of connection and collaboration. As pointed out by the media scholar Quentin Schultze, cyberspace in general and social media in particular is 'the largest functioning anarchy in the world' (2002, p. 19). Subscribers to social media networking platforms operate and play along the lines of anarchist fundamentals: self-initiative, mutual-cooperation and non-hierarchical structure (Milstein, 2010, pp. 13, 25). Still, the digital realm continues to grow in one beautiful chaos. While surveillance and censorship in some closed countries manage to erect a firewall to keep its citizen from joining the party, it has very little power to shut the windows or extend its grip to the rest of the world. All these should encourage the local theologian that the digital environment serves as a happy host to a diversifying theological discourse with no clear centre as point of reference.

Global Christianity's Pentecostal Identity

'Christianity is a global religion that is at the same time incarnational' says Melba Maggay (2017, p. 124). What she means is that:

> There is a sense in which we are 'global', an interdependent community of God's people all over the world who bear a family resemblance. This does not mean, however, that we cease to be creatures of our cultures, in much the same way that we do not cease to be male and female, rich and poor, even as we are one in Christ. Each local body of believers, in its very peculiarity, forms part of that picture of renewed humanity that Christ is re-creating. (p. 126)

Accordingly, a global theology made up of local theologies should not resemble the Tower of Babel, where everyone speaks the same language and agrees on the same tool to reach God in the heavens. Instead, Pentecost shows the direction and path of global Christianity – where everyone shall hear the Gospel in his or her language. The Jerusalem Council pointed out that there is little baggage that shall stand in the way. And Paul, in his various letters, showed how the Gospel would look after incarnating itself into a particular context and communicating through a particular medium. His epistles showed us how a medium can amplify and amputate a particular culture's sensibility and faculty. Again, Professor Andrew Walls reminds us:

> [m]ission involves moving out of oneself and one's accustomed terrain, and taking the risk of entering another world. It means living on someone else's terms, as the Gospel itself is about God living on someone else's terms, the Word becoming flesh, divinity being expressed in terms of humanity. And the transmission of the Gospel requires a process analogous, however distantly, to that great act on which the Christian faith depends. (2002, p. 170)

There have been efforts to create a respectable platform for the diverse voices of local theologies to gain a hearing such as the *Global Dictionary of Theology: A Resource for the Worldwide Church* (Dyrness and Kärkkäinen 2009). But to appreciate the beauty that resides in the subtle nuance of diversity, one has to learn how to give local cultures and ethnic theologies what the French sociologist Pierre Bourdieu calls 'the pure gaze' (1979). This is a 'mode of artistic perception or aesthetic disposition that gives one the capacity to consider in and for themselves, not only legitimate works of art but also everything in the world, not yet consecrated as such' (p. 3). After all, the earth – and everything derived from it – is the Lord's. And as God gazed upon His last great masterpiece, He exclaimed, 'It is very good' (Gen. 1.31). Pure gaze. Gaining fluency with this optic capacity is important lest the inclusion of theologies from the non-Western world will be made not for the inherent value of its contribution but merely for 'ornamental' purposes it can serve (Rajeshakar 2015, para. 14).

Digital Theologizing in the Philippines

Having been reared in a print culture shaped by a Protestant-evangelical dismissal of the visual, what defined the Filipino evangelicals' notion of Jesus were letters, pages and books. Yet as Paul writes in his letter to the Colossians, Jesus is the very 'image of the invisible God' (Col. 1.15). The intangible Word spoken at the beginning of creation and prophesied in the written scrolls of the Old Testament assumed a visual form in Nazareth and was nailed on the cross. 'In the beginning was the Word ... and the Word was made flesh,' says John the Beloved (John 1.1, 14). However, today, two thousand years later, most evangelicals know Jesus only through printed texts or at best through colouring-in materials used in Sunday Schools.

Andrew Walls offers a missiological insight that may expand spaces for reimagining portrayals of Jesus in today's context to include the digital: the Gospel possesses an 'infinite translatability'. He writes, 'This principle (of translatability) brings Christ to the heart of each culture where he finds acceptance; to the burning questions within that culture, to the points of reference within it by which people know themselves' (1996, p. 23). When Jesus physically left the earth, he left behind a visual image that the world can feel, see and touch – the Body of Christ, revealed in physical persons formed of flesh and blood. As Bishop Graham Cray says, 'The body of Christ is called to bear the image of the biblical Christ' (2013). Throughout history, Christ came to people in the guise of a crusading army, an invading colonial power, a struggling but armed minority yearning for liberation, and even as an entrepreneur marketing the faith with tenacious profitability. But now the body of Christ has assumed a digital mode of existence. In 2004 Walter Wilson termed it the 'Internet Church' and since then the online community of faith has surfed and dived into the waves of digital technology. In this, his latest incarnation, Jesus' arms, hands and feet have taken on a digital form. Jesus' extended presence on earth, the church, is now seen on YouTube channels and in a variety of social networking sites with profiles and avatars for all the world to see.

In the Philippines, this digital presence of the church is manifest in small groups and discipleship networks meeting and multiplying through video conferencing platforms. One church calls it 'Skypleship!' This is becoming the fresh face of the church in the Philippines that has gained traction over the years, building well on the local culture's internal wiring for social connectedness. Long before social media rocked the private world of Western individuals and pushed them to become more 'social' and 'communal', Filipinos were already 'social' and 'communal'. Thus, it should be no surprise that the Philippines became the world's 'Social Media Capital'. Facebook and Instagram merely amplified these cultural habits to global proportions.

Surely, this digitalization of church ministries presents both exciting opportunities for growth and at the same time concerns for possible alterations if not altogether distortions in the very DNA of the Body of Christ. From his own study of the history of technology, the communication critic Neil Postman offers a sharp diagnosis:

> New technologies alter the structure of our interests: the things we think *about*. They alter the character of our symbols: the things we think *with*. And they alter the nature of community: the arena in which thoughts develop. (1992, p. 20)

Indeed, there is 'a heavy cost' that comes with the bountiful gifts of technology (1992, p. xii). Jesse Rice, in his book *The Church of Facebook* rightly identified that the challenge really is to step into the digital world of social networks with 'eyes wide open' and with keen attention to the many ways community could get redefined (2009, p. 216). The waves that social media calls us to navigate are definitely not easy. But such concerns not only stir up fresh challenges, but also provide viable content for theological reflections in the Philippine context. Hopefully, changing modes of digital communication and the contemporary social discourse surrounding it will continue to inform the conceptualization and formulation of local theologies. Pardue and Gener issue an apt reminder: 'the theologian is a servant of the church, if the church's questions are different from what they used to be, then the books and presentations that theologians offer need to change as well' (2015, p. 60).

But inasmuch as Timoteo Gener's recommendation that 'good theology is a biblical response to particular (i.e., local) socio-cultural issues and experiences' and that 'contextualized theology means ministry in context' (2005, pp. 4, 9) continues to resonate well with Filipino theologians, then the issue of digitalization of church communities in the Philippines will find its place at the forefront of local theologizing. All the more necessary as Gener argues that the way for the Philippine church to advance local theologizing in the twenty-first century is to ensure that 'local theologies will be generated by local churches as they faithfully engage in proficient mission and biblical discipleship with a culture-transforming outlook' (p. 9). It is this grassroots rooting of theologizing that makes for an intrinsic connection between local theology and missional engagement down at the community level which has grown and extended into the digital sphere.

Furthermore, Gener argues that for local theologizing to have a strong grounding in ministry, it cannot remain the province alone of professional theologians in the academe. Instead, the emphasis has to be that 'every believer is a theologian because theology arises from ministry and for the sake of ministry' (p. 9). This conviction paves the way for deep biblical reflections on theology, missiology and technology, towards what Gener calls a kind of 'people-of-God theology' constructed not only by theologians but by people working with and those simply immersed in today's digital technology (p. 16). In a way, the motivating force of contextualization to include the ministry of the people of God and their self-reflection is what retrieves the missionary nature of theology (Maggay 2013, p. 7).

To close, the encouraging words of Calvin Chong sketch a hopeful picture for the future of digital theologizing,

The dramatic developments in communication networks, platforms, and technologies in the twenty-first century have paved the equivalent of the first century's roads in Rome ... Together with these developments have come new opportunities for ministry and service. New media and communication platforms bring with them greater awareness of global and local happenings, knowledge of what's trendy in popular culture, access to information databases, and resources, connections to communities, growth in learning opportunities, avenues for creative expressions, and rich multidimensional solutions to complex problems. In addition, they open doors for individuals and organizations to build communities, share stories, collaborate on projects, build social capital, advocate for causes, pool resources, and effect personal as well as social change. Thus the church cannot ignore new communications networks, platforms, and technologies, in its ongoing work of nurturing spirituality and furthering the work of justice in the world. (2015, pp 51–2)

References

Asia Theological Association, 2020, *Asian Christian Reflections on Society and Spirituality*, https://across.ataasia.com/introducing-a•cross/, accessed 1 July 2020.
Bourdieu, Pierre, 1979, *Distinction: A Social Critique of the Judgment of Taste*, trans. R. Nice, 1984, Massachusetts: Harvard University Press.
Castells, Manuel, 2010a, *The Rise of the Network Society*, 2nd edn, Chichester: Wiley-Blackwell.
Castells, Manuel, 2010b, *The Power of Identity*, 2nd edn, Chichester: Wiley-Blackwell.
Castells, Manuel, 2010c, *End of Millennium*, 2nd edn, Chichester: Wiley-Blackwell,.
Chong, Calvin, 2015, 'The impact of global flows on spirituality and justice', in Ringma, C., Hollenbeck-Wuest, K. and Gorospe, A. (eds), *God at the Borders: Globalization, Migration, and Diaspora*, Metro Manila: OMF Literature, pp. 59–75.
Clayton, Philip, 2010, 'Theology and the Church After Google', *The Princeton Theological Review*, Vol. 17, No. 2, pp. 7–20.
Cray, Graham, 2013, 'On not knowing the end at the beginning', *Journal of Missional Practice*, Spring 2013, https://journalofmissional practice.com/on-not-knowing-the-end-at-the-beginning/, accessed 25 May 2020.
Crizaldo, Rei Lemuel, 2019, 'When the great commission goes digital', *Evangelicals Today*, Vol. 44, No. 2, pp. 10–12.
Dahle, Lars, n.d., 'Why the Reformation anniversary matters for media engagement', *Lausanne Media Engagement Network*, https://engaging media.info/reformation-anniversary-media-engagement/, accessed 1 July 2020.
De Mesa, J., Padilla, E., Lanaria, L., Cacho, R., Cipriano, Y., Capaque, G., Gener, T., 2017, *Ang Maganda sa Teolohiya*, Manila: Claretian Communications Foundation.
Dyrness, William and Kärkkäinen, Veli-Matti (eds), 2009, *Global Dictionary of Theology: A Resource for the Worldwide Church*, Downers Grove: InterVarsity Press.
Fabella, Virginia and Sugirtharajah, Rasiah S. (eds), 2000, *Dictionary of Third World Theologies*, New York: Orbis Books.
Friedman, Thomas, 2005, *The World is Flat: A Brief History of the Twenty-first Century*, New York: Farrar, Straus and Giroux.
Gener, Timoteo, 2005, 'Every Filipino Christian a theologian: a way of advancing local theology for the 21st century', in Acoba, E. et. al., *Doing Theology in the Philippines*, Metro Manila: OMF Literature, pp. 3–23.

Gener, Timoteo and Pardue, Stephen (eds), 2019, *Asian Christian Theology: Evangelical Perspectives*, Carlisle: Langham Global Library.

Gener, Timoteo, 2019, 'Divine revelation and the practice of Asian theology', in Gener, T. and Pardue, S. (eds), *Asian Christian Theology: Evangelical Perspectives*, Carlisle: Langham Global Library, pp. 13–38.

George, Susan, 2006, *Religion and Technology in the 21st Century: Faith in the E-World*, London: Information Science Publishing.

Giddens, Anthony, 2004, *Runaway World: How Globalisation is Shaping Our Lives*, London: Profile Books.

Hipps, Shane, 2005, *The Hidden Power of Electronic Culture: How Media Shapes Faith, the Gospel, and Church*, Grand Rapids: Zondervan.

Hjorth, Larissa and Arnold, Michael, 2013, *Online@ Asia Pacific: Mobile, Social, and Locative Media in the Asia Pacific*, Abingdon: Routledge.

Jenkins, Philip, 2009, *The Lost History of Christianity: The Untold Story of the Church's First Thousand Years*, New York: HarperOne.

Kemp, Simon, 2020, 'Global Analysis', *Digital 2020 Report*, https://wearesocial.com/blog/2020/01/digital-2020-3-8-billion-people-use-social-media, accessed 25 May 2020

Kwon, Jin-Kwan and Kuster, Volker (eds), 2018, *Minjung Theology Today: Contextual and Intercultural Perspectives*, Leipzig: Evangelische Verlagsanstalt.

Lausanne Movement, 2011, *The Cape Town Commitment*, Peabody, MA: Hendrickson Publishers.

Lule, Jack, 2012, *Globalization and Media: Global Village of Babel*, Plymouth: Rowman and Littlefield Publishers.

Ma, Wonsuk, 2019, 'Lord and giver of life: The Holy Spirit among the spirits in Asia', in Gener, T. and Pardue, S. (eds), *Asian Christian Theology: Evangelical Perspectives*, Carlisle: Langham Global Library, pp. 119–38.

Maggay, Melba, 2013, 'The task of contextualization: Issues in reading, appropriating, and transmitting the faith', in Maggay, M. (ed), *The Gospel in Culture: Contextualization Issues through Asian Eyes*, Metro Manila: OMF Literature, pp. 1–56.

Maggay, Melba, 2016, 'Drawing these chapters together', in P. Bazzell and A. Penamora (eds), *Christologies, Cultures, and Religions: Portraits of Christ in the Philippines*, Metro Manila: OMF Literature Inc., pp. 184–9.

Maggay, Melba, 2017, *Global Kingdom, Global People: Living Faithfully in a Multicultural World*, Carlisle: Langham Global Library.

McLuhan, Marshall and McLuhan, Eric, 1988, *Laws of Media: The New Science*, Toronto: University of Toronto Press.

McLuhan, Marshall, 1962, *The Gutenberg Galaxy: The Making of a Typographic Man*, Toronto: University of Toronto Press.

McLuhan, Marshall, 1964, *Understanding Media: The Extensions of Man*, Reprint 1994, Massachusetts: MIT Press.

Media Center of the College of Mass Communication, 2010, *Facebuking: Uncovering Filipino Culture in Facebook*, Quezon City: University of the Philippines.

Milstein, Cindy, 2010, *Anarchist and Its Aspirations*, Oakland: AK Press.

Mburu, Elizabeth, 2019, *African Hermeneutics*, Carlisle: Langham.

Palakeel, Joseph, 2011, 'Theology and the technologies of communication', *Media Development*, No. 4, pp. 32–40.

Pardue, Stephen and Gener, Timoteo, 2015, 'Global theology: Where to from here', in Ringma C., Hollenbeck-Wuest, K., and Gorospe, A., *God at the Borders: Globalization, Migration, and Diaspora*, Metro Manila: OMF Literature, pp. 59–75.

Pertierra, Raul (ed), 2007, *The Social Construction and Usage of Communication Technologies: Asian and European Experiences*, Quezon City: The University of the Philippines Press.

Postman, Neil, 1992, *Technopoly: The Surrender of Culture to Technology*, New York: Knopf.

Rajeshakar, J. Paul, 2015, 'Theological education in an era of globalization: Some critical issues', *Journal of Lutheran Ethics*, Vol. 15, No. 1, www.elca.org/JLE/Articles/1069, accessed 25 May 2020.

Rice, Jesse, 2009, *The Church of Facebook: How the Hyperconnected Are Redefining Community*, Colorado Springs: Cook.

Russel, John, 2013, 'The Philippines leads the world in social networking', in Berlatsky, N. (ed.), *Social Networking: Global Viewpoints*, Michigan: Greenhaven Press, pp. 17–21.

Schreiter, Robert, 2004, *New Catholicity: Theology Between the Global and the Local*, Orbis New York: Books.

Schultze, Quentin, 2000, *Communicating for Life: Christian Stewardship in Community and Media*, Grand Rapids: Baker Academic.

Schultze, Quentin, 2002, *Habits of the High-Tech Heart: Living Virtuously in the Information Age*, Grand Rapids: Baker Academic.

Schwarz, Jonas Anderson, 2014, *Online File Sharing: Innovations in Media Consumption*, New York: Routledge.

Universal McCann, 2008, *Power to the People: Social Media Tracker Wave 3*, https://web.archive.org/web/20080921002044/http://www.universalmccann.com/Assets/wave_3_20080403093750.pdf, accessed 25 May 2020.

Van Hoozer, Kevin, 2006, 'One ring to rule them all?', in Ott, C. and Netland, H. (eds), *Globalizing Theology: Belief and Practice in an Era of World Christianity*, Grand Rapids: Baker Academic, pp. 85–126.

Villanueva, Federico, 2014, 'The challenge of Asian biblical interpretation today', *Journal of Asian Evangelical Theology*, vol. 18, no. 1, pp. 5–17.

Walls, Andrew, 1996, *The Missionary Movement in Christian History*, New York: Orbis.

Walls, Andrew, 2002, 'Christian scholarship and the demographic transformation of the church', in R. Peterson and N. Rourke (eds), *Theological Literacy for the 21st Century*, Grand Rapids: Eerdmans.

Walls, Andrew, 2002, *The Cross-Cultural Process in Christian History: Studies in the Transmission and Appropriation of Faith*, New York: Orbis Books.

We Are Social, 2020, *Digital 2020: Global Digital Overview*, https://wearesocial.com/digital-2020, accessed 25 May 2020.

Wilson, Walter, 2004, *The Internet Church*, Nashville: Thomas Nelson.

PART 2

Missional Practices

5

Finding Jesus Online:
Digital Evangelism and the
Future of Christian Mission

STEVE HOLLINGHURST

Early Christian mission was aided by writing, so travelling evangelists could carry books of the Bible and Christian literature. The invention of the printing press enabled the mass production of Bibles and Christian literature, so the evangelists of recent centuries could not only carry but distribute literature as part of evangelism. Radio and TV enabled new global broadcasts of evangelistic messages. Media and mission have always gone together. This mediation always becomes part of the message; the way we find Jesus. So how does the digital media revolution affect evangelism? What is the gospel online? Who is the digital Jesus and where and how can we find him?

I approach these questions as a missiologist, used to thinking about intercultural mission and what it means in each culture and context to follow the commission of Matthew 28.19 to 'make disciples of all peoples'. In essence, digital media is 'just another way people can communicate' rather than a place or a culture we are called to inhabit as digital missionaries. Yet this is not quite true. The nature of digital media changes how we communicate and also who we communicate with. This has important consequences if we are seeking to fulfil that 'great commission'. Digital media is probably the most important development facing Christian mission. This requires a digital missiology not just digital action.

Cultural Change and Communication Media

In his 1991 book *Transforming Mission*, David Bosch describes a series of paradigm shifts in mission history. These correspond to major shifts in culture (see also Hollinghurst 2010). Changes in communication technology have played a crucial part in these shifts. The first predates Christianity but was important in the spread of the early Church, the shift from an oral to a literary culture with the development of writing. In Phaedrus, Plato records Socrates speaking very negatively of this shift. He argues that writing, like a painting, stands alone from its creator and is fixed and unresponsive, unable to teach as a teacher does a student. However, as Walter Ong points out, while Plato expresses his unease about the shift from oral to written discourse in both Phaedrus and his Seventh Letter on writing, Plato's own thought was dependent on a written form (2012, pp. 24, 78–80). In this, Plato illustrates the power of text to communicate across time and space and reach a far wider audience than spoken words. Yet, the power no longer lies with the speaker, but with the reader and interpreter of the text. This idea is important in contemporary communications theory. So, John Fiske states 'the meaning of the message is not "contained" in the message itself but is the result of an interaction or negotiation between the receiver and the message' (2011, p. 45). It ultimately only has the meanings the receiver's context makes possible, and that context may be very different to the author's. For this reason, Charles Kraft suggests that 'one might question whether the "same" message presented in several different situations would indeed be the same message' (1991, pp. 58–9). This affects the early spread of the Christian message. What began as the oral witness of the first evangelists is eventually left in a text, the Bible.

The next communication revolution was the printing press. Ong notes that printing finally established the shift from oral to literary culture; from a hearing-based culture to a seeing-based one. The act of printing a book made the book finalized in a way the written manuscript was not. It also, he argues, enables a privacy of communication with texts not aimed at specific audiences but as an abstract self-expression. This in turn aids the increasing individualism of modernity. This, Ong suggests, enabled the philosophical and intellectual developments of the Renaissance to become permanent in Western culture (2012, pp. 95, 113–14, 129–35, 174–6.)

Printing made the Reformation possible. Instead of people depending on priests for the reading and interpretation of scripture, people could have a Bible in their own language to read for themselves. Post-Reformation faith was also informed by the textual finality of print culture and the individualism it fostered. In this way the shift to printed text became part of a paradigm shift in mission and the expression of Christian faith, not simply a change in how it was communicated (Bosch 1991, pp. 239–345; Hollinghurst 2010, pp. 159–64).

Printing also enabled the mass production of tracts to be used in mission. These ranged from tracts produced by Luther through to the 'penny sermons' of Charles Spurgeon and twentieth-century tracts like Bill Bright's 'Four Spiritual Laws' and Norman Warren's *Journey into Life*. These gave resources to hand out by individuals who might otherwise not engage in evangelism.

Another important issue in communication is the difference between broadcast media which is general and aimed at a mass audience, and narrowcast media which is more personal and aimed at a specific audience. Personal conversation or personal correspondence is more open to discussion. Broadcast media is far less open, and as audience size and reach increases it has to be less targeted (Kraft 1991, pp. 52–66; Neil Thompson 2011, chs 6 and 8). This is reflected in the difference between mass evangelism and personal evangelism.

Public preaching and the use of tracts in evangelism are broadcast media. They suggest an understanding of the evangelistic message as universally applicable. A tract like *Journey into Life* might be translated into different languages but is not altered to reach specific audiences or cultural contexts. The development of broadcast media would later enable sound and vision to accompany mass evangelism via television and radio. These dramatically increased the reach of evangelistic preaching but also in broadening the audience decreased any possible focus on a specific audience. Over time mass production could allow some variation in packaging, enabling a choice of tracts or videos designed for a more targeted appeal. However, the presentation of 'the gospel' was usually dictated by modernist assumptions about a 'universal humanity' (Hollinghurst 2010, pp. 158–62). As Bosch points out, this formulaic approach was also true of global mission in which the spread of Western culture and civilization were part of spreading 'the gospel' and following the right formula a guarantee of success. But as Bosch goes on to note, as the twentieth century developed, it was becoming apparent to many, especially in the global mission field, that this approach was not working (1991, pp. 342–4).

Digital Media and the Cultural Context for Mission in the Twenty-first Century

Marshall McLuhan, writing in the latter half of the twentieth century, famously coined the phrase, 'the medium is the message' (1964, pp. 3–12). McLuhan's point is that we naturally focus on the content of the message but miss the subtle and therefore potentially powerful effect the medium has on us. For instance, putting a play on television changes our relationship to the characters who feel closer and more intimate when actually they are no longer present. Ong notes how new media changed political debate. In the 1850s Lincoln delivered an hour-long address before a responsive live audience of 12–15,000 people. In contrast, the modern TV debate enables millions to get 'up close' to the candidates beamed into their living rooms but the candidates are not really present to their audience (Ong 2012, p. 135).

Ong, having spoken of the printed text as marking an end of oral culture, speaks of electronic media, TV film and radio, as creating a 'secondary orality'. This was not a return to primary orality; it was still dependent on printed text. However, it created new oral and visual formulas and patterns and an imme-diacy not possible in a book. This enabled new group identities which were larger than those of traditional oral cultures, being part of what Ong refers to as 'McLuhan's "global village"' (pp.133–4). Ong's observations have been taken up by others in exploring the impact of digital media. John Hartley explores this in his chapter at the end of the revised edition of *Orality and Literacy* (Ong 2012, especially pp. 207–9). Hartley cites Tom Pettit's point that the rise of digital media marked the era of printing as a 'Gutenberg Parenthesis' (Pettit 2012). Hartley goes on to note that

> It is only with the growth of the digital interactive media that this 'parenthesis' can be seen as a discrete period of history, rather than an inevitable evolutionary step. In the era of the internet vastly more people can make use of literacy, including print-literacy, by publishing it for themselves. So we are in a time of unprecedented *convergence* among oral, written and print-literate modes were oral forms like phatic communication are migrating to the web, the turn-taking modes of speech are augmented by links, photos and file sharing, private conversations are also global publications, text is literally hyper-inflated, and these multi-modal uses of multimedia literacy extend across much wider sections of the population than heretofore. (Hartley in Ong 2012, pp. 208–9)

The idea of a new orality is also explored by Frida Mannerfelt elsewhere in this volume, highlighting the interactive nature and potential for instantaneous discourse fostered by digital media.

The idea of a 'Gutenberg Parenthesis' also points to the social significance of digital media as part of a paradigm shift to a new era that Bosch refers to as postmodern (1991, pp. 349–67). This paradigm shift combines changes in philosophy, science, culture and technology as did the paradigm shift into modernity. The rise of digital communication is central to this and both partially effects and reinforces these other changes (Hollinghurst 2010, pp. 9–64).

A major shift in this new paradigm is from religious to non-religious as the culture of Christendom collapses. Some saw this as a European phenomenon, but it is now clear that the US is following suit. For recent global figures showing the rise of 'no religion' especially among young adults see the 2018 publication by the Pew Forum (Pew Forum 2018). In regions like Africa where being religious remains the norm, there is evidence that globalization may lead to a pick and mix approach to religion in which a surface adherence to Christianity or Islam hides an eclectic practice of traditional African religion and global New Age style beliefs (Hollinghurst 2010, pp. 65–97). This is aided by growing access to digital media in places that have never been connected to other media. Satellite driven smartphones are not only extending the reach of global digital media but also the blending of visual and textual media referred to by Hartley. Not everyone is connected to the internet, but the number who are is significant and growing rapidly. Internetworldstats gives a figure of 58.7% of the world's population accessing the internet, ranging from 39.3% in Africa to 94.6% in North America (2020). Globally these figures are over ten times as high as in the year 2000, and over 100 times as high in Africa.

The emerging 'postmodern' paradigm is also characterized by a shift from 'big stories' to personal ones; from a culture that defers to experts to one in which each individual values their own expertise; from a culture that values a common humanity often defined by concepts of evolutionary progress to one that values difference and cultural specificity and finally defines truth according to personal experience rather than a notion of objective rational universal observation (Hollinghurst 2010, pp. 25–40; Bosch 1991, pp. 349–62). Within this paradigm New Spiritualities have arisen as affiliation to religion has declined. These have grown in a culture in which people seek to create their own religious path, often borrowing from a variety of global beliefs and practices. The majority of those who see themselves as 'non-religious' hold some sort of spiritual belief, often associated with these New Spiritualities, even if many could not be counted as committed adherents. These New Spiritualties have become normal in contemporary society and have grown through digital media in both of which they are very much 'at home' (Heelas, Davie and Woodhead 2003, pp. 170–82, 229–47; Hollinghurst 2010, pp. 41–64; Hollinghurst 2003).

While digital media are an increasingly global phenomenon and creates elements of a shared global culture it also enables considerable diversity and arguably a 'new tribalism'. High levels of choice are enabled by the possibility of globally gathering people who share niche interests. This has led to the idea people operate on social media in 'bubbles' or 'echochambers'. A research team at MIT show that people naturally like to associate with like-minded people and therefore digital interactions tend to reinforce already held opinions. When confronted with different views to those usually heard this tends to generate angry reactions rather than dialogue (Gillani, Yuan, Saveski, Vosoughi and Roy 2018). On the other hand, Elizabeth Dubois and Grant Blank argue that many such studies are within single platforms. They see evidence that across different platforms people access different media on the same issue and argue that this dissipates the effect of the echo chamber (2018). I note that while Dubois and Blank record that people do come across diverse opinions on social and other media, they don't address the issue raised by the MIT team that encountering diverse views may lead to negative responses and a reinforcing of existing views.

Pam Smith, citing the work of Aleks Krotoski (2013), suggests that digital media can lead to the formation of genuine human communities. Interest groups and gamer meets become social spaces where people develop relationships, interest in people's wider lives and spaces for socialization beyond the reason the group has formed (2015, pp. 89–91). As we noted, Ong argued that in a situation of a 'secondary orality', these communities may also develop their own distinct group cultures, reinforcing group identity.

Another feature of digital media is the place of anonymity and pseudonymity. Brady Robards in his study of tribalism on Reddit points out that 80% of those who access the site never log on or contribute but remain listeners (2018). John Suler in his exploration of disinhibited behaviour on the internet, offers several explanations. First, there is a dissociative anonymity in which people feel their actions 'online' are not traceable to them, they can be someone else and don't have to take responsibility. This is especially so if they are using a pseudonym or have a very common root to their email address. Second, there is a related phenomenon of invisibility. This may be as Robards describes, the ability to be a hidden observer or listener. Suler also notes that in text-based social media the fact people cannot be seen or see others means we are always 'looking away'. Third, on text-based social media platforms there is not necessarily an instantaneous response, unlike face to face communication. This asynchronicity means people can do an 'emotional hit and run', posting then 'running away'. Fourth, Suler refers to the impact of solipsistic introjection in which we imagine others and play out scenarios with these imagined others in our own heads. This can lead to communicating online as if it were an imaginary conversation. Fifth, these conditions can create a dissociative imagination in which the online world is perceived as not real, and people dissociate 'online fiction' from 'offline fact'. In this regard Suler cites the unpublished research of Emily Finch, a criminal lawyer exploring cybertheft, who noted criminals treating their actions as a computer game with no real victim. Finally, Suler argues that the internet is designed to be a network that resists control and over which it is hard to exert authority. This creates a feeling that no-one is in charge and encourages things to be said that might otherwise not be. Suler goes on to discuss if disinhibition means people are more 'truly themselves' online. As a psychologist he concludes this is an illusion based on an assumption there is a 'repressed self' within. Rather, he concludes, much online behaviour is better seen as experimenting with different identities (2004).

Suler's study of online disinhibition was based on the use of text-based media which created a level of distance that affected how people related online. Since then, there has been increasing use of video conferencing, especially as I write in the spring of 2020 during the Covid-19 pandemic. In a video conference you can see others and you are communicating in real time. However, a video meeting is not just like meeting face to face. Scholars argue that about 65% of our communication is non-verbal, consisting of things like facial expression, posture, hand gestures, etc. (Haiyan Wang 2009). When we can see someone, we expect to be able to read these non-verbal signals but in video conferencing we lose many. This means we must work harder to correctly understand people (Sklar 2020).

Suler's observations are that people treat online communication as at least one stage removed from offline communication and sometimes as if it is not real. Yet other research shows that online behaviour has very real impact offline. So, Heather Underwood and Bruce Findlay found that online relationships were negatively impacting people's offline primary relationships (2004). Faye Mishna, Alan McLuckie and Michael Saini in their study of cyber abuse among teens found those teens considered online relationships as real and important, often forming romantic relationships online. Yet they expressed a level of mistrust of those online relationships compared to offline relationships. These online relationships were a mixture of people known offline and those met only online. Levels of disinhibition were shown in that young people often quickly offered intimate secrets online. Also, disinhibition was shown in levels of abusive behaviour, shaming and sometimes stalking or sexual pestering (2009). Mishna, McLuckie and Saini argue we need to understand that online relationships for young people are not only real but largely neutral or positive. The importance of this for digital evangelism is that when we communicate online it is really someone offline that we relate to. Online disinhibition may make it easier to do online evangelism but may also make it easier to do it offensively or abusively unless we remember the offline person we are communicating with.

Heidi Campbell in her opening chapter to *Digital Religion* notes the language shift from 'religion in Cyberspace' to 'online religion' and finally a current growing consensus in the use of 'digital religion' (2013, pp. 1–21). This is a move from understanding the internet as a place in which virtual communities and virtual religions can be formed, to a platform by which offline people and communities and religions connect via online communications. Campbell goes on to state:

> Based on this I suggest that the term 'digital religion' describes the technological and cultural space that is evoked when we talk about how online and offline religious spheres have become blended or integrated. We can think of digital religion as a bridge that connects and extends online religious practices and spaces into offline religious contexts, and vice versa. This merging of new and established notions of religious practice means digital religion is imprinted by both the traits of online culture (such as interactivity, convergence, and audience-generated content) and traditional religion (such as patterns of belief and ritual tied to historically grounded communities). This echoes assertions made by Hoover and Echchaibi (2012) that discussion of 'the religious digital' requires a recentering of our attention on the shape of religion in light of the digital. They suggest that when lived religious practice and digital culture meet a 'third space' emerges, a hybridized and fluid context requiring new logics and evoking unique forms of meaning-making. (pp. 3–4)

In summary, digital media while employing text in websites, blogs, emails and chat rooms, mixes these media with imagery and video. In this way social media utilize both broadcast and narrowcast communication and blur the distinction between them, crucially making them interactive, unlike print or broadcast media. There is a 'secondary orality' that reintroduces traits of oral communication culture that help form groups and communities. However, this communication exists at one stage removed, leading to disinhibition. This can enable people to explore new ideas and ways of being and build solidarity between strangers, but can also foster antisocial behaviour that people would not countenance offline and in some cases enables people to commit crimes with no sense of any potential consequences. While this dissociation occurs, it is real offline people who are having real communication and building real relationships via online platforms. Not surprisingly, as the advent of digital communication is part of a paradigm shift to an emerging 'postmodern' paradigm, offline culture and religion bear close resemblance to online cultural and religious expressions. Digital media act, as Campbell describes, as a bridge that creates a 'third space' in which new meanings are formed. Indeed, as Campbell notes, Mia Löuheim

concludes that scholarship demonstrates that religious identity online is not that different nor completely disconnected from religious identity in everyday offline life. This means that, while the Internet enhances the possibility that individuals may practice religion outside institutional contexts, digital media also provide a space for anchoring one's religious identity and helping one connect the online and offline in order to find and negotiate personal meaning in everyday life. (Campbell 2013, p. 13)

Digital Media and Contemporary Missiology

Bosch outlines an 'emerging ecumenical missionary paradigm' within the context of an emerging postmodern paradigm shift (1991, pp. 368–510). Bosch notes that in Western thinking, a distinction was drawn between mission which happened abroad among those who had never been Christian and evangelism which happened at home among those who were no longer Christian. However, by the late twentieth century that distinction had broken down as the majority 'at home' became increasingly those who were never Christian and there were many abroad who were no longer Christian (p. 410). In effect everywhere was increasingly a foreign mission field. This insight led writers like Bosch and Vincent Donovan (2001) to apply post-colonial approaches to mission abroad in countries with a Christian heritage. This approach to foreign mission had moved away from assuming mission should result in the exporting of European or American Christianity along with European or American culture. Instead, the emphasis was on seeking to express Christianity within the culture and context of local people so that an indigenous expression of faith emerged.

Applying foreign mission methods to countries with a Christian heritage was highlighted in the UK by the *Mission-Shaped Church* report (Cray 2004). This described how 'fresh expressions of Church' emerged from contextual mission within distinct cultures and people groups rather following a pre-determined model. The report quoted from Donovan in support of this approach, citing the application of what he learnt from mission among the Masai to his native New York. 'Do not try to call them back to where they were, and do not try to call them to where you are, beautiful as that place may seem to you. You must have the courage to go with them to a place neither you nor they have been before' (Donovan 2001, Preface). That is, mission requires a third space to be created by both the missionary and those they are in mission among so that an indigenous expression of Christianity can emerge. This approach is often referred to as 'intercultural' as it is reliant on an exchange between people of different cultures in which both parties contribute and come to a new understanding of faith. This is similar to Heidi Campbell's comment that digital religion exists in a third space between offline religion and online ways of operating (2013). Campbell cites things common to the internet such as interactivity, convergence and audience-generated content. These are general factors due to the nature of the technology, enabling high levels of interactivity and allowing anyone to 'publish' in a way that was previously not possible. However, as content is developed for niche interest groups and social media enable niche interest communities to form, there is much cultural diversity on the internet. In addition to this, there are the diverse local cultures represented in the online 'global-village'. To take an intercultural mission approach to digital evangelism therefore not only requires a dialogue with the cultural distinctives of the internet overall as pointed to by Campbell, but also the cultures of specific social media platforms and the specific cultures of its different groups and websites.

In 2010 I wrote a book I called *Mission-Shaped Evangelism* precisely because the shift in thinking among missiologists about mission in countries with a Christian heritage had shown little impact in the world of evangelism. Much evangelism still presented a single gospel message with no attention to context or the growing lack of knowledge of Christianity and Christian terminology. As was noted by John Finney in his research on adults coming to faith (1996), most of those who responded to evangelism were people with Christian backgrounds, whereas the 24% who came to faith from non-Christian backgrounds did so over time, not on the whole in response to evangelistic events but due to personal relationships.

The 'Talking Jesus' research carried out by Barna group in 2015 surveyed faith sharing by Christians with non-Christians (Talking Jesus 2015). One question listed the reactions of non-Christians to Christians sharing faith with them. These were largely people they knew: only 13% were strangers. There are not surprisingly both positive and negative reactions. In only one category out of six was the experience more positive than negative, with 51% feeling comfortable with a Christian sharing faith with them whereas 33% felt uncomfortable. In other areas negative reactions were often much higher than positive. So, 18% said they wanted to know more about Jesus Christ after hearing a Christian talk about their faith but 60% did not want to know more about Jesus after this has happened. Similarly, after hearing a Christian talk about their faith in Jesus, 16% felt sad they did not share their faith, but 43% felt glad they did not share their faith. One would not expect everyone to respond positively and the research does not tell us why people are more likely to respond negatively to people sharing their Christian faith. Finney's research suggests that positive reactions came from those with a faith background, negative reactions from those with no faith background.

Finney's research helped support the idea that people needed to 'belong before they believed' and process evangelism within social contexts became popular. Programmes like the Alpha Course not only offered several weeks to explore Christian faith, but crucially a discussion group in which to do this following a shared meal. This enabled a more interactive approach to evangelism but much of the language remained little different from that used in mass evangelism events. In his research into Alpha, Stephen Hunt noted that only about 8% of those attending Alpha had no church background while just over 62% were already church members (2004, pp.169–71). Those with no church background found an expectation of a level of Christian knowledge they did not possess (pp. 173–87). Many evangelism methods assume the kind of Christian knowledge which used to be common when most people were raised in church, which may be why they are largely not effective with those raised with no religious background (Hollinghurst 2010, pp. 9–24).

All our evangelism will increasingly need to be shaped by the principles of intercultural mission. There will need to be an understanding of why Christianity is 'good news' for these people in this place rather than assume the same message can be delivered. We need to recognize with Kraft that it will not be the same message in different contexts. We must try and become at home in each context and seek to discover what authentic Christianity looks like with those who are part of each community. This will be especially true for digital evangelism where those we meet may be more postmodern and post-Christendom. When I began thinking about digital evangelism in the late 1990s, I assumed the 'virtual world' of cyberspace was a place to enter as a foreign missionary and plant churches in 'online culture'. I no longer think this way; rather I see digital evangelism as a bridge, using Heidi Campbell's term, through which we meet offline people who find it easier to explore faith online because of the way it disinhibits people and enables experimentation. We meet them online not only within the culture of the internet but also in their own niche culture groups and their offline cultural homes. Hubs of faith may spring up online to support people's faith journeys but I increasingly suspect these will ultimately support people's offline faith, and this accords with what we find about the way people relate the online to the offline. The people we meet online are always offline, flesh and blood human beings and it is important to remember this.

The relationship of offline and online faith exploration is well illustrated by a video posted on Dutch YouTube page mijnverhaalmetgod (my story with God) by Kimberly in 2012 entitled 'I found God on the internet' (Mijnverhaalmetgod 2012). As a new student from a non-Christian background, Kimberly began asking questions about life she did not have answers for. She was impressed by Christians she met at university but felt she could not talk to them. Instead, she began putting her questions into internet search engines. She doubts she would have ever explored them without this option. She found a website explaining Christian faith and a prayer to pray if you wanted to know God. She did not fully understand this but felt it was what she was looking for and prayed the prayer. This demonstrates the value such web based evangelistic resources provide; they enable people to explore faith anonymously without having face to face conversation or feeling any human pressure. As John Edminston says: 'People do their secret thinking on the Internet, and because of that people explore things on the Web – such as who Jesus Christ is – that they can't or won't explore in public' (quoted by Von Bueseck 2010, p. 26). Kimberly's next step, however, was to join an Alpha course and through that a local church. Kimberly found God on the internet, but both before and after it was non-digital approaches to faith that were important. Noting Hunt's research, Kimberly's online research may have prepared her, as someone from a non-religious background, for the level of Christian knowledge required by Alpha.

There are further lessons from Kimberly's story. She had started university and began asking questions about life. Changes in circumstances can put people in 'liminal states' between worlds which are places often associated with exploring religion (a classic anthropological text on this is Victor Turner 1969). At this time, she met Christian students at university who impressed her. Had she met them instead in a Facebook group, what kind of behaviour online might impress somebody so they wanted to explore Christian faith? Before the advent of digital media, Kimberly might have gone to a library to do such research. Compared to that, the internet offers vastly more material much faster. However, her search engine would have prioritized the order she saw material according to her search history, with paid for advertising also highlighted. Websites with good designers can also search optimize their sites so they appear high in the ranking. It is likely Kimberly chose the pages to look at from the first two pages on her search engine. The website she found was designed to lead people to faith, which is why it had a prayer for her to pray if she wanted to know God. In one sense the site was a digital tract. However, unlike a tract it would be more interactive, enabling her to choose the content she wanted to see. It may have contained audio or video. It might have had links to other pages to explore. In this way Kimberly had far more control over her exploration of Christian faith. What was essentially a broadcast medium, like printed material, was far more interactive due to digital technology. It is interesting to note she felt she didn't properly understand the site; we don't know what content it contained but it might not have been easily accessible to someone like Kimberly who had no Christian background. This website, however, gave her enough information to find an Alpha course and through that join a church.

This story shows how digital evangelism might reach people with whom pre-digital approaches might not work. It demonstrates how digital evangelism enables a bridge between online and offline faith development and how digital evangelism can make broadcast media interactive in a way print media, television or radio cannot. Some digital evangelism will be personal evangelism conducted as intercultural mission and very narrowcast. However, broadcast media can also be effective in digital evangelism if they can be a bridge to enable people to connect with others either online or offline and become part of a Christian community. To enable this kind of connection the Christian Enquiry agency, of which I am a trustee, adds to its site Christianity.org.uk the possibility of requesting prayer or interacting with people who will exchange emails and if wanted connect people with a church. Other organizations like Christian Vision make high quality videos for individuals or churches to use in online evangelism (www.cvglobal.co).

Missio Dei and Digital Evangelism

A crucial theme in the emerging missionary paradigm is the role of God in mission expressed in the concept of *missio Dei*. As the twentieth century progressed; mission was increasingly seen as an attribute of the Trinity. It was no longer the Church's mission but God's mission in which the Church was invited to participate. This also declared that God in mission acted directly in the world not just through the Church. Those who advocated this view did not see it as an innovation but a return to the approach of the early Church. This idea was taken by some to mean that the Church had no role in mission, that God alone acted in mission and did this through secular history. Most however, saw the Church as sent by Jesus to join in with God in mission in the world (Bosch 1991, pp. 389–93). This idea helped a convergence of mission thinking between the Catholic Church, the World Evangelical Alliance and the World Council of Churches (World Council of Churches 2011).

What then is the relationship between digital evangelism and *missio Dei*? First, mission is a wider category than evangelism; it is concerned with the coming of the Kingdom of God on earth as in heaven. So, the digital mission of God is much broader than digital evangelism, seeking to work for justice and the salvation of creation online not just people coming to faith through online Christian witness. However, the salvation of creation and bringing in God's justice will involve the transformation of individual lives, communities and societies and that is what people are called to through evangelism. This is the approach to mission and evangelism contained in the Anglican Five Marks of Mission:

The mission of the Church is the mission of Christ:
1) To proclaim the Good News of the Kingdom
2) To teach, baptize and nurture new believers
3) To respond to human need by loving service
4) To transform unjust structures of society, to challenge violence of every kind and pursue peace and reconciliation

5) To strive to safeguard the integrity of creation, and sustain and renew the life of the earth (Anglican Communion 2012).

The Five Marks are closely linked to Matthew 28.16–20 in which the Apostles are sent to make disciples of all nations. However, *missio Dei* calls us to see God at work in mission not just in the sending of the Church as Christ's Body, but also in the work of the Spirit beyond the Church in the lives of those the Church is sent to witness to. Equally, the Church's evangelistic message will not simply be a call to personal salvation, but to participation in the coming Kingdom of God.

Alistair McGrath uses the analogy of bridge building for an approach to Christian apologetics (1992). The idea is to look for 'points of contact' in the lives of others which can then become a place to 'build a bridge' to the Christian faith. McGrath's approach assumes these points of contact would be universal states of the human condition in quite a modernist and I think Christendom-orientated way (Hollinghurst 2010, pp. 171–5). McGrath has since adapted his approach to take more account of a postmodern post-Christendom context (2012), but the metaphor of bridge-building is helpful when thinking about *missio Dei* and evangelism. The advocates of *missio Dei* believed it was present in pre-Christendom mission but lost in Christendom so it is helpful to look at examples of God's mission from creation through the early Church to understand what it might look like in digital evangelism after Christendom (Hollinghurst 2010, pp. 101–52).

A key figure in the early development of *missio Dei* was Justin Martyr. He had prior to his conversion studied under Platonist philosophers and saw links between Greek philosophy and Christianity so that Greek philosophy was preparing people to receive Christ. He based this on the identification of Jesus as Logos, John 1.1–14, and the concept of the Logos in Greek philosophy. Heraclitus had taught that the Logos was the source of life and the fire in all the living. This idea had been developed further by Plato. For Justin, the philosophical concept of the Logos was also linked to the pre-existence of Christ who was the Logos with God in creation. He also believed that 'seeds of the Logos' dwelt within everyone enabling them to perceive what was good and true, but only partially until the full revelation came in Jesus (see for instance Justin's first 'apology' chapter 44 and the second 'apology' chapter 10). Therefore, he could speak about Jesus within the terms of Greek philosophy, believing God to have inspired its partial revelation. Likewise, Paul speaking in the Areopagus, Acts 17. 21–34, used the debate the philosophers had started among the Greek intelligentsia about whether there was one God as opposed to many. In this he quoted Greek poetry in praise of Zeus as the one creator God as a way of connecting the ministry of Jesus to the concept of the true creator God (Hollinghurst 2010, pp. 122–4). Similarly, evangelists in the Roman province of Asia, largely modern Turkey, used statues of Orpheus, a shepherd with a sheep over his shoulders, to link the well-known story of Orpheus who returned from the land of the dead, to the story of Jesus the 'Good Shepherd' who rose from the dead (p. 138). These all worked on Justin's principle that in pagan religion and culture there were seeds of the Logos pointing to Christ. Digital evangelism will need to be looking to find the 'seeds of the Logos' within elements of online culture and within the social media groups it hosts. This theme is explored further in John Drane and Olive Fleming Drane's chapter in this volume. Digital evangelists will need to be looking for concepts and ideas that can be bridges to explore Christian faith. As with other areas of the online world these will often relate to the offline world, but within online contexts may be explored more openly.

Possible 'seeds' may be climate change; people who feel nature is spiritual; animal welfare; art music and poetry; the battle of good and evil in video games or games in which players build civilizations; the repeated sharing of news on social media and the problems of 'fake news'; explorations of the supernatural; the politics of race, immigration and globalization; human nature as witnessed in online community, and many more.

Finding Jesus Online

The importance of 'third spaces' has been a common theme in talking about digital media. It also surfaces in research into how people from non-Christian backgrounds come to faith and become part of Christian communities. First, contact between Christians and non-Christians is more likely to lead to faith conversations if that connection exists in more than one place. In terms of digital evangelism, then, the people you are part of several groups with are more likely to have faith conversations with you. Therefore, it is better to invest in groups that have related interests rather than try and spread yourself across very different groups. This is also a more natural form of behaviour and will be more likely to mean Christians online are part of groups they naturally enjoy. Second, in offline situations, the journey from faith conversations in secular spaces to joining a Christian community is for most people with no church background too big culturally. Projects that succeed in enabling people from non-church backgrounds to become members of a Christian community often do so by creating a third space in which relationships can be deepened but also subjects linked to things like spirituality, worldview, life choices etc. can be explored. These spaces are not usually explicitly about exploring Christianity. For example, the Alpha course is probably too far to be an effective third space (Hollinghurst 2010, pp. 225–44; Hollinghurst 2013). In digital evangelism this principle is perhaps easier to apply; joining and creating groups online is simple. Little commitment is required, making it easier for people to experiment with groups. Groups that already exist may also be suitable forums to explore the kind of discussions third spaces are designed to facilitate. The challenge is to connect online groups to offline churches. However, many places have things like Facebook pages for local residents, enabling the possibility that online relationships can become offline ones too. Online Christian communities may help this or online enquirers' courses. Several churches are currently running online Alpha and it will be interesting to see how that works. Setting up more culture-specific courses online will be much easier than doing so offline. Of course, some of the social aspects of an offline enquirers' course cannot be replicated, but there are other things like ease of joining that are advantages.

The 'digital Jesus' can therefore be encountered online in three ways and these are key to digital evangelism within a holistic approach to mission as God's mission. He will be found through his Body the Church being online both through broadcast media like Christian websites and videos and through individual Christians building relationships via social media. However, Jesus will also be found online working within non-Christian social media groups, memes, videos and webpages. Discovering what the gospel is in each context will be based on how Christians and non-Christians explore these 'seeds of the Logos' and from them form an indigenous Christian faith in which people can become disciples of Christ.

The advent of digital media is a communications revolution within a paradigm shift from the modern the postmodern era. It makes communication interactive and empowers people to be authors of media in a way that was not possible before. It is creating online communities with a secondary orality that is part of an increased diversification of culture and calls for new modes of intercultural mission. It builds bridges between people offline and enables them to explore online things they would not have the courage to explore otherwise. As such it is a major force in forming our culture and our lives. If Christians want to be a part of forming our culture and allowing God to transform people's lives, communities and world, then digital evangelism is going to be increasingly important.

The medieval mystic Teresa of Avila wrote a famous prayer expressing the idea that we were the way the world encountered Christ, and in a similar vein we are the presence of Christ online. This is how we are online. This is why how we are online is as important as what we tweet, message or share. Yet it is only part of the story. *Missio Dei* tells us that as we go online Jesus is already there waiting to be found. He will already have been sowing 'seeds of the Logos' in the videos, social media groups, webpages and posts. These are there not just for those of no faith to find Christ, but if Christians are to be effective in digital evangelism, they, too will need to find Jesus online, see what he is doing and join in.

References

Anglican Communion, 2012, 'Five Marks of Mission', www.anglican-communion.org/mission/marks-of-mission.aspx, accessed 17 June 2020.
Bosch, D. 1991, *Transforming Mission*, New York: Orbis.
Campbell, H. A. (ed.), 2013, *Digital Religion*, London: Routledge.
Cray, G., 2004, *Mission-Shaped Church*, London: Church House Publishing.
Donovan, V., 2001, *Christianity Rediscovered*, London: SCM Press.
Dubois, E. and Blank, G., 2018, 'The echo chamber is overstated: The moderating effect of political interest and diverse media', *Information, Communication & Society*, Vol. 21, No. 5, pp. 729–45.
Finney, J., 1996, *Finding Faith Today*, London: Bible Society.
Fiske, J., 2011, *Introduction to Communication Studies*, New York: Routledge.
Gillani, N., Yuan, A., Saveski, M., Vosoughi, S. and Roy, D., 2018, 'Me, My Echo Chamber, and I: Introspection on Social Media Polarization', in WWW 2018: The 2018 Web Conference, April, pp 23–7.
Gould, M., 2013, *The Social Media Gospel*, Collegeville: Liturgical Press.
Heelas, P., Davie, G. and Woodhead, L. (eds), 2003, *Predicting Religion*, Aldershot: Ashgate.
Hollinghurst, S., 2003, *New Age, Paganism and Christian Mission*, Cambridge: Grove.
Hollinghurst, S., 2010, *Mission-Shaped Evangelism*, Norwich: Canterbury Press.
Hollinghurst, S., 2013, *Starting, Assessing and Sustaining Pioneer Mission*, Cambridge: Grove.
Hunt, S., 2004, *The Alpha Enterprise*, Aldershot: Ashgate.
Interworldstats, 2020, *The Big Picture*, www.internetworldstats.com/stats.htm, accessed 17 June 2020.
Kraft, C., 1991, *Communication Theory for Christian Witness*, Maryknoll: Orbis.
Krotoski, A., 2013, *Untangling the Web*, London: Faber and Faber.
McGrath, A., 1992, *Bridge-Building*, Nottingham: Intervarsity Press.
McGrath, A., 2012, *Mere Apologetics*, Grand Rapids: Baker Books.
McLuhan, M., 1964, *Understanding Media*, New York: Mentor.
Mijnverhaalmetgod, 2012, 'I Met God Online', www.youtube.com/watch?v=i7pWcO7cHxo, accessed 12 November 2014.
Mishna, F., McLuckie, A. and Saini, M., 2009, 'Real-World Dangers

in an Online Reality: Examining Online Relationships and Cyber Abuse', *Social Work Research*, Vol. 33, No. 2, pp. 107–18.

Ong, W. J., 2012, *Orality and Literacy*, revised 30th anniversary edition with additional chapters by J. Hartley, Oxford: Routledge.

Pettit, T., 2012, 'Media Dynamics and the Lessons of History: The "Gutenberg Parenthesis" as a Restoration Topos', in Hartley, J., Burgess, J. and Burns, A. (eds), *A Companion to New Media Dynamics*, Oxford: Wiley-Blackwell, ch. 3.

Pew Research Centre, 2018, 'The Age Gap in Religion Around the World', www.pewforum.org/2018/06/13/the-age-gap-in-religion-around-the-world/, accessed 17 June 2020.

Robards, B., 2018, 'Belonging and Neo-Tribalism on Social Media Site Reddit', in Hardy, A., Bennett, A. and Robards, B. (eds), *Neo-Tribes: Consumption, Leisure and Tourism*, Cham, Switzerland: Palgrave Macmillan, pp. 187–206.

Sklar, J., 2020, '"Zoom fatigue" is taxing the brain: Here's why that happens', *National Geographic*, 24 April.

Smith, P., 2015, *Online Mission and Ministry*, London: SPCK.

Suler, J., 2004, 'The Online Disinhibition Effect', *CyberPsychology & Behavior*, vol. 7, no. 3, Mary Ann Liebert, Inc., pp. 321–6.

Talking Jesus, 2015, 'Talking Jesus: Perceptions of Jesus, Christians and evangelism in England', https://talkingjesus.org/wp-content/uploads/2018/04/Talking-Jesus.pdf, accessed 17 June 2020.

Taylor, B., 2016, *Sharing Faith Through Social Media*, Cambridge: Grove.

Thompson, N., 2011, *Effective Communication*, Basingstoke: Palgrave Macmillan.

Turner, V., 1969, 'Liminality and Communitas', in *The Ritual Process: Structure and Anti-Structure*, Chicago: Aldine Publishing, pp. 94–130.

Underwood, H. and Findlay, B., 2004, 'Internet Relationships and Their Impact on Primary Relationships', *Behaviour Change*, Vol. 21, No. 2, pp. 127–40.

Von Buseck, C., 2010, *Net Casters: Using the internet to make fishers of men*, Nashville: B. & H. Publishing Group.

Wang, H., 2009, 'Nonverbal Communication and the Effect on Interpersonal Communication', *Asian Social Science*, Vol. 5, No.11, pp. 155–9.

World Council of Churches, 2011, Pontifical Council for Interreligious Dialogue and the World Evangelical Alliance, *Christian Witness in a Multi-Religious World*, www.oikoumene.org/en/resources/documents/wcc-programmes/interreligious-dialogue-and-cooperation/christian-identity-in-pluralistic-societies/christian-witness-in-a-multi-religious-world, accessed 9 September 2020

6

The Sword of the Cherubim: Do Algorithms Inhibit Our Access to the Knowledge of God?

Google and *Missio Dei* in a Digital Age

CHRISTIAN GRUND SØRENSEN

The Sword of the Cherubim

The preliminary metaphor of the cherubim relates to Genesis 3 and depicts a situation where access is denied. When Eve and Adam were expelled from the Garden of Eden they were not only expelled from the presence of the Almighty and the unfallen version of creation. They were also restricted from the information needed for perceiving the full truth about the 'Answer to the Ultimate Question of Life, the Universe, and Everything', to borrow from Douglas Adams and his novel *The Hitchhiker's Guide to the Galaxy*.

Having eaten from the fruit of the tree of the knowledge of good and bad (Gen. 3.6) a new individual understanding emerged. It may be argued that the orthodoxy of the pure, unfallen worldview was suddenly challenged by a legion of different concepts, ideas and assumptions. Choice, in a radical sense, came into the world. It can be argued that Genesis 3 'is a comment on the ontological insecurity that derives from freedom' (Nyoyoko 2016, p. 223). And such richness of choice in a philosophical understanding may constitute the scaffolding of the heterodox thinking so typical of late modernity.

Humans were due to circumstance separated from the immediate vision of God. In a broad Christian theological understanding, humans are therefore incapable of reaching back to the original, intuitive and infallible recognition of God. In the biblical narrative, angels, cherubim and a flaming sword prevent Eve and Adam from returning to Paradise lost.

Within the scope of this chapter, the cherubim and the flaming sword refer to the limitations and information curation facilitated by the search engine companies and similar agents. Just as Eve and Adam were prevented from accessing divine knowledge, so sons of Adam and daughters of Eve may encounter technological restrictions in acquiring essential knowledge of the divine. This analysis is based on the Pauline assumption that 'Consequently, faith comes from hearing ...' (Rom. 10.17a). So, the reception of information is a philosophical, theological and psychologic prerequisite of faith in an adult and reflected sense.

This chapter presents and discusses some of the challenges posed to the Church in relation to mediating the gospel of Christ in a digital age. The central focus will be on three aspects:

1 The biblical and theological necessity for unbiased information in the process of mediating Christ.
2 The challenge of bias in relation to the Search Engine Manipulation Effect and a discussion of the role of search engines as curative agents in mediating Christianity.
3 Suggestions for the Church to establish a sustainable strategy and framework for mediating Christ in a digital environment.

The chapter is interdisciplinary in nature and depends on insights from theology, digital theology, sociology, computer science, ethics and epistemology. Realizing that the topic of algorithmic bias is part of a rapid technical, ethical and political development, the focus is not primarily on describing current algorithms and curation. Present search engine tactics may suddenly become obsolete. Nevertheless, the overall strategy, the paradigmatic approaches and the dynamics of persuasion in the tailoring of information is certain to be relevant for the foreseeable future.

The Knowledge of God

How can we know about God? This is not only the postmodern question posed to any traditional religious authority, it is also the existential echo of the 'quid est veritas?', 'what is truth?' of Pontius Pilate on Good Friday (John 18.38). The question of epistemology is always at the centre of our reflection on God. How do we know?

Fundamentally, what humanity needs may be enlightenment through information and by the Holy Spirit. While the work of the Holy Spirit is intangible from a perspective of immanence, the material content and mediation of information is not. From a traditional Christian perspective, the Almighty did not rely on spiritual revelation alone, or even the incarnation of Christ, but also put trust in the biblical tradition and in the explanations and testimonies of the saints, known as τό εὐαγγέλιον, the Good News. In classic Pauline theology a prerequisite for faith is information and knowledge. 'Consequently, faith comes from hearing …', signifying that faith is not merely a construct of imagination and emotion, but rather a consent to and applauding of revealed truth.

Thus, the dissemination and reception of the knowledge of divine matters is a vital part of the *missio Dei* in a digital age – and in any age. However, fundamental changes in paradigm are happening and some of these are related to the way in which information and knowledge is encountered. This chapter discusses the role of algorithms in search engines and the impact of these in relation to acquiring the knowledge of the Good News and encountering the Church.

In the twenty-first century, a growing complexity and societal dependency on symbol-analytic work generates immense amounts of digital data. Matters of the Spirit and the Church are by no means exempted from this. Finding the right path in the spiritual journey of life may require valid digital signposts along the way in the form of reliable information. Therefore, digital findability is a vital aspect in the *missio Dei* in a digital age.

To an increasing extent, search engines impact the way in which we approach and select information. The verb 'google' has become synonymous with information seeking and retrieval, suggesting answers to many everyday questions. At the same time, information is shaped differently and at times adheres to a questionable concept of truth.

In the fields of mathematics and computer science, results are most often perceived to be precise. Imagine, however, a situation where 2 + 2 does not every time equal 4; if the result of this simple addition varies from 3 to 5, determined on past mathematical skills and achievements. Furthermore, this bias is not transparent or immediately predictable for the mathematician. The mathematical example is not related to complex theories of quantum physics. Surely, everyone would discard this imaginary calculator. We expect data processing to be reliable, transferable and replicable.

However, in other cases it is more difficult to confirm valid truth, especially when this is dependent on probability or less precise aspects of Aristotelian logic such as the rhetorical enthymeme, dependent on persuasion: it is a 'degenerate ... deduction that can be applied to contexts where conclusive proof is not to be had' (Burnyat 1996, p. 99). Here results may for good reason display a margin and may still be credible. This is a conceptual example of the inconsistency of data feedback present in search engines such as Google.

For example, a customer searches the web for a new car. Not all cars can be presented. The search engine then may select colour dependent on the viewer's past history of car watching. Anyone with a previous preference for blue cars, in the future will be exposed to a further majority of blue cars, though some cars will still have the colour expression of the rest of the rainbow. Now, imagine asking this blue-car biased person about the prevailing frequency of car colour. In a closed environment, this person may give an answer literally coloured by the biased impression of reality, thinking most cars are blue. In fact, the prevailing car colour in Europe is white.

These examples visualize some simple consequences of information that is neither untruthful nor fully true. They are expressions of a tailoring that creates a search engine bias. Some of this selected information is hardly very significant or problematic. The assumption of most cars being blue hardly diminishes quality of life unless the user is a professional car manufacturer or car dealer. For some people, some lack of precision is insignificant. In the mathematical example, consequences may be more critical. Since the bias is of a more fundamental nature from an ontological point of view, consequences may scale accordingly. A bias in 2 + 2 may result in tax and banking systems breaking down, loss of trust in in society and social unrest. If 2 + 2 is biased the consequences in a space mission will most likely be fatal.

The Trustworthy Computer

It is apparent that search engines, Google in particular, to some extent have taken over much of the authority from pre-digital sources such as teachers and books and other written material. Perhaps some of this new authority stems from not only the search facility in itself, but also from the machine.

Computers are often associated with a certain kind of consistent and trustworthy function. Few people add up their bank statement manually once the balance has been carefully calculated by the bank computer system. As long as the correct information is inserted, the computer is expected to output infallible truth, at least in the fields of economy and engineering. In the area of self-driving cars there is less trust in digital technology; however, many drivers already rely on an adaptive cruise control and traffic sign recognition. B. J. Fogg argues that the traditional role of the computer as a tool of humans is changing into roles of authority:

Today computers are taking on a variety of roles as persuaders, including roles of influence that traditionally were filled by teachers, coaches, clergy, therapists, doctors, and salespeople, among others. We have entered an era of persuasive technology, of interactive computing systems designed to change people's attitudes and behaviours. (2003, p. 1)

Digital systems gradually supplement or occupy the roles of human experts. From the perspective of *missio Dei* it is interesting that Fogg includes clergy and teachers in his analysis or vision of computer agency. The tasks of preaching and teaching have historically been in the centre of human wisdom and competence. Now it is suggested that competence and authority is transferred to technological platforms. For Fogg this is not a rejection of traditional knowledge, but rather a reflection on the role of technology in mediating and facilitating it.

From a Church perspective, it often appears natural to engage in technoclastic grievances, claiming that everything was better in the media situation of the goose feather or the mechanical typewriter. In its radix, the computer understood as a simple Turing-machine is neither good nor bad but, like humans and most tools, it includes the moral potential of both or none. However, in the era of the information society, digital technology is connected not only with communication and commerce, but also with culture. Everything that is important to humanity should be important to the Church. The computer as the basic technological tool and icon of the age is highly important and should be treated accordingly. Ecclesiastical festivals might meaningfully be complemented with multimedia and coding events, celebrations of gratitude in a digital age.

Challenge of Digital Media

In the twenty-first century, much printed tradition has given way to digital information. While the Holy Spirit is presumably unaffected by this, it is obvious that the divine Good News of the millennium often comes in a digital mediation.

Therefore, the mission of the Church is not least to facilitate access to this vital Good News through available platforms and applications. At the same time, it is correspondingly vital that this information is relatively truthful and unbiased, since faith comes from hearing.

We are, however, conceptually and to some extent chronologically at the end of an era of a first naivety in relation to unbiased information search and information presentation in digital media. Naturally, critical source evaluation has always been central in handling any media type, books, TV, newspapers. However, the fascination of new media in some cases appeared to overshadow the critical sense. This has changed gradually by our familiarity with digital media. As our point of departure, we now often distrust digital information, and simultaneously experience society and individuals as often quite dependent on digital media. The optimistic notion of an 'information superhighway' or an 'infobahn' of the final years of the last millennium has been replaced by an experience-based recognition, that information in a contemporary digital landscape may also be fluctuating, untruthful, or biased.

Obviously, this is the nature of every media type mediating the Good News, new or ancient. However, for every new media type it is imperative to develop literacy and interpretational skills as well as understanding the dynamics of the medium. The future of the Church is dependent on accessible, truthful information. This, however, proves problematic in a digital age. Digital communication differs from other media types in several important aspects.

Media types	Oral tradition	Manuscript	Printed	Broadcast	Digital
Agency	Dynamic	Fixed	Fixed	Fixed	Dynamic
Personalization potential	Yes	No	No	No	Yes
Bias check potential	Little	Yes	Yes	Yes	Little

Table 1: Properties of selected media types.

This model displays selected media types and selected properties. First, agency is defined as either dynamic or fixed. Dynamic agency describes that content may be altered or reshaped in the course of the communicative event. In an oral tradition, the storyteller reads the reception of their narrative with the audience and selects content and style from experience. This is also the case with the experienced preacher, able to leave the manuscript and follow a lead of intuition. Thus, there is a potential for personalization and, from a negative perspective, the spontaneous, fluctuating character of speech makes it difficult to rewind and check up on unwanted bias. At the same time, an oral narrative is hardly expected to be unbiased. The colouring of content by the narrator is part of the communicative event and often appreciated.

Media in writing or broadcast is generically fixed. Words do not change in written material or files of sound or video, except for rare cases of forgery. Information is fixed, and therefore there is no possibility for personalization. These media types are not interactive. There may be reflections on target groups and recipients but, after codification, they remain unchangeable. Therefore, these media types may be subject to extensive check for bias or coercion.

Digital media are different. In appearance, digital media often resemble written media or broadcasts. There are, however, fundamental and important differences. Digital communication may well be fixed in its appearance, but at the same time be dynamic in relation to agency. Where first-generation websites, etc., provided a consistent text, now digital media may generate numerous diversified texts. This personalization is motivated by a tailoring intention aiming, at its best, to serve and please the user. The personalization potential in some ways supersedes the potential in the oral tradition since digital mediation also supports the implementation of various types of multimedia. At the same time, the potential personification and tailoring of content, creating different texts complicates the bias check. The textual material for such a control may be less consistent and therefore less trustworthy.

In this article, it is not the intention to discuss all aspects of general possibilities and problems of interactive digital media and bias. Focus is on a corner of the challenge, the role of search engine bias. As suggested in Table 1, the issues of personalization and limited bias check are generic of all interactive digital media types. However, in the context of search engines such as Google, consequences may be extensive, not least for searches in relation to spiritual matters and religion.

Search Engines

Since the 1990s, the growing number of binary information elements passing the user has grown at an ever-increasing speed. Gordon Moore's prediction of the doubling capacity of silicon chips every two years has proved to be not too far from reality. The number of web pages has grown from approximately 17 million in 2000 to a staggering 1.6 billion in 2018, a growth of almost 10,000% (Internetlivestats 2019). Obviously, the immense number of individual web pages shows the need for extracting the needle of relevant information from the haystack of miscellaneous messages.

Several search engines eventually emerged. The early search engines such as Yahoo and Altavista were to a large extent based on the topical categorization known from classical library ontologies. This was helpful for many well-defined organizations such as churches. For example, the category 'church' at a given location would be helpful in navigation to the index page of the local church. By 2001, Google's rating and ranking system for web pages was launched. The Google algorithm, however, proved to be superior in daily use and gradually became the favourite search engine for the average digital user.

The Google algorithm relies less on categorization and more on the results of an immense number of deep searches analysing website content. This does not always construct the same neat, manageable categorization as the older search portals did, but proves to be very helpful in finding even text strings in documents located in a subfolder at a website. This was previously quite difficult.

Google is the dominant market leader of general search engines with a frequency of 92% of searches. The challenger, Bing, is down to 2.6% (Statcounter 2019). From this perspective, it is obvious that Google almost monopolizes general searches. Google's position as the globally preferred search engine has remained quite unchallenged for at least a decade. At the same time, the volume of content accessible through digital systems has increased exponentially, making access to vast data volumes of different text and media types possible. This access, however, is by no means intuitive, since information is not labelled, categorized or structured coherently. Questions of navigation, procurability and overview are essential.

Besides the general search engines, different specialized search services help navigate more limited digital environments. Apart from spin-offs from Google such as Google Scholar, these search engines are most often linked to a certain multimedia or social media environment. For example, YouTube is owned by Google but offers an apparently independent search engine whose results are limited to media content available in the YouTube universe. Facebook also offers an independent search engine with queries limited to relevant social media content. Linkedin is owned by Microsoft but features a search engine that is apparently unrelated to Bing. Even smaller digital knowledge providers such as The Kaj Munk Research Center feature a search engine, mostly facilitated for deep searches in archives of rare documents and manuscripts.

Search engines can be discussed from several observation points, the most important being the aspect of the seeker and the aspect of the provider.

- The seeker requires relevant, valid and current information. The seeker wants to find. This could be a seeker looking for a church or a meaningful presentation of the Good News.
- The provider has a message or commodity to share. The provider wants to be found. This could be a church wanting to present itself or a meaningful presentation of the Good News.

Success is where the objectives of both seeker and provider are met. This could happen in several ways as described in Table 2.

Type	Description	Requirements
Direct traffic	Precise address in browser	Knowledge of address and idea of content
Referral traffic	Link from other website or media	Link from other content providers
Search engine traffic	Link from search engine result	Reasonable priority in search engine results

Table 2: Properties of different types of online traffic.

Table 2 shows several ways to access a website. Direct traffic refers to a seeker accessing a website directly. This requires knowledge of the website or a certain expectation from the seeker, as well as a manageable domain name or the user previously bookmarking the web page. Referral traffic is important since it is recommended from another website. This could be from a portal such as a central denominational website or the website of a partnering organization or a grateful user. Search engine traffic is linked from e.g. Google and obviously it is important to be easily findable in the search engine suggestions. Referral traffic and search engine traffic are highlighted because they are largely dependent on external factors.

Customization and Bias

Since search engines are meant to unite seeker and provider there should be little conflict in relying on them for the good of the Church. However, this is not entirely the case. Different aspects of search engine dynamics challenge this perceived benevolent partnership, some of them being:

- A major challenge for the search engines is to limit the number of results, constantly optimizing the suggestions through seeker customization and personalization. The manageable cognitive load of information processing is limited.

- The business model of search engines is advertisements, and priority in visual placement may promote bias. Research suggests that fundamental conflicts of interest appear: 'In general, interests will be aligned on some products and misaligned on others ...' The identity of the products misrepresented depends on the actual business model (Burguet, Caminal and Ellman 2014, p. 45).
- The role of political and/or religious restrictions and censorship. In the recent corona virus pandemic, some public authorities appeared reluctant to allow the publishing of critical health information. Also Facebook filters and fake news monitoring may limit the potential 'to connect people with information they are likely to want to consume, by making some items easier to access than other items, resulting in a personalized stream of content [that fails to offer] users a set of alternatives to choose from' (Rader and Gray 2015, p. 175).

In this chapter, only the first of these challenges is discussed at length. There is an ongoing discussion about the role of the Search Engine Manipulation Effect (SEME). To what extent do search engines present accurate, trustworthy, unbiased results? The precise answer to this question is for several reasons difficult. It is, however, apparent, that problems do exist:

In relevant academic research, there is little disagreement that Search Engine Manipulation Effect is a factor to be reckoned with. Algorithms that filter, rank and personalize online content are playing an increasingly influential role in everyday life. Their automated curation of content enables rapid and effective navigation of the web and has the potential to improve decision-making on a massive scale. (Epstein 2017, p. 42:2)

The dynamics that facilitate effective searches on Google build on the implementation of search history and user segmentation in order to procure the statistically most desired suggestions. This means, in a limited interpretation, that anyone with a history of great interest in blue cars will be presented with a majority of blue cars every time the person searches for a car. If this person aims to continue this rather special interest, the tailoring of results is both helpful and unproblematic. If, however, the person wants to change or expand interest, it will take some time to recalibrate the search engine to the new search preferences.

Evolution psychologist B. J. Fogg argues in his discourse on persuasive technologies that this very tailoring of content to the individual user is the foundation for some of the positive implementations of digital systems in information management:

> Tailoring technologies make life simpler for computer users who don't want to wade through volumes of generic information to find what's relevant to them. Psychology research has shown that tailored information is much more effective than generic information in changing attitudes and behaviors. (2003, p. 37)

While Fogg's argument is undoubtedly true, it also poses some important questions about validity and bias. Even with the best of intentions tailoring, customization and personalization produces individualized search results that may in turn be biased in the sense that the user receives more of the same. At the same time the algorithms of Google are not transparent or public. There is little possibility for observing the search algorithm functions apart from conducting case studies. One such study undertaken for the sake of this chapter is discussed below.

From the user's point of view search algorithms may be perceived to be unbiased; however, the combination of data together with tailoring some kind of bias can be expected. As Goldman suggests:

> Due to search engines' automated operations, people often assume that search engines display search results neutrally

and without bias. However, this perception is mistaken. Like any other media company, search engines affirmatively control their users' experiences. (2008, p. 121)

Big data is collected on a routine basis from numerous systems and applications. Google search algorithms are not restricted to obtaining data from search history alone. Data from Gmail, YouTube and even social media might be taken into consideration. In recent years, these volumes of big data are being monitored by a system of general artificial intelligence searching for the not-so-obvious correlations between data sets, and may be paving the way for bias in future search results. This has been highlighted by Baeza-Yates, who observes:

> From a statistical point of view, bias is a systemic deviation caused by an inaccurate estimation or sampling process. As a result, the distribution of a variable could be biased with respect to the original, possibly unknown, distribution. (2018, p. 54)

The algorithms of the search engines are the black box of the Search Engine Manipulation Effect (SEME). Engineering these systems has a primary focus on function and seeker satisfaction. 'However,' Epstein argues, 'algorithms are human inventions, and as such, characteristic human elements – such as intentions, beliefs, and biases – inevitably influence their design and function' (2017, p. 42:2). In this understanding algorithms often feature an undesired, anthropomorphic psychological component: 'Recent research has shown that society's growing dependence on ranking algorithms leaves our psychological heuristics and vulnerabilities susceptible to their influence on an unprecedented scale and in unexpected ways' (p. 42:2).

The pilot study below highlights some of the problems around search engine customization and bias. Does the Google search algorithm constitute a conceptual sword of the Cherubim, as this article suggests? It may be possible that algorithms both facilitate and complicate our access to knowledge of God.

Pilot Study: Three Religious Characters on Google

With the objective of shedding light on the role of past search activities, a pilot study was executed during three weeks in April 2019. Three pseudonymous profiles were created on Google, intended to fit three fictive people of three different worldviews, a traditional Christian, a traditional Muslim and an atheist. For the sake of ensuring as valid data as possible, the fictive people were designed as quite narrow-minded representatives of their respective worldviews. All user behaviour targeted topics of perceived interest in the relevant worldview.

Obviously, designing these roles is ethically problematic since they display a reductionist approach to people of different worldviews. However, this reduction of complexity was necessary to create a reasonably valid test environment, avoiding factors that might influence the test result too much. Another concern was also to trigger the Google algorithm to record inconsistencies in search results. With a limited three-week test period it was imperative that a bias could be revealed quite soon and results would not be polluted by random search traffic.

The pilot study is consciously limited in volume and complexity. The research question is simple: is it possible to confirm a search engine manipulation effect in the field of religion? Manipulation is here not linked to coercion but rather to tailoring and curation. The study does not take account of other worldview representations and it does not enter into a discussion about semantic fields and definitions. The research design is based on the informed judgement that a small and simple study is sufficient to confirm or discard the assumption that the SEME may actually be confirmed in using Google for searches on religion. The study is therefore not designed to research a quantitative and aggregated effect.

The three characters were completely fictive and were designed as digital test dummies.

- Ludvig From represents a traditional Christian. His name is inspired by a fictive theology student in Søren Kierkegaard's writings. 'From' means pious in Danish.

- Achmad Islam represents a traditional Muslim. His name is inspired by a Google search on common Muslim names. 'Islam' means submission in Arabic.
- George Nocreed represents a traditional atheist. His name is a conjunction of 'no' and 'creed'.

As mentioned, the objective of creating these characters was to reveal a possible religious bias in the Google search engine. The research question is this: to what extent do past activities on Google and YouTube affect search results when posing the common question: 'Who is Jesus?' This question is chosen since it may be relevant for all three fictive characters.

However, in order to calibrate the fictive users for a religious or worldview labelling in Google, it was necessary to develop a limited search history. Internet sites, news providers and video-feeds from You Tube and several queries on Google should feed the algorithm with suitable information.

	Pseudonymous profiles:			
	Ludvig From	Achmad Islam	George Nocreed	Interactions
News sites	Christianity Today	Al Jazeera	Atheist Republic	3 stories
YouTube	How to read the Bible	How to read the Quran	How to read Nietzsche	3 videos
Google ?	What is Eucharist?	What is jihad?	What is atheism?	5 links
Google ?	Christian prayer	Muslim prayer	Atheist ethics	5 links
Google ?	Christian home	Muslim home	Atheist home	5 links
Google ?	Christian household and rules	Islamic household and rules	Atheist household and rules.	5 links

Table 3: Table of prior interactions.

Interactions are made as close to each other as possible, recognizing the difference of the three worldviews. Obviously, atheism stands out as not being a religion. Interactions resemble the number of times the fictive character is accessing a certain content, this being recorded in the personal Google profile, which was totally empty until now.

	Pseudonymous profiles:			
	Ludvig From	Achmed Islam	George Nocreed	Change
Question	Who was Jesus?			
Objective	40%	40%	45%	5%
Critical Western	10%	10%	15%	5%
Christian	25%	25%	20%	5%
Sectarian	15%	10%	10%	5%
Jewish	10%	10%	10%	Unchanged
Muslim	–	5%	–	5%

Table 4: Table of categorized results.

Table 4 shows the results of the common query. From a human perspective, it is obvious that the question 'Who was Jesus?' may be answered differently from the premise of the different worldviews. However, an unbiased digital algorithm should display no such difference, merely displaying the same results, which have been assessed and ranked as helpful for everyone.

However, the results indicate that the suggested webpages are not identical. From a list of the first 20 not-sponsored results, there is a notable though not overwhelming difference. The categories of websites are defined thus:

• Objective: refers to websites dedicated to offer ideally unbiased information, such as Wikipedia, encyclopedias, university content and similar.
• Critical Western refers to websites promoting an atheist or generally critical approach to religion.

- Christian: refers to websites of an Evangelical or Catholic origin and content.
- Sectarian: refers to websites linked to groups such as Jehovah's Witnesses with a connection to the Christian tradition.
- Jewish: refers to websites of a clearly Jewish origin and content.
- Muslim: refers to websites of a clearly Muslim origin and content.

As shown in Table 4, the differences are notable though not groundbreaking in this pilot study:

- The Christian character is presented with more sectarian content and a reasonably high level of Christian content. No Muslim content.
- The Muslim character is presented with a reasonably high level of Christian content but as the only one also with definitely Muslim content.
- The atheist character is presented with less Christian and sectarian content. There is more objective and critical Western content. No Muslim content.

The conclusion of this pilot study is not very surprising, but yet revealing. After just 26 selected interactions on Google the three fresh profiles appear already to be involved in a certain search engine bias. This bias is hardly political or religious in nature, but originates from the search engine algorithm analysing and curating content on the basis of search history.

The Tailored Truth

This limited pilot study shows differences in search results depending on search history. Differences may be expected to be more substantial over time, feeding the algorithm with not only 26 selected interactions, but dedicating years of search history to calibrating a more or less unique pattern.

A recent Danish newspaper article discussed a similar question. High school teachers experience students not being able to locate the same content as they do. Due to search algorithms and search history, students and teachers are fixed in different knowledge subsystems. Chairman of High School Teachers Union Niels Jakob Pasgaard argues, 'As a society it is a problem that we no longer encounter the same things when we are seeking information. You will not be challenged in your beliefs, you will become spiritually lazy' (Mainz 2019). Obviously, encountering a common corpus of information might also limit critical engagement. Political propaganda in a totalitarian society is an example of this. However, Pasgaard's argument may still be valid since tailored content appears even more persuasive than omnibus communication.

Even though Pasgaard probably does not use spiritual in a Christian, Trinitarian sense, his message is also meaningful, not least in the perspective of *missio Dei*. Trustworthy and relevant information is a prerequisite for both professional and existential reflection. Spiritual laziness is the result of remaining unchallenged or even confirmed in one's own preconceptions.

Reflecting on the hermeneutic circle (or spiral) of Hans-Georg Gadamer (2004), it is obvious that new information in some form must be present to challenge old preconceptions. In Hegelian philosophy of history, it is evident that an antithesis must be present in order to challenge the existing thesis. Only then is it possible for a synthesis to develop, ideally integrating aspects of old and new. In general learning taxonomies, it is imperative that the student is given access to new material intended to be internalized and operationalized accordingly. More of the same usually produces more of the same, a presumption that problematizes the usefulness of the tailored truth.

It is probably safe to assume that tailored information may unwillingly reduce the potential of acquiring new knowledge and inspiration, thereby minimizing the potential for a renewed religious reflection. In this sense, algorithms on one hand maximize the potential for acquiring relevant knowledge, and on the other hand make it less likely to enter into the heterogenic discourse of faith change.

Search Engines Define Religion

One question is: how do search engines inhibit or curate the access to knowledge of Christianity and, eventually, to the knowledge of God? Another question is: how do search engines actually have an agency in shaping thoughts of religion and faith? In his book *The Third Reformation: From State Christendom to Google Buddhism* scholar in religious studies Morten Thomsen Højsgaard connects the dominant Danish conception of Christianity with the technology of the Google search engine. The background for suggesting this connection is the postmodern cultural inclination for exploring the world through a digital lens. 'What is the new understanding of Christianity in a changed, modern world, where Google has replaced Gutenberg, all about?' (2011, p. 65).

'Google Buddhism' is for Højsgaard a description of a late modern religiosity supported by two pillars. The first pillar refers to contemporary epistemology. Knowledge stems primarily from easily accessible digital sources, identified as Google. The second pillar is related to Buddhism and the tradition of yoga. Buddhism in the West is characterized by being a religious system that requires little active devotion. It is a religion helpful for the religious who reject the conception of a personalized God.

While the concept of Google Buddhism obviously eludes the inherent complexity of modern religion, it meaningfully combines two important aspects of faith: the actual religious outlook, and the medium by which this is mediated to the individual.

Google here symbolically represents the complex mix of information which the individual himself in this electronic age seeks out, finds, and assesses quality. As it is for the great search engine it is for faith in the electronic age, you do not seek in depth but for the most accessible, popular, applied, or recommended. Google is in this respect not only an image but also a very important co-player in the religious search. People who today want to seek out information about religion, in practice first and foremost use search engines like Google to seek knowledge about the content of faith. (Højsgaard, p. 129)

Højsgaard suggests it is not possible to define Western Christian belief as Church Christianity or Bible Christianity. The latter was historically often the characteristic of Christian revivals. However, today 'Google religion' or 'Google Christianity' may be helpful descriptions that capture the current state of religion. As a consequence of the algorithmic curating of information discussed above, this view of faith and religion may, however, prove to be reductionist in nature. The tailored truth may inhibit the individual from achieving a genuine religious encounter. At the same time it may be questioned whether Højsgaard's expression is entirely helpful since search engines and information curation are not limited to any one company or structure.

It is also possible that Højsgaard's perspective is somewhat too negative in relation to the Church and the *missio Dei*. Obviously, 'Google Buddhism' has been a dominant religious approach for some time, at least in Denmark. At the same time the art of googling cannot be unlearnt, and the Eastern religiosity that is now dominant may soon be considered old fashioned and obsolete. In that sense, Google may be both a threat to traditional religion and also a medium for anonymously exploring the depths of Christianity, with the caveats of tailoring discussed above.

The Sword of the Cherubim

Having confirmed that search engine bias is a challenge, how may the Church surpass the Cherubim? In the biblical narrative, it may appear impossible to surpass. The paradise of unbiased or non-manipulatory information is forever lost. However, biblical narrative also informs us, that it may be possible to change these presumably manifest and unchangeable conditions by looking in other directions. The incarnation of Christ is an example of divine out-of-the-box thinking. Paradise lost is accessible not through going back past the Cherubim, but by changing the game altogether, paving the way along Calvary for the New Jerusalem instead of the outdated Eden.

It is not likely that the Church or any church will be able to influence or persuade Google or other major digital platforms and/or systems into releasing unbiased information about Christianity. Even with the best of intentions, the complexity of search engine algorithms does already, or will soon, derail the single computer scientist, leaving much of the future development and calibration to artificial intelligence implementing big data. Humanity will most likely lose the overview. One reason for this is that the human capacity for handling complexity does not grow in correspondence with the growth of data and digital content. Search engine developers will therefore need to compress information even more in a funnel-like conceptual construction allowing a modest fraction to reach the seeker.

At the same time political and/or religious interests might for different reasons inhibit unbiased searches. Some regimes in the Middle East and the Far East appear to work in this direction. But also the media companies themselves may have incentives to limit search possibilities. Some political and religious groups are not welcome on YouTube, which is actually part of the Google Corporation. In case of political turmoil, it is not entirely unthinkable that Google may at one time exclude groups or views from the general search engine as well. That could be certain religious groups, or limiting the search possibilities altogether to secular worldviews only, not to favour one religious group for another.

The Church, however, is not without viable possibilities in this situation. It needs to supplement the digital information strategy for local churches, denominations and organizations away from a single-tracked strategy of dependence merely on dominant search engines. As mentioned in Table 2 (properties of different types of online traffic), general search engines are only one possibility. Direct access traffic is helpful together with referral traffic from friendly sites.

- Churches may design applications that are interesting enough for people to download and keep an eye on, using a mobile device. Apps should support easy access to lots of faith-relevant material, ideally linking to a common bank of Good News content.
- Churches may cooperate with positive, perhaps nonreligious stakeholders in building a scaffolding of referral traffic that is not vulnerable to changes in search engine politics or dynamics.
- Churches may develop a common, ideally international web-based platform for connecting with spiritual content and information.
- Churches may develop websites suited for bypassing the current search engine bias. This may be done adding specific content and headlines supporting findability for users with a different search history.

Some of these suggestions require cooperation. Churches need to express humbleness towards theological, political, historical and hierarchical differences.

How can we know about God? *Quid est veritas?* – 'So faith comes from hearing ...' (Rom. 10.17a). Enlightenment in a Christian sense includes the enlightenment of information as well as the enlightenment of the Holy Spirit. The Good News may flow from many media streams, even digital ones, but it definitely springs from the same analogue well in Christ.

References

Baeza-Yates, Ricardo, 2018, 'Bias on the Web', *Communications of the ACM*, Vol. 61, No. 6.

Burguet, Roberto, Caminal, Ramon and Ellman, Matthew, 2014, 'In Google we trust?', *International Journal of Industrial Organization*, Vol. 39, March 2015.

Burnyat, M. F., 1996, 'Enthymeme: Aristotle on the Rationality of Rhetoric', in Rorty, A. O. (ed.), *Essays on Aristotle's Rhetoric*, Berkeley, CA: University of California Press.

Dyck, Ed, 2002, 'Topos and Enthymeme', *Rhetorica: A Journal of the History of Rhetoric*, Vol. 20, No. 2.
Epstein, Robert, Robertson, Robert E., Lazer, David and Wilson, Christo, 2017, 'Suppressing the Search Engine Manipulation Effect (SEME)', *ACM Hum.-Comput. Interact.*, Vol. 1, No. 2, Article 42.
Fogg, B. J., 2003, *Persuasive Technology: Using Computers to Change What We Think and Do*, Burlington, MA: Morgan Kaufmann.
Gadamer, Hans Georg, 2004, *Truth and Method*, London: Continuum.
Goldman, E., 2008, 'Search Engine Bias and the Demise of Search Engine Utopianism', in Spink, A. and Højsgard, Morten Thomsen, *Web Search*, Berlin, Heidelberg: Springer-Verlag.
Mainz, Pernille and Nissen, Marie, 2019, 'Google-søgning kan spænde ben for elever', *Politiken* 11.11.2019.
Nyoyoko, Vincent G., 2016, 'The fall story of Genesis 3: the experience of the culture of alienation, anxiety & violence', in Ejizu, Chris (ed.), *Readings on Religion & Culture in Africa*, Port Harcourt, Nigeria: M & J Grand Orbit Communications.
Rader, E. and Gray, R., 2015, 'Understanding user beliefs about algorithmic curation in the Facebook news feed', in: Begole, B. and Kim, J. (eds), *Proceedings of the 33rd Annual ACM Conference on Human Factors in Computing Systems*, Seoul, Republic of Korea.
Zimmer, M. and Spink, Amanda (eds), 2015, *Web Search: Multidisciplinary Perspectives*, Information Science and Knowledge Management series, Vol. 14, Berlin, Heidelberg: Springer-Verlag.

Web

www.internetlivestats.com, 2019www.statcounter.com, 2919.

7

Interactive Technologies, *Missio Dei* and Grassroots Activism

ERKKI SUTINEN AND
ANTHONY-PAUL COOPER

Introduction

Interactive technology refers to digital technologies that have been designed with the active roles of users in mind, rather than designs based mainly on users receiving (authorized) information from digital outlets. The example of television clarifies the distinction between non-interactive and interactive technology. While early television users were merely consumers, following programmes at times determined by broadcasting companies, an interactive television experience transforms the experience of users, so that as well as consuming content, they also take on the roles of producer or director: they are able to participate in interactive programmes at times of their own convenience, with the inclusion of their own interventions, reactions, or even self-recorded materials.

In contemporary society, grassroots activist movements, exercised globally as a counter-phenomenon to hierarchical, centralized power houses, whether religious, political, economic or digital, have drawn their influence from, largely, interactive technology. Even in the era of intentionally analysing individual users' digital behaviour, often without their consent, and misleading others by misusing the results, interactive technology is a unique way for an individual activist to get their voice heard by billions of people within a time frame that never before in history was even remotely possible.

Of course, grassroots activism can require courage and risk taking. While a previously unknown person can become a global influencer within a matter of a few months, their activism can be detected using technology much more quickly than previously. This can lead to such activists being targeted and disrupted; in countries with disputable human rights records, this can include risk to personal safety. Even in countries with strong human rights records, this targeting can take the form of trolling and harassment. However, while interactive technology can pose risk to out-of-the-mainstream users, its potential benefits can surpass the expected troubles, especially when stakes are high and critical. Young climate change activist Greta Thunberg, for example, has been the target of much personal criticism online, but has persevered in pursing climate change reversal.

The tension between those in power and those far from it is also evident in the realm of faith. While traditional religions have tended to use equally traditional channels to spread their messages, individuals living at the grassroots of the fast-changing world, and usually far from the epicentres of the religious elite and decision making, have started to challenge the conventions, in both content and communication.

This chapter focuses on the challenge of designing interactive technologies that could facilitate constructive, active and, possibly, critical participation for those historically considered to be only passive consumers and followers of their faith. Therefore, the chapter offers suggestions for how current and future interactive technologies can and ought to facilitate the participants of *missio Dei* in their activism at the very grassroots.

While the ideas, considerations and recommendations of the chapter have been devised for the Christian context, many of them could be applied and contextualized to other faiths as well.

The Why: Background and Motivation

The success story of Christianity is far from straightforward. In his book, church historian Bart D. Ehrman (2018) investigates how a grassroots movement led by a few uneducated young men in the remote, rural periphery of the Roman Empire transformed within a short timeframe of a few hundred years into a dominant influencer of society – the Catholic Church.

Ehrman identified two main factors for the success of the early church: the movement was exclusive and missionary. By being *exclusive* the Church distinguished itself from most other religious traditions at the time and thereby precluded the possibility that Christianity could be added as another ingredient of a pluralistic religious identity. To be a member of the Church demanded a rejection of one's earlier affiliation.

By being *missionary*, the Church actively aimed at reaching out of its limits. During this time, there were other faiths that were exclusive, such as Judaism. However, that faith's inward orientation meant that its adherents tended not to place a focus on proselytizing: it did not grow in the same way as Christendom, in terms of members.

The interplay of being closed by exclusive participation or membership, and open by a missionary approach had two noteworthy consequences. First, within the Church, the exclusivity of faith that a Church member was supposed to spread to those outside defined their religious *identity*: a Christian was an active messenger of their unique message. Second, the emerging movement assumed a societal role outside of the boundaries of its communities. This engagement was motivated by an *ethics* based on the premise that the teachings of the Church needed to encompass all aspects of its members' lives. The spiritual message was to concretize in their lived experiences. These two consequences highlight clearly how, even in its beginnings, the Christian movement was focused on the application of communication techniques to spread the message of Christ to others. Jumping ahead to Christianity in the twenty-first century, this remains clear to see – as digitization extends possible approaches to communication, so too technology can extend this core Christian behaviour of relaying the core message of faith to others.

In his book on the Church at the grassroots level (in Finnish: *Ruohonjuurikirkko*), bishop emeritus and former missionary to Tanzania, Erik Vikström (1986) shows how Christianity, from its very beginning since the early refugees – not missionaries – in Antioch (Acts 11.19–26), was spread to new people in new areas by ordinary people who migrated to places outside the Christian presence, to work in their profane roles, destinies and professions. Their identity as exclusive-inclusive Christians, together with their strong ethics, attracted attention and curiosity among the people they met naturally in their professional lives and societal encounters. As a result, Christianity found new terrains as a fruit of latent grassroots activism. *Missio Dei* has been a bottom-up movement where the Holy Spirit has opened unplanned, improvised (with no strategy) new encounters where ordinary Christians end up opening and sharing their faith with other people.

The non-denominational movement that in many ways characterizes emerging Christianity in the global South adds force to the grassroots activism inherent within the Church. Although many non-denominational churches would be based on volunteerism, they still follow a top-down, strategic organization. So, while many of them, especially locally organized independent parishes, can be labelled 'grassroots' relative to the traditional, hierarchically and globally organized churches, their activism might not be that of the members, but rather delegated to them from the elders or local leaders.

According to Bosch, the concept of *missio Dei* reinstates mission as the very attribute of God (1991, pp. 389–90). *Missio Dei* assumes that the essence of the Church is its mission which consists of a range of actions that are instances of the triune God's work in his creation, 'a movement from God to the world'. Rather than being the goal of mission, the Church is an instrument of God's continuous mission in the world. Technology is but one of the tools that is available, as an example of God's continuous creation, to the Church when it participates in *missio Dei*. The core of the *missio Dei* is exclusive as coming from God alone and derived from the nature of God, whereas its individual concretizations, instruments and tools reflect the context where it takes place; they need to change with time and place so as to be able to convey the unique message in a way and form meaningful to the context. The conventional use of digital technology was to make the existing processes in a given application area of technology more *efficient*, measured by the consumption of time, space or other resources, without rethinking or changing the processes, or activities, themselves. Further, conventional use of digital technology was based on *automating* a given set of user processes. For example, the early booking systems of airlines helped in ensuring that the planes could fly with as many passengers as possible; or an invoicing system of a given business made sure that the losses caused by delayed payments were as low as possible. In the church realm, various member record systems would monitor the attendance of the members at church events, and remind them of key events, when need be. However, while all these systems would streamline existing services, the activities themselves did not change: the planes flew the same routes, the companies continued offering the same services, and churches were busy running the activities and social provision they had done for the past two millennia. Undisturbed by the digital technology, it was business as usual.

This is in stark contrast with the modern application of digital technology – in which case we mostly speak of interactive technology – which aims to positively change, rethink and even *disrupt* existing processes and users of the technology. While automation might come with occasional incremental innovations of user processes, disruption calls for radical innovation that changes the processes themselves. In this sense, the key question arising in the context of the modern application of digital technology is how technology might enable new *designs* to enable offline activities and processes to happen in completely different and potentially transformative ways. When considered in this way, the question might shift, for example, from how churches might better count, administer and contact attendees using automation to how church might exist in an online space and thereby increase participation, access and inclusivity. In the secular example, social media has been a key tool for customers to exchange their observations of the airlines, their prices and services, and has thus helped to change the global airline business, forcing many traditional airlines into bankruptcy. Similarly, data science allows a company to analyse its customer base using invoice data, and thus renew their services or offer novel or tailor-made products to existing customers. In the same way, this modern and transformative approach to technology might see churches eventually closing their existing places of gathering and worship as the use of new and redesigned physical or digital spaces enables the Church to better provide for existing demand while also reaching and catering for previously undiscovered demand. Indeed, early instances of this phenomenon are already beginning to emerge, albeit under forced conditions, at the time of writing this chapter. The Covid-19 pandemic which has caused loss of life and large-scale disruption around the world has seen churches in many countries close their doors and switch to an online-only mode of operation with only days to plan. As the pandemic is ongoing, it is unclear what long-term effects this experience might have on church use of technology. However, early qualitative research conducted in three countries (Cooper et al. in press 2020) has found the Church to be responsive and quick to adapt to new uses of technology, often making great use of the laity in designing the offering of online church content. The process of user-centred re-design, or co-design, not only offers the potential for increased participation (in business services in the secular examples and in worship in the church example) but also for increased democratization. Where technology responds to the requirements of users, it enables users to partake in direction-setting and help shape the service/offer they receive. In this sense, this modern approach to applying digital technology to the Church offers a unique opportunity to not just better cater for churchgoers, but to more closely involve them in religious life and practice. In the specific example of the Covid-19 pandemic, it has allowed churches to continue to offer regular, but renewed, acts of worship, at a time where physical gatherings have been impossible.

Hence, *missio Dei* calls its instrument, the Church, to a radical and continuous change, and it is clear that one of the critical methods today is the disruptive use of interactive technology; one that requests creative and open-minded design. This demands an openly innovative curiosity about how interactive technology reshapes the concretization of mission, and therefore the Church, at its very grassroots, the loci where *missio Dei* concretizes into actions.

Let us have a look at how the distinction between automation and disruption of services applies to church leadership. While Christianity has established itself in various organizational forms, most of them are highly hierarchical, contrary to the historical success story of Christianity as a bottom-up movement of *missio Dei*.

From the viewpoint of digital technology, a hierarchical organization can be made more efficient by automating its key processes with conventional, database-type solutions. In comparison, a distributed organization grows in effectiveness by distributed digital designs that are implemented in comprehensive co-design schemes with groups that consist of stakeholders and diverse actors, not only leadership and management. Co-design is understood within this paper to be a subset of participatory design, in which designers collaborate with users in the design of digital technology. In their paper on the application of co-design to the design of services, Trischler, Pervan, Kelly and Scott observe that co-design allows the combination of 'customer insights into latent user needs and in-house professionals' conversion of promising new ideas into viable concepts' (2018, p. 75). In the same way, co-design has the potential to allow those involved in grassroots missionary activity to contribute their needs for digital technology into the design process from the outset.

The conventional approach leads to conservative technical solutions that fix the current processes, although as automated versions; for example, through efficient membership managements systems. By contrast, the co-design process starts from heterogeneous stakeholders' expectations, wishes and requirements and crowd-sources the demands into services that might not have existed before at all; say, mobilizing Christian education as gamified Bible studies led by those earlier ignorant of, but inherently interested in, the Bible.

At a time when the world is transitioning from the information age into the imagination age, or the fourth industrial revolution or Life 3.0 (Tegmark 2017), the role that interactive technology could have for the Church increases dramatically. The different characterizations of the arising era are based on the changes that robotics and artificial intelligence have for extending the human situation. Whereas during the information age the main focus of technology was to provide faster access to information (that remained *outside* of its user, as an object), the imagination age shifts the focus to *integrating* the human and the machine, allowing for subjective technology that transforms its user to break the limits of not only time and space, but also many restrictions caused by disability or other binding conditions, paving the way to living the imagined. Whereas the business models of the information age were based on information as the main source of livelihood, the imagination age lives from what can be imagined, which early examples like the games industry give indications of.

Hence, while today's technology, answering to the challenges of the information age, still mainly provides faster access to available, often authorized information, in the near future it will be actively transforming the whole landscape of information. The process takes place in a dynamic information ecosystem at the limits of our existing knowledge, opening a horizon for imagination that is enhanced by artificial intelligence. In theological terms, this shift parallels the transition from sermon to prophecy, from doctrine to vision, from dogmatism to mysticism, from ecclesiology to eschatology. These shifts are all aligned with moving from information transfer towards shared imagination and dialogue; from 'to' to 'in between'.[1]

The Who: The Owners and Customers of the Challenge

This section outlines the field and different conceptualizations of digital theology. As an emerging field of research, definitions of digital theology have not yet reached a steady state and new definitions continue to be proffered, providing various nuances and details around the scope of the subject. One early definition proposed that digital theology was 'an integration of technology into the understanding of the concept of God and the nature of religious ideas' (Kolog et al. 2016, p. 1). A more recent definition (Phillips et al. 2019) provided a more comprehensive definition of this emerging field, which included four levels of digital theology:

> DT1: The use of digital technology to communicate or teach theology as a traditional academic subject (p. 37).
> DT2: Theological research enabled by digitality or digital culture (p. 38).
> DT3: Intentional, sustained and reflexive theologically-resourced engagement with digitality/digital culture (p. 39).
> DT4: A prophetic re-appraisal of digitality in the light of theological ethics (p. 39).

Since digital theology is, inspiringly, still in its infancy, our relatively loose and still evolving definitions allow us to focus this section on one aspect, or task, of digital theology, namely design. The design challenge takes us to the most critical factor of most successful design processes: identification of the targeted users. In our case, they are the grassroots activists participating in the *missio Dei*.

In keeping with other digital theology research studies, this chapter considers theology in a broad sense to encompass areas of study and research which may be found in any typical university department of theology and religion – 'from the analysis of religious texts to issues of faith practice' (Cooper et al. forthcoming, p. 4).

Digital Theology as a Design Exercise

As part of digital humanities, digital theology as a research field can be described as having a threefold agenda:

1 To apply existing digital interactive technologies and/or design novel digital interactive technologies to challenges of a theological nature.
2 To apply theological principles or methods to the design or evaluation of interactive technologies.
3 To pursue digital theology research as a hybrid of theology and interactive technology research.

As a meeting point of theology and digital technology, we can position various tasks of digital theology within a quadrilateral. Table 1 gives examples of four different research approaches that all tackle the same challenge of expressing faith-related issues on an interactive platform, making use of social media.

	Objective	Subjective
To know or understand	(Post-)positivistic questions of What: What are the emerging faith-related contents within social media in a given context at a certain time period?	Interpretive questions of Why: Why do certain faith-related concepts emerge in social media?
To change	Design agendas of How: How to design an AI-based social media platform that would support a constructive faith-related dialogue?	Emancipatory agendas of Do: Make a digital community that would allow Christians under risk to share their faith.

Table 1: Examples of questions and agendas of digital theology research.

In this chapter, we focus on digital theology from the viewpoint of *designing* digital technology for a particular, theologically defined challenge, i.e. to facilitate *missio Dei* by an interactive platform for grassroots activism. In fact, we consider digital theology and digital design to be so closely interrelated, we propose that professionals in digital theology, often referred to as digital theologians, could just as accurately be referred to as theological designers.

Thus, we regard digital theology as a research, development and innovation (RDI) field that investigates, designs, implements and productizes tools, techniques and approaches that allow their users to express faith by digital means. The definition, inspired by the constructive agenda of one of digital theology's parents, computing, emphasizes the field's function *outside its own realm*, to those that are in need for expressing their faith digitally, but in a theologically sound way. This function cannot be handled without the contribution of the other parent of digital theology, i.e. theology. Hence, digital theology lies in the intersection of computing and theology, but cannot be reduced to one of them only.

Users in the Design Process

For the innovative design aspect, we need to identify the users that we have in mind for what we design. The users will have a key role in defining the goals of the interactive technologies, and the criteria for evaluating their functionality, i.e. how well the technologies meet with the required goals. Evaluation can also be formative, in which case representatives of the users need to be available throughout the lifetime of the designed technologies.

For the purposes of an innovative design process, we divide the users into individuals and communities, like churches or congregations. Users can be categorized as laypeople and clergy, both of which might be technologically conservative or radical. The same applies to communities of two kinds: traditional or denominational, and non-denominational. It is important to note that a technologically conservative church or individual might be theologically liberal, or the other way around. However, within this chapter we focus on users that can be described as activists – a grassroots activist might be an individual layperson, an ordained minister or an instance of a larger community. What all the activists share is that they have assumed an active role in their geographically or digitally determined surroundings; they have a mission – an instance of the *missio Dei* that they participate in – that they are struggling to fulfil.

All of the user groups have theological issues, tasks or challenges where they require interactive technology. In this chapter, we focus on the expectations or goals of activists. We can summarize the expectations as follows:

> *messaging*: clarifying or making sense of the exclusive, core message;
> *inviting*: requesting other people to join them; and
> *practising*: exercising and promoting the life required by their message.

In some cases, users might struggle with self-contradictory or conflicting expectations. The phenomenon leads to trade-offs. For example, while 'inviting' requires visibility and publicity, the concerns for privacy might limit the ways that activists can or are willing to invite others in a carefully monitored digital environment.

Similar trade-offs apply to 'messaging' and 'practising'. While an exclusive message helps activists to profile or distinguish themselves within a diversity of digital contents, too sharp a message might lose the point of a wider Christian gospel. In a Christian praxis, the key principles of faith, hope and love might have almost opposite manifestations based on what is correct behaviour in a given cultural environment, i.e. what is interpreted as an act of faith, hope, or love.

There are also disparities between individual and community users. Independence versus dependence can concretize within different dimensions, such as religious, political, economic, or digital independence. A Christian community might enjoy religious freedom, far away from that of its individual members. Churches can be public and visible, whereas some individual Christians might prefer to stay invisible. An activist Christian community might consist of enforced passivists.

There is one further division among the users which is important to keep in mind. A primary user of a given technology, whether an individual or a community, is a user who cannot carry out – at least without unnecessary difficulty – their tasks without the technology in question; the technology is crucial for a meaningful function. A secondary user may use the technology but would succeed in their tasks almost equally well without it. To take an analogy from a musical instrument: a church musician in several churches is a primary user of an organ, whereas a laymen's music group as its secondary user might perform without it. A grassroot activist should be a primary user of any functional technology that we might call *missio Dei technology*.

The various aspects and trade-offs of the users, described briefly above, are manifest or latent in the users' expectations from the technologies to be designed. Usually, it takes a long time to form the trust between the users and the designers, needed for designing disruptive technologies by following a radical innovation process. Without such mutual trust, users' shyness, modesty, concerns, or, occasionally, their outright resistance, will lead to conservative solutions. This could serve to make innovation incremental, if achieved at all.

The How: User Requirements Elicitation, Design Science, and the Method of Correlation

In this section, we introduce the approaches and methods that would inform how to design an interactive platform for grassroots activism in *missio Dei*. The key for any design assignment is the identification of users, as discussed in the previous section. In particular, we will develop a novel design approach that combines methods of designing interactive technologies with the theological method of correlation as understood by Paul Tillich. We will investigate the two approaches one after another, and conclude by developing an integrated design approach that makes use of both.

INTERACTIVE TECHNOLOGIES, *MISSIO DEI* & ACTIVISM

Designing Interactive Technologies by Participatory Approaches

In any design process the targeted users of the artefact to be designed have a key role to play. In early approaches, especially when automating existing processes without any idea or demand for rethinking them, the users were mostly regarded as objects in the design process. The designers and researchers collected data by observing, surveying, or interviewing users and later analysed that data. The process has usually been rather straightforward and linear and therefore has occasionally been referred to as the waterfall model or, more typically, as user requirements elicitation.

Conversely, designing interactive technologies that have a disruptive impact on the users' organization requires a significantly stronger role from the users. Participatory design is the generic term for design approaches that engage users. Participatory design centres on considering how to involve users in the design of digital technology and is rooted in the ideals of democracy in design (Smith et al. 2017, p. 65). Any participatory design process is by nature iterative: the hopefully constructive yet critical feedback of the users leads to taking a few steps back in the design process. Often, even the very demand for the technology is far from clear at the outset of the process and would certainly change over the iterations. Therefore, users, or their representatives, are also engaged in analysing the user requirements throughout the process. A participatory design process does require a certain level of awareness of the potential of the technology or else the users would not be able to envisage its potential and could settle for less advanced products than are possible.

Co-design belongs to the family of participatory design. It requires a high level of active participation from a range of stakeholders throughout the democratic design process. Therefore, everyone needs to contribute to the concept, functionalities, user interfaces, user experience and interaction design. It is not necessary for everybody involved in co-design to have technical experience; indeed, in their paper on the new

landscapes of design, Sanders and Stappers note that one definition of co-design is 'the creativity of designers and people not
trained in design working together in the design development
process' (2008, p. 6). Co-design demands the use of agile methods that can instantly show early prototypes of the final design
artefacts. Indeed, agile methods fundamentally place control
in the hands of users, through daily user-designer interactions
(Highsmith 2002). Taking this approach allows design projects
to fail fast where a design project has taken the wrong approach
or has failed to correctly grasp the user requirements, while
allowing successful projects to evolve quickly from merely
usable products to fully developed solutions. Other schools of
design are, among others, contextual design, emphasizing the
importance of societal and cultural factors in the design, and
inter-contextual design that is contextual design taking place
in parallel in diverse contexts, where the processes are intertwined with each other.

While co-design sounds an appealing design approach,
because of its pragmatic, engaging practices, it might be exercised as a regulated and almost technocratic process. The end
users, or for that matter other co-designers, might be either only
superficially heard or listened to as much as the questions posed
to them would allow them to speak up. The recent emphasis
on empathy towards every participant in the co-design process,
however, is the key for designing successful, functional solutions. Empathy means that everyone in the co-design team can
assume the role of anyone else, to understand or interpret the
expectations of others, from within them, so that what cannot
even be listened to, because of missing dialogue or just plain
difference in the backgrounds, can anyway be heard or sensed
in another way.

To summarize, in the design process of interactive technology,
in this case specifically for the purposes of grassroots activists
participating in the *missio Dei*, a participatory approach aims
at ensuring the functionality of the end product or service.
That is, the digital outcome of the design process has to match
the original design question, as expressed in the requirements
which are refined over the iterative co-design process. This can

be lengthy – understanding the critical demand, or the original question, can be time-consuming work. Thus, participation in *missio Dei* by technology requires participation throughout the technology's design process.

Designing Theological Solutions Through Dialogue

To a certain extent, the process leading to a meaningful theological answer to an existential question shares similarity with the participatory design process. For example, empathy is a critical asset for theologians, the designers of theological answers, to understand the core of the existential question, so to frame and relate it to their theological expertise.

In what follows, we apply Paul Tillich's method of correlation (Tillich, 1951–1963, p. 8) to outline a process leading from existential questions to their theological answers. Tillich's scheme requires that a theologian be capable in both uncovering the often-latent essence of the question and finding a relevant, matching answer to it, a process that usually would require what we call a *theological design* process. In fact, the method of correlation is a functional cornerstone of digital theology, because it extends or reminds us of, depending on our entry point to theology, the task of theology as a design discourse. A digital theologian is a theological designer, who, in an existential dialogue, designs interactive technologies based on theological elaboration.

Individual existential questions are related to one's existence and its boundaries and, in particular, the finitude of an individual life. Usually, an existential question, or in fact the reason that causes it, can be understood as a small death that restricts oneself, whether illness, losing one's job, meaningfulness, or, of course, the loneliness at the proximity of one's own death.

Although existential questions have usually been understood as those of individuals, the recent discussion of, for example, climate angst or flight shame serves as a reminder of their more extended scope. Hence, we will introduce existential questions of and in the contemporary world that are beyond individual questions, and divide them into two additional categories.

Local existential questions are related to social aspects that threaten not only an individual's life but the life of those within a given social context. So, a local existential question is a shared one, although it concerns each of the social context's members differently. Causes for local existential questions are diverse, such as being detached from the community, marginalization, unemployment, outsiderness, being misled by disinformation, disbeliefs, dis-faith or the lack of digital freedom.

Local existential questions emerge due to fast changing social contexts, where the interplay of individuals' identities causes challenges to knowing one's changing self over the course of time (Harari 2018). At the same time, a digital social context makes use of the emerging opportunities of assuming a digitally fabricated role that releases one's physical restrictions or dis-abilities – significant causes for social isolation – to participate in the physical social life. The story of a physically disabled but digitally abled Norwegian, Mats Steen, is an example of local existential questions that can find digital existential answers (Schaubert 2019). Mats Steen's life is a paramount indication of the coming imagination age.

Global existential questions are related to the threat by, or the vulnerability of, the physical realm, like global virus outbreaks, causing threat for possibly the whole of humankind, or the changing climate making the planet as we know it vulnerable. A global existential question, even if is instantiated within an individual, is primarily a question shared by everyone on the planet.

Global existential questions force individuals to extend their scope from their individual or local existence to the global scene. An experience of frustration for not being able to influence a global threat transforms the question also into an individual and compelling one. At the same time, science as a globally available and advancing resource and community empowers especially younger minds' imagination to take up the universal challenge of mortality, an ultimate existential question since times immemorial. An illustration is the nine-year-old Laurent Simons, one of the youngest ever (almost) university graduates, whose dream is to solve the problem of mortality, by creating artificial organs (Peltier 2019).

While it is evident that a given existential question can belong to several categories, the three-level scheme reminds the theological designers, the experts in the method of correlation, to keep sensitive to ever arising, novel and diverse questions of existential character. Moreover, the interplay between the categories, like a global existential question related to climate change generating individual angst, is a challenge for designing interactive technologies that help to identify, alert on and prepare for a complex fabric of events and phenomena evoking existential questions, and essentially, to find answers for them.

The above categorization of existential questions mainly in the physical reality can be further refined to remind of similar questions in the physical and digital realm, as Table 2 shows.

	Physical	Digital
Individual	Fear caused by a terminal illness.	Fear of being digitally forgotten.
Social	Marginalization of one's ethnic group when migrating to a new country.	Experiencing hate speech in social media based on one's orientation.
Global	Threat by a virus outbreak.	Losing privacy in the internet.

Table 2: Categories of existential questions, with examples.

The What: Interactive Technology for *Missio Dei* at the Grassroots

This section presents early design ideas for a set of interactive technologies that can serve in grassroots activists' digital tool boxes in support of their participation in *missio Dei*. The design ideas can be further designed and implemented following the hybrid method devised on pages 143–4.

Design Ideas

Table 3 maps the set of early design ideas to both the background existential questions and the key tasks of grassroots activists in *missio Dei*, i.e. messaging, inviting and practising.

Design name	Existential question	Grassroots activist's primary user role
Mobile catechism	Dis-faith, ignorance	Messaging
Jesus on the lake	Climate	Inviting
Interfaith dialogue	Social detachment	Practising
Mission bottom-up	Identity	Practising
Sea of glass	Indifference	Messaging
From mediated to immediated faith	Belongingness	Inviting
Life before Death	Individual mortality	Messaging, practising

Table 3: Example designs for grassroots activists in missio Dei.

Mobile catechism refers to a learning community – rather than a traditional, physical learning material such as a book – using mobile technologies for understanding the core of the Christian message, by interactive navigation tools such as faith maps. The intended target participants of the learning community are especially located in the global South. In that region, mobile technologies, more than printed materials, are ubiquitous, even at the grassroots of society. Furthermore, theological education, while authoritarian, is sometimes lacking as a result of biases due to ignorance or inadequate training. This occasionally results in false promises and enforced domination by those exercising religious power. Mobile catechism would be a bottom-up community, pedagogically based on constructivism, where technology helps the members of the community in their elaborating together theologically sound, mutually agreed upon understanding of key faith issues.

Jesus on the lake is a virtual reality application for co-telling an interactive Bible story within extended reality. The first prototype was coded by a team of University of Turku students in the extended reality laboratory of the Department of Future Technologies. The users were represented by the experts from the Finnish Bible Society. The application can be used as a background story for discussing the impacts of the global climate change, bringing in the viewpoint of God's presence.

Interfaith dialogue is getting an increasing demand at the era of conflicts with religious bias, causing global marginalization and social detachment. Timo Honkela, a professor in human language technologies and artificial intelligence, has suggested in his book *Peace Machine* (2017) how modern technology can be used for purposes of peace building, rather than war making.

Mission bottom-up explores how technology facilitates shared leadership within the Church. This is a key prerequisite for grassroots activists, enabling them to participate in *missio Dei* on a delegated basis, with a full mandate also from their leaders. A bottom-up leadership strengthens the identity of the activists.

Sea of glass refers to the diversity and multiple layers essential for expressing faith in a way that is aligned with one's personality. It got its name from a student referring to the Sea of glass in Revelation 4.6 or 15.2 (NKJV): 'For me, it is important that a religious term, like Sea of glass, gives inspiration for thought and openness in interpretation.' A one-interpretation-fits-all approach, sometimes mixed up with the exclusive core message as a key for *missio Dei*, contradicts the inclusive, missionary demand for diverse interpretations, causing indifference among those invited.

From mediated to immediated faith is a design idea for digital theology at the Kairos, or the event of God's appearance to a human being. Interactive technology can intensify the immediacy of the Kairos experience. An experience conveyed by digital presence might extend that of physical presence, not only for digital natives, but also people in restricted personal or societal situations. For instance, not all people have the senses, like sight, needed to experience a physical sacred space, or means to get there.

Life before Death is a project for designing an application for those who are approaching their own death. It allows for exploring and elaborating the questions and answers of life and death by interactive tools.

While the design ideas above feature a diverse range of possible applications, they share the essential characteristics of interactive technologies for facilitating *missio Dei* as grassroots activism.

First, each of the design ideas is based on an existential question that has been collected in Table 2. For instance, while the extended reality version of the gospel story of Jesus in the storm might touch the contemporary concerns of the limitations of the planet and the unexpectedness of its climate, it can also relate to or release from the indifference or detachment of modern people from the existential questions of people at the time of Jesus, struggling with their fears of drowning and dying.

Second, each design supports activities, or activism, at and from the grassroots. It is important to note that *missio Dei*, as grassroots activism, can take place by messaging, inviting and practising, or any combination thereof, especially when the use of interactive technology is involved. For example, while *interfaith dialogue* calls for practising Christian love by respecting and being curious to those of other faiths, it can also help an open-minded Christian partner in the dialogue to deepen their own identity and interpretation of their faith. Thus, we can say that the application helps in messaging.

All of the sample applications are interactive, not just digital.

It means that they call the user to an active role of elaboration. While at times demanding, as for instance for a person weakened by the proximity of their own death, interaction might be the only way to engage people with their existential questions in a personal way. The function of digital theology applications, such as the ones described above, will often require a special sensitivity and empathy from the designer, necessitating strong contributions from representatives of the targeted users within the design process.

An example of the design process applying a hybrid method of participatory design and correlation

This section outlines one possible design scenario of an interactive technology for *missio Dei*. Because of the design team's continuous participation and contribution throughout the design, the stages of the process cannot be scheduled or devised beforehand. Table 4 illustrates how to apply a hybrid method to design the *Sea of Glass* application.

Aspect	Application in the Sea of Glass design process
Uncovering the existential question	Comprehending the importance of imagination and multiple interpretations of the key concepts of faith and how they make use of cognition for tackling existential questions
Identifying the co-design team	A team of inspired higher education students with diverse backgrounds in, and attitudes to, religion and discipline, plus a theologian and a software designer
Preparing the team	Team building for trust, story sharing and getting familiar with related software
Meetings with agenda	Agile development meetings over one year, using a focus group from a church outreach organization

Table 4: The aspects of a possible design process of Sea of Glass.

To make sure that the design process succeeds, it is important that the co-design team features a representative cross-section of grassroots users alongside the requisite competent individuals with design and development expertise. It is also vital that the co-design team organize their work as a goal-oriented project. Transparency of the process to the general public and challenging them to give feedback would yield better results than working only within the team. A particular challenge is to iterate the directions, plans and versions on a regular basis, including the very existential question that the design aims to find a solution to.

It is crucial that the iterations of the technical design and the search for the key existential question and its answer go hand in hand. They are but two complementary sides of one process, a hybrid of the method of correlation and participatory design.

Discussion: Interactive technologies release the multiple talents within the Body of Christ for *missio Dei*

A serious dialogue – at the grassroots, between people from different backgrounds – is an essential factor for the co-design processes. Dialogue is critical for the process towards mutual understanding: between a user and an expert and between laymen and clergy. A co-design process requires that everyone involved is able to contribute, though. This might be as demanding within a theological as in a technological process. Co-design requires co-learning. On the technical side, projects such as co-designing digital stories for HIV and AIDS education with students of poor Tanzanian rural schools indicate potential benefits as long as there is will, time and opportunities.

Correlation processes leading to theological answers to existential questions seem, on the face of it, very different to design processes aiming at interactive technologies for identified challenges. However, their similarities have allowed a hybridization of the two, scaffolding the iterative process aiming at co-designing interactive tools to be used by those participating in *missio Dei* in the contemporary world. Iteration as the modus operandi of the process is critical because the first expressions of existential questions and design challenges usually do not capture the final essence of either. Iterations require open discussion for constructively critical feedback, and open discussion requires trust.

In many ways, the disruptions facilitated by the brave and open-minded designs of interactive technologies have a parallel in the reformations caused by the grassroots activism of the *ecclesia militans* – a key instrument of *missio Dei*. But the parallels do not end here.

For example, platform economy – where a given digital service, like one for travelling, can been organized as an interplay of multiple, even competing service providers – can be seen as a technical parallel to the Body of Christ which consists of diverse members. In a digital age, or even more in the emerging imagination age, what would be more natural than to digitalize the mission of the Body of Christ as a set of services by which all the members of the whole universal, but distributed, church can participate in *missio Dei* by the unique strengths, talents and resources of each and every one?

Democracy is critical for maintaining a creative tension between the hierarchical and the grassroots approaches. Throughout its existence, the Church has suffered from the power play between clergy and laity. The balance of the creative tension requires that people with different statuses, assignments, experiences, knowledge and competences are, symbolically, at the same eye level. Interactive technology can contribute to the balance by offering a channel, occasionally anonymous, for both laymen and clergy to express their, at times, critical ideas and suggestions to the discussion. These would often indicate a weak signal of what needs to change within the Church, its theology or practice. The role of the clergy, in the open process at the grassroots, is to analyse the signals and correlate them to the theology in a way transparent and relevant to everyone concerned.

Democracy requires freedom and equal participation. Though

there are a myriad of diverse roles in a digital society, democracy requires digital freedom. In turn, digital freedom requires skills, competences and awareness of the opportunities and limitations of digital technology. It is important to consider here how digital technology has the power to increase both online and offline inclusion. By opening up spaces of theological thought and discussion online, technology allows individuals who might not otherwise have engaged with the discourse via traditional means a space to be heard and included. But this will only work to the extent that offline barriers or blocks to inclusion are mitigated and prevented from facilitating online disruption. This is why we should not underestimate the need of technological education for those involved in grassroots activism within *missio Dei*.

'Quality is the relevance of contents', is a voice from a retired vice-chancellor of a Mozambican university. Interactive technologies that would facilitate *missio Dei* need to make sense in the grassroots context that they will be used in. Participation throughout their co-design process is a key to their quality.

Conclusion

A few years back, on his sabbatical at St John's College, Durham University, the lead author Professor Erkki Sutinen was talking about digital theology with the Bishop of Cambridge. He suggested, or maybe envisioned, that the digital and thus the more interactive technology would have major impact both on the content and on methods of theology, comparable only to that of the printing press at the time of the Reformation.

The Reformation was a critical step to make the sacred, authorized texts accessible to lay people, in their own language, and that required the then equivalent technology of Web 1.0, i.e. the printing press, for sharing information freely.

The digital revolution takes us further, especially when understood as interactive. Besides providing access, the technology, in the spirit of Web 2.0, allows the users to become creators, or activists, if you will, having ownership well beyond access.

That will certainly have an impact on theology, not just in practice but also in content.

Missio Dei as God's continuous action within the world that he created concretizes at the grassroots, within the activism where Christians participate in God's mission. In this chapter, we have paid a particular attention to how it takes place by messaging, inviting and practising. We have also derived a method that scaffolds the process to design such technologies, as a hybrid of the theological method of correlation and the participatory design scheme of digital artefacts.

Further research is critical not only to analyse the phenomenon but to design tools that allow the grassroots activists to take their role as critically constructive in a way that animates the core of the Christian faith, ever crystallizing in the continuous elaboration by the enthusiasts that transform the message to the future generations. Maybe even in the form of Web 3.0, or Web x.0, for that matter?

Acknowledgements

The authors are thankful to Bishop Erik Vikström for his encouraging comments and critical observations on the manuscript.

Note

1 Erik Vikström refers to the common mistranslation of Acts 20.7 ('Paul ... spoke *to* them', NKJV), emphasizing information transfer, whereas the original Greek wording διελέγετο should be translated as talking or discussing *with*, pointing out the ambience of sharing or imagination between those who were together. The emphasis on mutual relationship or between-ness is the essence of interaction (and, thus, interactive technology) that, according to Vikström, is the work of the Holy Spirit; he refers to Taylor (1972). How the Holy Spirit makes use of the interplay of imagination and interaction by technology provides an interesting topic for further research, but also the renewal of church by technology.

References

Bosch, David J., 1991, *Transforming Mission: Paradigm Shifts in Theology of Mission*, Maryknoll: Orbis Books.

Cooper, Anthony-Paul, Jormanainen, Ilkka, Shipepe, Annastasia and Sutinen, Erkki, forthcoming, 'Faith Communities Online: Christian Churches' Reactions to the Covid-19 Outbreak', *International Journal of Web Based Communities*.

Cooper, Anthony-Paul, Mann, Joshua, Sutinen, Erkki and Phillips, Peter, 2020, 'Understanding London's church tweeters: A content analysis of church-related tweets posted from a global city'. Submitted for peer review.

Ehrman, Bart Denton, 2018, *The Triumph of Christianity: How a forbidden religion swept the world*, New York: Simon & Schuster.

Harari, Yuval Noah, 2018, *21 Lessons for the 21st Century*, New York: Spiegel & Grau.

Highsmith, Jim Robert, 2002, *Agile Software Development Ecosystems*, Boston, MA: Addison-Wesley.

Honkela, Timo, 2017, *The Peace Machine*, Helsinki, Finland: Gaudeamus.

Kolog, Emmanuel Awuni, Sutinen, Erkki and Nygren, Eeva, 2016, 'Hackathon for learning digital theology in computer science', *Modern Education and Computer Science*, Vol. 8, No. 6, pp. 1–12.

Peltier, Elian, 2019, '9-Year-Old Prodigy Pulled from College Over Degree Delay', *The New York Times*, www.nytimes.com/2019/12/11/world/europe/laurent-simons-university.html, accessed 15 May 2020.

Phillips, Peter, Schiefelbein-Guerrero, Kyle and Kurlberg, Jonas, 2019, 'Defining digital theology: Digital humanities, digital religion and the particular work of the CODEC Research Centre and Network', *Open theology*, Vol. 5, No. 1, pp. 29–43.

Sanders, Elizabeth B.-N. and Stappers, Pieter Jan, 2008, 'Co-creation and the new landscapes of design', *CoDesign: International Journal of CoCreation in Design and the Arts*, Vol. 4, No. 1, pp. 5–18.

Schaubert, Vicky, 2019, 'My disabled son's amazing gaming life in the World of Warcraft', *BBC News*, www.bbc.com/news/disability-47064773, accessed 15 May 2020.

Smith, Rachel Charlotte, Bossen, Claus and Kanstrup, Anne Marie, 2017, 'Participatory design in an era of participation', *CoDesign: International Journal of CoCreation in Design and the Arts*, Vol. 13, No. 2, pp. 65–69.

Taylor, John V., 1972, *The Go-Between God: The Holy Spirit and Christian Mission*, London: SCM Press.

Tegmark, Max, 2017, *Life 3.0: Being Human in the Age of Artificial Intelligence*, Westminster: Penguin.

Tillich, Paul, 1951, *Systematic Theology*, Vol. I, Chicago: Chicago University Press.

Trischler, Jakob, Pervan, Simon J., Kelly, Stephen J. and Scott, Don R., 2018, 'The value of codesign: The effect of customer involvement in service design teams', *Journal of Service Research*, Vol. 21, No. 1, pp. 75–100.

Vikström, Erik, 1986, *Ruohonjuurikirkko: Evankelioimisen teologia*, Helsinki: SKSK-Publishing Ltd.

8

Amusing Ourselves to New Life? Strategic and Pastoral Reflections on Digital Media and Contemporary Spirituality

JOHN DRANE AND

OLIVE FLEMING DRANE

Introduction

Neil Postman was one of the early pioneers of media studies, and in his influential book *Amusing Ourselves to Death* (1987; Postman 1993), he speculated about the impact of electronic media on both public and private discourse. In predicting future trends, he wondered whether it would be George Orwell or Aldous Huxley whose insights would prove to be correct. One of them foresaw a future dominated by the triumph of oppressive totalitarian systems (Orwell 1949), while the other imagined a scenario in which we would be the creators of our own catastrophe by distracting ourselves with a form of narcissistic consumerism in which almost everything became a plaything pandering to our natural tendency to choose self-indulgent idleness whenever the opportunity presents itself, creating a world in which we know the price of everything and the value of nothing (Huxley 1932). With the benefit of hindsight, we might argue that to varying degrees Orwell and Huxley were both right. From the perspective of his own time, however, Postman clearly believed that Huxley was the more right of the two and his analysis of societal trends is dominated by the conviction that the fabric of society was most likely to unravel into a dystopian tangle as a consequence of our own inclination to prioritize trivia. In this scenario, civic life would be diminished by turning it into a form of entertainment, and intelligent discourse would be downgraded by rewarding the sort of infantile behaviour that would distract us with infinite possibilities for our own amusement. Marx might have thought that religion was the opiate of the masses, but Postman argued that our own propensity for idle pleasure was more than enough to anaesthetize us from the realities of what he called 'culture-death'.

Many people today would agree with Postman's analysis, and point to the popularity of digital media as evidence of the cultural implosion of which he wrote. Spending hours looking at screens for no apparent reason other than their accessibility is indeed one of the temptations of this generation, and though online behaviour reflects the same capacity for good and evil that has characterized human relationships since the beginning of time, Christians can sometimes be especially negative about the online world. It is not uncommon to find even close friends insisting that they will never join us on social media and explaining their reasons in language that conveys some sense of moral superiority on their part, with the accompanying implication that our engagement with such things automatically diminishes our intellectual or spiritual maturity to such an extent that friendship itself could be under threat. Most have never heard of Neil Postman, but if they had they would agree wholeheartedly with his conclusion.

Much of what happens online is undoubtedly chaotic. It can be damaging and exploitational, and it certainly encourages the self-indulgence with time-wasting trivialities that Postman identified so eloquently. But from a theological and missional perspective we need to ask a different question. Could it be that the digital world might also be life-giving – not because Postman was wrong but because, regardless of its temptations, this is a space where we can encounter God? That might sound like a question akin to speculation about angels dancing on pinheads, but it is actually foundational for a meaningful Christian understanding of this environment. By implying that there are places where God cannot be found – in effect, no-go areas for the divine – we are not only creating significant missional prob-lems for ourselves but are arguably denying an essential truth of the faith. If, as the first page of the Bible claims, this is God's world then we must be able to find God at work in it. A core conviction of biblical faith is that everything relates in some significant way to God, which means that there is nowhere that God cannot be found. The online environment is not only a major element of today's culture: for digital natives it is the dominant culture, and if the psalmist could declare that God is present even in the depths of Sheol (Ps. 139.8) we can be certain that signs of God's activity – the *missio Dei* – will be found in our websites and social media posts. Since God is the life-giver *par excellence*, it must be possible to identify how, rather than amusing ourselves to death, God may be engaging us here in ways that can lead to new life.

Defining the *Missio Dei*

Olive has previously argued that 'While the notion of the *missio Dei* has become a catchphrase of contemporary mission the-ology, it is not always clear what it might look like in practice' (Fleming Drane 2017, p. 38). A report by the Global Mission Network of Churches Together in Britain and Ireland went further, characterizing it as a 'gloriously inclusive term' with 'an inherent, if not deliberate vagueness … It can be made to include anything under the sun that anyone considers a Good Thing' (Richards 2010, pp. 53–5). It follows that if we are to identify where God is at work in the digital – or any other – world, we need to have some idea of how we might recog-nize the *missio Dei* when we see it. Pragmatic understandings tend to be along the lines of 'find what God is doing in your context and then get alongside it', while theological explan-ations rarely focus on practical outcomes. Michael Moynagh's exposition of the theme is typical, with vague statements that nobody is going to object to, but which are hardly transparent in relation to offering much guidance as to what the *missio Dei* might amount to in practice: 'Mission is ... not a consequence of God's being. In God's will it is fundamental to God's being' (2012, p. 121).

That sort of definition surely raises a further (and more fundamental) question, namely how can we identify something as the work of God? Spiritual discernment clearly plays a part, but what if our vision is limited by our previous experience and expectations? In particular, when we look for signs of God at work from an existing perspective that is defined by what is already familiar to us from the world of conventional ecclesial religiosity, are we in danger of imprisoning God in a circumscribed space that is determined by our own assumptions of what we think God *should be doing* – something that can often amount to little more than what we are prepared to approve of because it is within our personal (or institutional) comfort zone?

Exile is a fashionable metaphor for the state of today's church among both academic and popular writers (at least in the global North) and is helpful to many (Brueggemann 1997; Frost 2006; Bell 2008; Thompson 2010; Beach 2015; Cox-Darling 2019). At the same time, it easily becomes a way of perpetuating a limited vision that sees the future as a restoration of what was lost – a future that will no doubt be much diminished by comparison with what went before, but one that will ultimately involve a revival of the old familiar ways. This is undoubtedly a comforting vision for a struggling church, and it can even be supported by an appeal to the New Testament (Phil. 3.20: Heb. 11.13; 1 Peter 2.11). But what if there is a better biblical paradigm than exile, based not on random proof-texts but on what is perhaps the most disruptive and compelling narrative at the heart of the gospel?

At the most formative point in the emergence of the early church, between Easter and Pentecost, the *missio Dei* consisted entirely of things that the first disciples neither understood nor believed in. A new community was in the process of coming to birth, and nothing at all made sense by reference to the inherited wisdom of the past. All the assured beliefs and expectations regarding 'what God is doing' had crumbled. The idea that the Messiah might be crucified was anathema to the disciples (Matt. 16.21–23), and after the unthinkable had happened it was beyond belief that he might be resurrected (Luke 18.31–34). The only people who believed in any sort of afterlife were the Pharisees, and the disciples clearly shared the opinion (widespread among the rest of the religious population) that resurrection was not possible and believing in it might even be heretical. Thomas was not the only one with questions (John 20.24–29).

In that post-Easter period, they found themselves navigating entirely new territory, and though they eventually acknow-ledged the reality of both cross and resurrection the disciples behaved as if they were entering a new age of exile rather than the age of new possibilities that was about to dawn. Their immediate instincts were to preserve what they had enjoyed previously and to plan for its continuation with the appoint-ment of Matthias (Acts 1.21–26). They felt comfortable with that, but the divine plan was more ambitious, involving a com-pletely new landscape where anything was possible, in which the signs of God's presence – and the future of the community – would be totally reimagined. If we transpose that into the context of the emerging digital world, is this where we find ourselves today – in a space where whatever God is doing will look so different from anything that we have seen so far that it will potentially lead to a reframing of almost everything?

Of course the experience of Pentecost did not emerge from nowhere and the entire history of the people of God, from Old Testament times through to the present day, demonstrates that no matter how radical a form the *missio Dei* might take at any given moment, there is always a discernible continuity with what has gone before. That is the sense in which God can be said to be 'the same, yesterday, today and forever' (Ps. 90.2, James 1.17, Rev. 1.8), though continuity with the past is not the same as replicating it. With the benefit of hindsight, the apostles realized that Pentecost and what followed was (like the primal act of creation in Genesis 1) not creation from nothing, but a new form of divine order emerging from the uncertainties of chaos and inaugurated by the same Spirit. In searching for signs of divine activity in the digital environment, we can assume some essential continuity between what we know of God from the past and present, and what may yet come to birth, even in other worlds.

How then might we recognize any new manifestation of the *missio Dei*? In exploring that we were reminded of the work of Chinese missiologist Raymond Fung, with whom we worked during his tenure of the evangelism desk at the World Council of Churches. His identification of Isaiah 65.20–23 as a central text for mission in our times was one of the more original contributions to late twentieth-century missiological understanding (1992). The specific statements of what he called the Isaiah Vision are firmly rooted in the physical world and are as relevant today as they were in Old Testament times. But how might they be transposed into values that will be appropriate to the digital environment? This passage has four discrete though complementary aspirations:

- 'Children do not die in infancy': Divine activity is always life-giving and leads to growth: can we characterize this as being about presence and journey in the digital world, offering space for contemplation?
- 'Old people live in dignity': Divine activity enables flourishing and maturity: is authenticity a key value here, characterized by acceptance of the other?
- 'Those who build houses live in them': Divine activity creates a safe, trustworthy space. What might this look like in terms of hospitality in the digital environment through the intentional creation of spaces characterized by fairness and justice?
- 'Those who plant vineyards eat the fruit': Divine activity implies shared grace as good news and celebration. Might this combine invitation to join the party with the assurance of sanctuary for those who respond?

Working with these key themes, we might suggest that the *missio Dei* is located wherever there is the intentional creation of a life-giving space in which human flourishing is characterized by opportunity for contemplation, acceptance, intentionality and sanctuary. The inclusion of contemplation in this list and its relevance to the digital world will become clearer towards the end of this chapter, but for now it is worth noting that it was the essential framework for the vision in the time of Isaiah, a time when there seemed to be no possibility at all of the vision coming to fruition, and the only thing both prophet and people could do was to pray and wait. In what follows, we will view these characteristics through the prism of St Paul's encounter with the spiritual searchers of Athens (Acts 17.16–34), seeking to identify the 'unknown gods' of cyberspace. Our primary concern therefore is not with recognizably 'Christian' or even 'religious' spaces (for example, we have intentionally excluded online churches or evangelistic websites from consideration here), but will involve the more radical approach of identifying spaces where echoes of the gospel can be found in what might seem to be unlikely places. That in turn has implications for the question posed earlier: what if the *missio Dei* looks so unlike anything we have so far imagined that our missional boundaries – not to mention our theological parameters – begin to be reimagined in some far-reaching ways? This involves exploration of an unlikely space that was identified through an online survey, before we share selected case studies that illustrate aspects of the *missio Dei* as it impinges on mission and pastoral engagement in the digital environment.

Online Spirituality

Between February and April 2019 we conducted a survey on attitudes to digital media in relation to matters of faith and spirituality, using Survey Monkey. We initially invited our own social media contacts to take part, and many of them then shared it with their own friends. Methodologically, this was clearly not a random sample by the usual definition, though with 537 responses the results can be claimed to have statistical significance, and the diversity of the respondents was not entirely untypical of many populations in Western countries today. Responses came from 297 females and 240 males, with almost equal numbers in all age groups from 18–65+: 61% were UK residents, 24% in the US or Canada, and 25% from elsewhere (mostly Asia, including Australia and Aotearoa New Zealand); 68% identified as Christian, in almost exactly equal male/female proportions, while 11% described themselves as either atheist or of no religion (predominantly male), 19% as pagans of various sorts (predominantly female), and 2% said they did not know if they were people of faith.

One question asked: 'Have you ever had an online experience that you would describe as transcendent or spiritual?' Of all respondents, 67% said they had, a clear majority of whom mentioned ASMR, with Headspace in second place and virtual reality experiences of Shinrin-yoku in third place. The designation of ASMR as 'Autonomous Sensory Meridian Response' was introduced by one of its early pioneers (Lopez 2018) and, at the point of writing, YouTube hosts almost fourteen million ASMR videos, with some sites having millions of followers. The most striking characteristics of ASMR videos are a whispered commentary alongside the replication of everyday sounds. These sounds tend to fall into two categories. On the one hand we find things like bottles being opened, hair being combed, fingers tapping on a table, crunching ice, popping a cork from a bottle, the clinking of utensils in a dishwasher (and literally hundreds of other similar everyday sounds), alongside images that often evoke washing (typical examples being the splashing or squishing of soap or shaving foam, towels or other fabrics being folded, often in the context of visits to a hairdresser or masseur). The combination of such everyday sounds alongside a whispered narrative is said to generate what practitioners describe as 'the shiveries', an experience similar to the sensation of one's 'hair standing on end', extending from the back of the head down the spine (the 'sensory meridian'). A typical ASMR video lasts for 40 minutes to an hour, though some are longer. ASMR is neither role-play nor visualization, though sharing some of the characteristics of both those experiences, and none of the empirical studies have been able to find any sexual element in it.

It is natural to wonder what is going on here. The studies carried out so far have tended to focus on the physiological effects of the experience rather than the feelings evoked, so any affective insights will be largely anecdotal and based on informed guesswork. One possibility is that these are all sounds and images that we typically encounter in our early years as babies and young children. Our parents introduce us to the everyday sounds of the world, often whispering to impart a sense of peace and security as part of the creation of an environment in which we can explore and discover while knowing that we are safe. There is no suggestion in ASMR of any sort of hypnosis or regression therapy, but could it be that the experience has the power to remind adults of simpler (maybe happier) times, moments of dependence and of security when someone genuinely cared for us in a self-giving way – or, for those many whose childhood was not like that, an invitation into an experience that was always longed for? In a world where we are increasingly wary of making physical contact with other people, there is an obvious attraction to the kind of virtual embrace that ASMR seems to offer. Something similar can be said about the absence of a sense of awe in today's lifestyles, with growing numbers of people searching for a still place in an increasingly noisy world, as evidenced by the unexpected (and growing) popularity of retreat centres. Perhaps ASMR offers an immediately accessible retreat, available on a regular basis in one's own space, and mostly free of charge. Does it function as a contemplative space shorn of any religious trappings or commitments, something that might have an obvious appeal not only to committed atheists but to the very many individuals for whom overtly religious language simply has no meaning?

Evidence of the popularity of ASMR was not especially surprising given the number of individuals who appear to create these videos as a full-time occupation, but it was more surprising to discover that while some 53% of respondents overall identified ASMR as their top transcendent online experience, the figure for those who described themselves as Christians was higher at 62% (with almost equal numbers of women and men, and across all age groups). Could it be that when encountered in the context of the Christian narrative, whether consciously or subliminally it also invokes images of divine parenthood, spiritual nurture, and that 'still small voice' of Elijah (1 Kings 19.11–12)? For now, that remains a matter of speculation as our survey offered no predetermined definition of what might constitute a transcendent or spiritual experience. Some respondents described ASMR in relatively mundane ways, as an aid to sleep or a way of reducing levels of anxiety and depression, while some claimed it as an antidote to loneliness and general feelings of isolation, and others more prosaically spoke of it as an enjoyable way to spend an hour. Empirical research supports all that and more. A report published in 2018 by a team from Sheffield University and Manchester Metropolitan University confirmed the findings of previous researchers, documenting beneficial impacts on both physical and mental health, including measurable decreases in heart rate and blood pressure as well as increased levels of positive emotions accompanied by reduction of anxiety and enhanced feelings of social connection (Poerio 2018; Barratt 2015; Fredborg 2017; Lloyd 2017; Smith 2017; Cline 2018). All this bears remarkable similarities to research that can be traced at least as far back as the 1970s, beginning with Harvard cardiologist Herbert Benson's investigation of the physiological effects of practices that included prayer and meditation alongside more active exercise and crafts such as knitting (1975; 2012). It also invites comparison with the work of neuroscientist Andrew Newberg, who identified similar outcomes when comparing the physiological effects of speaking in tongues with Buddhist meditation (2002; 2018). From an entirely different context, Richard and Lorimer Passmore describe detached youth work with teenagers in skate parks who intuitively characterized their experience of making the perfect jump as being an encounter with 'the flow' as a moment of transcendence and the starting point for an indigenous theology rooted in that experience (2013) – something that, without any conscious connection on their part, invokes echoes of the work of psychologist Mihály Csíkszentmihályi who used the same terminology to describe immersive states of consciousness in relation to music and art (1990). Complementing this, and from a different starting point again, is the work of zoologist David Hay, not only in his magnum opus *Something There: the biology of the human spirit* (2006) but also his report on *The Spirituality of those who don't go to Church* (2000). From a different perspective again, but converging on the same mind/body intersection, is *Sense Making Faith*, one of the most widely used resources from the ecumenical Mission Theology Advisory Group, designed to enable exploration of Christian faith through the senses (Richards 2007).

Exploring the connections between all these studies is beyond our scope here, but in relation to the experience of ASMR reported in the survey it is clear that this matches all four criteria of our earlier definition of the *missio Dei* as 'a life-giving space in which human flourishing is characterized by opportunity for contemplation, acceptance, intentionality and sanctuary'. Is this then part of the theatre of God's operation in digital space, and one of the 'altars to unknown gods' that we can acknowledge and affirm?

Spaces for Mission and Ministry

Before returning to that question, we need to say more about the four key online identifiers of the *missio Dei*: authenticity, hospitality, invitation, and presence and journey.

Authenticity ('enabling flourishing and maturity, characterized by acceptance of others')

Peter and Richard are siblings,[1] who over the years grew apart for no particular reason. They were raised in a strict Christian family, but in adult life Peter abandoned faith while for Richard it became a full-time profession. They both married and had children, who as they grew were naturally curious about their cousins. Peter protected his from Richard's family through a narrative that caricatured his brother as zealously fundamentalist, while (since they lived hundreds of miles apart) Richard's engagement with Peter and his spouse was limited to the exchange of Christmas cards and the very occasional brief encounter while visiting their aged parents. From the perspective of young adulthood, Peter's children were able to reflect more generously on the religious foibles of their grandparents and began to wonder what their uncle and his family might really be like. When Facebook came along that gave them an opportunity to find out without exposing themselves to what they imagined would be the condemnation of narrow-minded religious zealots. The online musings of Richard and his family revealed that they were indeed people of faith, but far removed from the stereotype of angry fundamentalists. In time, that led to a meeting between Richard and his family and the niece and nephew he scarcely knew, after which one of them posted 'I have met my family and they are quite normal'. A friendship developed on social media, not only with Richard but also between the cousins. One day out of the blue came a request from one of Peter's children, who was getting married and asked if Richard would conduct the ceremony. The couple described themselves as on a spectrum somewhere between Christian and pagan, and they wanted a ceremony that would take place on a major pagan festival and combine elements of both spiritual traditions. This relationship had clearly come a long way from the fearfulness of dealing with a fundamentalist uncle! Long hours were spent in conversation crafting an appropriate ceremony to include handfasting as well as the exchange of vows and other rituals, the sun shone on the day, and a new space for family reconciliation had been created that continues to flourish long after the event with regular interaction through social media that is often infused from both directions with spiritual values and concerns. All this came about through social media offering a space where the young generation could stalk their older unknown relatives to satisfy their curiosity, and the outcome has been a renewal of family relationships by skipping a generation, as Peter is still wary of connecting with his brother.

That story is by no means unique. Daniel Miller's research

identified many similar examples of friendships forged and families reconciled through engagement on social media (2011). Mentions of online stalking are often negative, but there can be a positive side to the ability to observe another's lifestyle at arm's length. Authenticity – being true to who you actually are – is perhaps one of the biggest challenges in the online world, where there is a constant temptation (and opportunity) to exaggerate and present oneself in a consistently good light, all of it encouraged by the ubiquity of fake news and 'alternative facts' in the wider culture. In this particular case it was ideological authenticity that played a key role, in particular those posts in which Richard and his family acknowledged their own struggles alongside their activities as enthusiastic and committed Christians while displaying an openness to learn new things, including from other spiritual pathways such as paganism. Authenticity opened a space that enabled flourishing, maturity and, in this particular case, reconciliation: a missional encounter by any other name.

Hospitality ('the intentional creation of spaces characterized by fairness and justice')

Social media offers endless possibilities of groups to join, and we are both engaged in many of them. They can be very demanding, and too easily end up in acrimonious arguments, especially if they involve religion or politics. In real life, the best invitations are often unplanned and spontaneous spur-of-the-moment ones. In early 2018, we mentioned on Facebook that we were planning to use the TV series *Broken* alongside a study guide produced by the Church of England's Birmingham Diocese (Gooder 2018). Olive was already committed to leading the course for one of our local churches, and the post was intended to encourage others to take a look at it. Neither of us had contemplated the potential of a pop-up group for Lent using social media, but in no time at all several others asked if they might join us – and since none of us lived anywhere near to one another it was going to have to be online. It worked so well for those individuals that they came back with a request for something similar in 2019. Some had previously met in real life, but they all followed each other online – another example of social media providing an opportunity to check out who might be a safe conversation partner. Theological safety turned out to be especially important: everyone in that self-selected group was involved in accredited pioneer ministry, both lay and ordained, and they were all people who, in one way or another, were no strangers to being told in real life that they were believing the wrong things, or were doing it the wrong way, or in some other respect were perceived as dangerous mavericks if not heretics. Observing one another's social media posts over an extended period reassured them that this would be a safe space where they might actually grow, and a space that was sufficiently intimate that it would be okay to be honest and open. That is just one example of the potential for offering hospitality in a space that can be trusted. Following Rachel Held Evans' tragic death in May 2019, something along those lines was a constant refrain in the many online tributes to her. The *New York Times* commented that 'Her congregation was online, and her Twitter feed became her church, a gathering place for thousands to question, find safety in their doubts and learn to believe in new ways' (Dias 2019), while Sojourners leader Jim Wallis described her blog as 'an internet sanctuary where people were welcomed, affirmed, encouraged, and lifted up' (2019). The potential for creating and sustaining life-giving community online is seemingly endless.

Invitation ('shared grace as good news and celebration')

Invitational mission is less popular than it once was, and in some circles would be actively discouraged. Long before the digital age, Martin Luther, William Booth and Sri Lankan theologian D. T. Niles were variously credited with defining evangelism as 'one beggar telling another where to find bread'. Regardless of who coined the phrase, social media platforms are easy places for that telling to happen. Sharing resources is a natural thing to do, whether it is a picture, a silly cartoon, a meme, a bizarre news story, lists of favourite books or films, or an invitation to an event. We expect our online friends to direct attention to whatever it is that they find to be of interest. That could include the story of Jesus, though identifying appropriate ways to do that can be more difficult than many would imagine. When our survey identified ASMR as a key source of transcendence for so many Christians, we wondered why something more obviously 'Christian' never featured, something like 'Christian Mindfulness' perhaps, which operates in the same mind/body space. It was easy to see why: huge numbers of websites and blogs emanating from Christians denounce anything containing the word 'mindfulness' as heretical, misguided, demonic, or worse. The gospel is good news, but so many self-proclaimed Christian websites and blogs manage to turn it into such bad news that searchers for spiritual wisdom are turned away before they get anywhere near the message of Jesus and his invitation to holistic love of God and neighbour (Luke 10.27). The possibility of vitriolic attack coming from other Christians can be a major reason why many find it hard to share faith stories as unselfconsciously as they might post pictures of their dogs or special meals. One project that we find helpful and will mention briefly below is Taketime which is the vision of Methodist minister Clive McKie. It is unashamedly focused on Jesus but, adopting the approach of Ignatian spirituality, also has clear connections to the mind/body world in which ASMR flourishes.

Presence and Journey ('be life-giving, leading to growth, offering space for contemplation')

In Isaiah 65 this is the first statement, but we come to it last here as in many ways it undergirds all the others. Isaiah looks to a time when children will no longer die in infancy, an aspiration that historically has been about infant mortality – and in many places it still is because of an absence of clean water and sanitation. Online, the issue is more likely to be suicide, often as a consequence of fake news, or shaming, or sexting, facilitated by the sharing of information about the technicalities of how to kill yourself. Olive recalls addressing this in a clergy conference for the Church in Wales diocese of St Asaph at a time when a number of teens had formed a suicide pact on social media, and in thanking her at the end of the session the bishop summed it up in the memorable phrase that 'people today are more afraid of living than they are of dying'. Since then, the challenge has grown exponentially, along with a fresh acknowledgement of the extent of mental illness. There is no one simple answer to what is increasingly being recognized as a crisis for many (and not only young people). In real life, children die because of the absence of clean drinking water and sanitation; online it can be the result of a toxic narrative that offers little hope of a better life. ASMR, along with mindfulness and other meditational techniques are often presented as the way to deal with the stresses of everyday life – and they do appear to work. But is the underlying assumption, that we need to learn how to deal with stress for ourselves, part of a false narrative that diverts attention away from the ultimate causes of personal struggle, which are systemic and cultural? Dana Becker argues that a societal obsession with what she calls 'stressism' intentionally conceals the real issue by suggesting that the problem is not with the way things are organized but is the fault of the hapless individuals who find it hard to keep up – and who as a consequence are offered a panacea that in the long run is no solution at all, but is itself a part of the problem (2012). There is no space here to expand on this proposition, though Ronald Purser sums it up well in the title of his book: *McMindfulness: How Mindfulness Became the New Capitalist Spirituality* (2019).

There are many ways of defining the *missio Dei*, and Raymond Fung's Isaiah Vision is only one of them. Another model that we could have used here is the Five Marks of Mission of the Anglican communion (Zink 2017). The thing they all have in common is an understanding that whatever God is doing will always be directed toward the creation of a better world, one that ultimately reflects the values espoused by Jesus himself. People of faith ought to be able to share a different narrative that is life-giving because it embraces the whole of life. Long before anyone had imagined social media, Clark Pinnock proposed that 'We should redefine heresy as something that ruins the story and orthodoxy as theology that keeps the story alive and devises new ways of telling it' (1990, p. 183). In another place, Olive has proposed that 'the story is the thing that denotes otherwise ordinary experiences as vehicles of divine grace', and suggested that 'the story' needs to include our own small stories alongside the big story that is Jesus (Fleming Drane 2017, p. 38). This is a major reason why we chose to highlight www.taketime.org.uk as the invitation to join in 'sharing grace as good news and celebration'. Though no empirical research has been carried out in relation to those who use this particular reflective space, it seems highly likely that the physiological and other effects produced will be similar, if not identical, to those experienced through ASMR, mindfulness, and other reflective practices previously mentioned. The one thing that is different is that Taketime is an unadorned narration of the gospel stories, in which the participant will experience every aspect of the story of Jesus, including his insistent call to make the world a better place as an essential component of authentic discipleship.

Storytelling is at the heart of the online environment, whether it is video streaming, music, gaming, or social media. We say that the story of Jesus is the greatest one ever told, and while it offers safe space to those who are struggling it also challenges those who hear it to radical action that will change the world. Sharing this message online will always involve vulnerability: our stories and dreams can easily be rejected and they might well be criticized or ridiculed, even (or especially) by other Christians. Identifying what God is doing in the digital space and joining in can sound simplistic but it is likely to be challenging, not only to us but to the cultural systems and structures in which we now find ourselves. Whatever else might be said, it will not be dull though it could be dangerous, and it will almost certainly look rather different from anything we could ever have imagined.

Note

1 This is a true story, though the names have been changed.

References

Barratt, E. L. and Davis. N. J., 2015, 'Autonomous Sensory Meridian Response (ASMR): A flow-like mental state', *PeerJ*, 3, e851, http://doi.org/10.7717/peerj.851.

Beach, Lee, 2015, *The Church in Exile: Living in Hope After Christendom*, Downers Grove: InterVarsity.

Becker, Dana, 2012, *One Nation Under Stress: The Trouble with Stress as an Idea*, New York: Oxford University Press.

Bell, Rob and Golden, Don, 2008, *Jesus Wants to Save Christians: A Manifesto for the Church in Exile*, Grand Rapids: Zondervan.

Benson, Herbert, 1975, *The Relaxation Response*, New York: Harper-Torch.

Benson, Herbert, 2012, *The Relaxation Revolution: Enhancing Health Through Mind Body Healing*, www.youtube.com/watch?v=KZ7JfC3_Zgc, accessed 9 September 2020.

Brueggemann, Walter, 1997, *Cadences of Home: Preaching among exiles*, Louisville: Westminster John Knox Press.

Cline, John, 2018, 'What is ASMR and why are people watching these videos?', www.psychologytoday.com/gb/blog/sleepless-in-america/201809/what-is-asmr-and-why-are-people-watching-these-videos, accessed 9 September 2020.

Cox-Darling, Joanne, 2019, *Finding God in a culture of fear*, Oxford: Bible Reading Fellowship.

Csíkszentmihályi, Mihály, 1990, *Flow: The Psychology of Optimal Experience*, New York: Harper & Row.

Dias, Elizabeth and Roberts, Sam, 2019, 'Rachel Held Evans, voice of the wandering evangelical', www.nytimes.com/2019/05/04/us/rachel-held-evans.html?fbclid=IwAR0ERDEYuSu13UDwyyb6bN8wFH_yW6DuKP27IwAs9ybOvSDtWKdJ9eCYeGs, accessed 9 September 2020.

Fleming Drane, Olive, 2017, 'Made in the image of God: Encountering the Creator through creativity', in Potter, Phil and Mobsby, Ian, *Doorways to the Sacred*, Norwich: Canterbury Press, pp.30–40.

Fredborg, B., Clark, J. and Smith, S, D., 2017, 'An Examination of Personality Traits Associated with Autonomous Sensory Meridian Response (ASMR)', *Frontiers in Psychology*, Vol. 8, No. 247, www.frontiersin.org/articles/10.3389/fpsyg.2017.00247/full, accessed 9 September 2020.

Frost, Michael, 2006, *Exiles: Living Missionally in a Post-Christian Culture*, Grand Rapids: Baker.
Fung, Raymond, 1992, *The Isaiah Vision*, Geneva: World Council of Churches.
Gooder, Paula, 2018, '"Broken" – A six week study course for Lent', www.cofebirmingham.com/news/2018/02/08/broken-six-week-study-course-lent/.
Hay, David and Hunt, Kate, 2000, 'Understanding the Spirituality of people who don't go to Church', A report on the findings of the Adults' Spirituality Project at the University of Nottingham, www.spiritualjourneys.org.uk/pdf/look_understanding_the_spirituality_of_people.pdf, accessed 10 September 2020.
Hay, David, 2006, *Something There: The Biology of the Human Spirit*, London: Darton Longman & Todd.
Lloyd, J. V., Ashdown, T. P. O. and Jawad, L. R., 2017, 'Autonomous Sensory Meridian Response: What is It? and Why Should We Care?', *Indian Journal of Psychological Medicine*, 39/2, pp. 214–15, http://doi.org/10.4103/0253-7176.203116, accessed 10 September 2020.
Huxley, Aldous, 1932, *Brave New World*, London: Chatto & Windus.
Lopez, German, 2018, *ASMR explained*, www.vox.com/2015/7/15/8965393/asmr-video-youtube-autonomous-sensory-meridian-response, accessed 10 September 2020.
Miller, Daniel, 2011, *Tales from Facebook*, Cambridge: Polity Press.
Moynagh, Michael and Harrold, Philip, 2012, *Church for Every Context*, London: SCM Press.
Newberg, Andrew, D'Aquili, Eugene and Rause, Vince, 2002, *Why God Won't go Away: Brain Science and the Biology of Belief*, New York: Random House.
Newberg, Andrew, 2018, *Neurotheology: How Science Can Enlighten Us About Spirituality*, New York: Columbia University Press.
Orwell, George, 1949, *Nineteen Eighty-Four*, London: Martin Secker & Warburg.
Passmore, Richard and Lorimer, with Ballantyne, James, 2013, *Here be Dragons: Youth Work and Mission off the Map*, Birmingham: Frontier Youth Trust.
Pinnock, Clark H., 1990, *Tracking the Maze*, San Francisco: Harper & Row.
Poerio, Giulia Lara, Blakey, Emma, Hostler, Thomas J. and Veltri, Theresa, 2018, 'More than a Feeling: Autonomous sensory meridian response (ASMR) is characterized by reliable changes in affect and physiology', *PLoS ONE* Vol. 13, No. 6:e0196645,https://journals.plos.org/plosone/article?id=10.1371/journal.pone.0196645, accessed 10 September 2020.
Postman, Neil, 1987, *Amusing Ourselves to Death: Public Discourse in the Age of Show Business*, London: Methuen.

Postman, Neil, 1993, *Technopoly: The Surrender of Culture to Technology*, New York: Vintage Books.

Purser, Ronald, 2019, *McMindfulness: How Mindfulness Became the New Capitalist Spirituality*, London: Repeater Books.

Richards, Anne Richards, 2007, *Sense Making Faith*, London: Churches Together in Britain and Ireland.

Richards, Anne et al., 2010, *Foundations for Mission: A Study of Language, Theology and Praxis from the UK and Ireland Perspective*, London: Churches Together in Britain and Ireland.

Smith, Stephen D., Fredborg, Beverley Katherine and Kornelsen, Jennifer, 2017, 'An examination of the default mode network in individuals with autonomous sensory meridian response (ASMR)', *Social Neuroscience*, Vol. 12, No.4, pp. 361–5, www.tandfonline.com/doi/abs/10.1080/17470919.2016.1188851, accessed 10 September 2020.

Thompson, James W., 2010, *The Church in Exile: God's Counterculture in a Non-Christian World*, Abilene: Leafwood Publishers.

Wallis, Jim, 2019, 'The overwhelming loss and legacy of Rachel Held Evans', https://sojo.net/articles/overwhelming-loss-and-legacy-rachel-held-evans, accessed 10 September 2020.

Zink, Jesse, 2017, 'Five marks of mission: history, theology, critique', *Journal of Anglican Studies*, Vol. 15, No. 2, pp. 144–66, https://doi.org/10.1017/S1740355317000067, accessed 10 September 2020.

9

Worship, Community and *Missio Dei* in a Digital Age

MAGGI DAWN

Missio Dei – a Discourse, Not a Shorthand for Mission

The term *missio Dei*, in many theological and ecclesiological contexts, has become almost interchangeable with the word 'mission'. Its usage implies an understanding of mission as God's self-giving action in the world, but what is sometimes lost is that the term entered into recent usage not merely to add nuance to missiological language, but as a significant and weighty cultural critique following the realization in the mid-twentieth century that mission had, in many instances, become intertwined with cultural domination. In a post-colonial world, any missiological framework had to indicate the ways in which God is at work in the world, without implying an ill-conceived and embarrassingly outdated concept of mission as the work of 'enlightened' Christians preaching to a remote, unenlightened, godless world. In its fullest sense, then, *missio Dei* is more than a shorthand term for mission – it is a powerful reminder that both ecclesiology and missiology must be properly located culturally as well as theologically.[1]

The *missio Dei* discourse was set in train by the great cultural seismic shifts of the twentieth century, and these, interestingly, were precisely the same conditions that accelerated and shaped the development of digital technology. '*Missio Dei*' and 'the Digital Age' therefore belong side by side, historically speaking. But just as the popular use of the term *missio Dei* dilutes its original meaning, so it is also noticeable that much of the discussion around the Church in the digital age often stays too close to the surface, focusing mainly on pragmatic concerns and aesthetic taste rather than deeper cultural, theological and anthropological implications.

Church practice has undeniably been slow to recognize that the impact of digital technology extends far beyond new methods of broadcasting information. Perhaps this is not surprising, given the social makeup of church communities, and the speed at which the digital revolution has brought about a transformation of everyday life. Even in the space of my own lifetime, phones have moved from the box at the end of the street, via the table in the hall, to your pocket or your wrist, and letters gave way to email, which itself is now beginning to seem quaintly old-fashioned. I wrote my own student essays by hand; the students I now teach deliver documents that are automatically spell-checked before being uploaded into anti-plagiarism software. Both the speed of change and the ubiquity of our devices make it easy to forget quite how quickly these changes have occurred. But not only is the speed of change breathtaking, so is its depth – for even in social settings like churches that are slow to adopt the full benefits of new technologies, the digital revolution has nevertheless transformed the way we write, think and speak, and altered the way in which both individually and as a community we inhabit our world and articulate our self-understanding. At the furthest edge of potential digital development lie visions of change that invoke ethical and anthropological discussions of what it means to be human, but even in terms of what is already prevalent in everyday life, the fact that personal and community relationships are now routinely conducted as much online as offline demands that we consider the implications of this for Christian theology and practice.

Among the range of discussions this opens up, what I want to address specifically is how the Church's self-expression, especially in worship, might be navigated in this ever-evolving digital culture. Discussions about digital culture in relationship to church life and ministry, and in particular the presence of digital technology in worship spaces, have often collapsed into binary arguments, limiting debate merely to whether one is 'pro' or 'anti' the embrace of digital technology within Church life. Those who have embraced digital culture passed the point some time ago where online and offline modes of engagement seem entirely distinct; we flow from one to the other without a second thought.[2] But while it is not impossible that those who are suspicious of the introduction of digital modes into worship are simply stubborn or obstructive, it is possible that their reservations may have some substance. The ideal would be for an ongoing critical examination of how technology may be more or less appropriate and helpful in particular contexts, without this undercurrent of opposition.

Taken separately, both these ideas – *missio Dei*, and church-related engagement with digital culture – can be oversimplified and lack engagement with their origins and complexities. But rather than begin with digital culture as a critique of missiology, I want to turn the conversation the other way around. I shall first trace the usage of the term *missio Dei* within twentieth-century missiology to see what it might have to say to cultures undergoing transformation, and what wisdom it might offer to help us navigate a creative course through digital culture. I shall continue with some enquiry into the relationship between digital and 'live' modes of communication specifically in the context of worship. Following on from this, I shall examine some ways in which, specifically in the practice of worship, the Church[3] might leave behind discussions that oppose digital and 'live' against each other, and move towards a more integrated understanding of these modes of engagement. The digital age brings with it a mixture, as Angela Gorrell puts it, of 'glorious possibilities and profound brokenness' (2019, p. 4), and if those possibilities are to flourish we need to shape the way in which we mediate worship in digital forms.

Missio Dei – a Twentieth-Century Cultural Critique

The term *missio Dei* was used by Aquinas in the thirteenth century, and the ideas it conveys can be traced all the way back to Augustine (Englesviken 2003, p. 482), but it was revived and reframed in the mid-twentieth century as a response by church theologians to how the unfolding events of that century cast new light on certain cultural assumptions embedded within western Christianity. This century of major cultural upheaval included two world wars, the rise of communism and the Cold War, and in the midst of all this established forms of Christian missionary work began to break down, especially in China. Missionaries began to leave China from the 1920s onwards, and as antipathy towards protestant missionaries increased, most of those who chose to remain were eventually imprisoned, including the teachers and pupils of an entire missionary school. Some died in prison and others were murdered, until eventually, between 1949 and 1953, all those remaining were expelled from China. The retrospective evaluation of the China Inland Mission is complex, and the stories of those who were imprisoned or murdered are nothing short of tragic. Nevertheless, the theological discourse that followed leaned principally and necessarily towards a sharp critique of nineteenth- and early twentieth-century missiology, and this critique came largely from insiders within those very missionary communities. One well-known example is Pearl S. Buck, who grew up in China as the child of missionary parents. On returning to the US in 1932 she wrote a series of books, including two biographies in a dramatized form – one of each of her parents – in which she developed the idea that foreign missions were a form of imperialism (Conn 1996, p. 149). Soon afterwards, a study entitled 'Rethinking Missions' was commissioned by J. D. Rockefeller Jr, the results of which were almost entirely negative towards the ethos of foreign missions (Bays 2011, p. 122). The collapse of mission in China, then, represented a huge crisis for missiology, and demanded a radical reconsideration of the relationship between the proclamation of the gospel and the imposition of western values and practices onto other cultures – in other words, all the concerns that have subsequently been developed under the umbrella of 'post-colonial studies' were nascent in this mid-twentieth-century *missio Dei* discourse.

Not much in twentieth-century theology escaped the influence of Karl Barth, and *missio Dei* was no exception. Barth insisted on the doctrine of God as the starting point for every detail of theological thought, and in a 1932 paper he laid out the idea that mission must be seen primarily as God's work in the world, and that any authentic mission undertaken by the Church must be a response to God's *missio* (Arthur 2010, p. 50). A series of theologians picked up both the phrase *missio Dei*, and the Barthian idea of locating mission in the doctrine of God. Hartenstein, Bosch, Newbigin, Moltmann and others gradually developed this as a corrective to earlier missiologies, shifting the principal location of mission from the doctrine of grace, to the doctrine of God (Hartenstein 1934).[4] A missiology based in the doctrine of grace made salvation a transactional process – a gift that, while offered freely, must be both mediated and received. It was a short step from this to perceiving salvation as being dependent upon the reception of the gospel in propositional terms, which in turn placed an urgency upon the Church to effect its communication through mission endeavours, Bible translators, evangelism, and so on. Reframing mission within the doctrine of God first emphasized that mission is primarily God's work, with the initiative and the work of mission belonging to God alone. Second, and in response to that, it shifted the Church's responsibility in mission from being the mediator of a message to becoming a participator in the work of a God already at work in the world. Theologically speaking this was not a new idea, but a corrective in emphasis, re-establishing the idea that God is everywhere present rather than a distant God who can be accessed only through the mediation of human ministers or messengers. But more importantly for that cultural moment, it began to open up ways of thinking about mission that do not carry the freight of cultural imposition.

Wider Context of *Missio Dei*

While the effect of *missio Dei* on foreign missions was swift and widespread in the post-war years, it also coincided with the decline of the Church in the West, so that home mission became a much bigger concern. The shift in thought from a transactional to a relational view of mission trickled down gradually, though not uniformly. Envisioning mission as an outflow of the work of God in the world, rather than a task given to the Church, brought into focus the wider doctrinal premise that not only mission, but all the work of the Church, is God's initiative.

Just as *missio Dei* saw distinctions breaking down between ideas that had previously been held in binary opposition, so there were corresponding shifts elsewhere in the theological landscape. First – and not for the first time in theological history – reconceiving mission as relational rather than transactional went some way towards undoing the privileging of idea over encounter, and served as a corrective to the notion of 'the gospel' as a set of propositions to be communicated and accepted as the prior condition of an experience of God. To claim experience without explanation could be seen as a hollowing-out of theology, a reduction of substance to mere personal feeling; the point, however, was not to reverse the order of priority, but to move away from a binary opposition. Australian poet-priest Noel Rowe, for instance, explaining why he had placed feeling as paramount in his religious poetry, wrote: 'The moment of transcendence is not made fully present in words ... Moments of transcendence have to be abandoned; we cannot hold on to glory or it turns from encounter to idea' (2005).

There was a further breakdown of binary oppositions in theological discourse as the division between sacred and secular began to lose currency,[5] and with it the distinction between worship and mission. *Missio Dei* served in part as a corrective to an unspoken assumption that church was sacred and the world secular, and that what Christians did in church was worship, while ministry in the world was mission – not unrelated callings, but differently oriented. Post-*missio Dei*, however, the sense that every part of the Christian life is rooted both in God's presence and God's initiative began to blur those distinctions. In the 1994 Didsbury Lectures, James Torrance explored the idea that the theology of worship must first be located not in liturgical practice, but in the life of the Trinity, where Father, Son and Holy Spirit have from eternity moved in constant mutual adoration and love, the result being that true worship occurs not out of our efforts to reach God, but from the overflow of the inner relationality of the Trinity (Torrance 1996). To put it in the vernacular, rather than conceiving of worship as taking gifts to God's door, knocking and hoping for an answer, imagine that the door is already open and the party has already started, and all we have to do is accept the invitation go inside and join in. Worship, in this vision, is what happens when anyone, whether consciously part of the church or not, joins in with a relationship of love and adoration that is now, and always has been, in flow within the holy and undivided Trinity.

This blurring of the distinctions between sacred and secular, and worship and mission, was already visible in practice. The later decades of the twentieth century saw multiple worship movements in which there was no longer any assumption that worship was not only an experience for the converted; instead, it was regarded as the most likely location of an encounter with God. The 'seeker sensitive' church movement, begun in Willow Creek,[6] was a practical outworking of the idea that mission is located in worship. The Alt*Worship movement, which first emerged in the late 1980s in the UK, was culturally in a very different vein, but similarly blurred the boundaries in terms of who was expected to participate. Alt*Worship was – by its very name – conceived of primarily as 'worship', but developed around the idea that an experience of God that was equally open to Christians with a developing spiritual life, people with no prior experience of faith, or those with the newly validated identity of ambiguous faith – the doubting believer, the post-evangelical, or the spiritual-but-not-religious. These new movements embodied the blurring of boundaries, fitting perfectly into the *missio Dei* mindset: it was now less the Church's responsibility to be the 'doctrine police', ensuring that people embraced correct ideas, than to create an environment for encounter. In the Alt*Worship movement (for which I speak from personal experience), the motivation was not principally towards mission, in the sense of seeking converts – in fact, it was characterized almost by an 'anti-mission' stance. Many of those inside the movement had come to question, not their faith *per se*, but the expression of church life they had thus far experienced, and Alt*Worship groups tended to form not (as has often been assumed) as a way of introducing the faith to those outside the Church, but to create a space for worship that felt authentic to those who no longer felt entirely at home with established and familiar expressions of church. This is not to deny that there was a good deal of spiritual mobility in the movement; some did convert to the Christian faith while others radically reframed their faith or gradually evolved out of faith altogether. And neither is it to suggest that doctrine and ideas were not important; the hours of discussion that accompanied those worship experiments, and the theological reading lists that were exchanged and discussed at length, out-ranked the theological depth of most church discussion groups I have encountered in traditional church settings. Nevertheless, for many the principal experience of Alt*Worship was learning to live with a degree of ambiguity, as they allowed their faith to evolve and develop in ways they could truly own.

These movements were, in different ways, also thoroughly intertwined with developments in digital technology – everything from TV clips to live video, moving image and digital music were present as the art and content of many typical Alt*Worship events. But while seeker services made use of livestreaming as a mode of delivering a message more widely, Alt*Worship tended not to, perhaps because it was more cyclical than sequential in form.[7] In a seeker-sensitive service, while the content might vary from one event to the next, the 'order of service' still remained sequential, led from the front, which lent itself to broadcasting. In Alt*Worship, however, there was no 'show' to livestream from start to finish, but a series of options which, while they could potentially be photographed or recorded and edited for broadcast, did not make for an easy livestreaming subject. Despite significant cultural and theological differences, then, these two worship movements that denied strict divisions between worship and mission, or sacred and secular, while concurrently engaging with digital technology in quite different ways.

So far, then, we have seen that *missio Dei* is far more than a re-designation of missiology as 'the work of God' – it was a radical re-thinking of missiology. Its major insight was that it is a catastrophic mistake to confuse mission with culture, and in particular to conflate Western culture with Christendom. The recovery of the theological truth that mission is God's initiative rather than ours was the first step towards a missiology of humility, in which mission was conceived of in terms of learning and encounter, rather than solely proclamation and teaching. Concurrent with (and perhaps, to some extent, emerging out of) the *missio Dei* discourse, was the development of a more cohesive and less compartmentalized view of the Christian life, and a blurring of the boundaries between church and world, mission and worship. *Missio Dei*, then, is not merely shorthand term for mission, but a radical rethinking of the relationship between the gospel and culture. How, then, might these observations offer us understanding and critique of the digital age in which we now find ourselves?

The Digital Age – Concurrent, Exhilarating, Terrifying

The juxtaposition of the twentieth-century *missio Dei* discourse with the Digital Age is not a forced one; as noted above, they emerged side by side chronologically, motivated by the same seismic cultural shifts and the political urgency of the inter-war years. It is unlikely, when we casually look at our smartphones twenty or thirty times a day, that we think of Bletchley Park; yet the cultural setting that triggered the *missio Dei* discourse was precisely the same set of conditions that that accelerated the digital revolution that is still unfolding all around us. And just as *missio Dei* began as a response to a single crisis but ended up part of radically transformed theological landscape, so digital culture, which began with specific and urgent developments in communication, is now understood as all-encompassing in its cultural consequences. The digital revolution has not merely improved the convenience of communication – having a phone in my pocket instead of having to wait at the phone box on the corner – it has changed us more fundamentally. Alistair Cooke was one of the first to recognize how the personal computer changed the way people write: in one of his famous *Letters from America* (2004) he remarked that early in his career as a journalist, he would gather his material, organize it in his head or on the back of an envelope, and then start writing at the beginning and keep going until he wrote the conclusion. 'No one writes like that anymore,' he wrote, 'now we write the middle first, and then the end, and the beginning last of all.' More recently, linguist Gretchen McCulloch has demonstrated the way in which the presence of the internet in our culture has begun to transform language, patterns of thought and human behaviour (2020).

It is one thing to observe change; another to evaluate it. And the benefits that accompany major cultural transformations always have a shadow side. David Bowie was a notable early adopter of internet technology; as the first major recording artist to release a song in online-only format (1996), in 1998 he launched BowieNet, offering public access to the internet via his own website. His engagement was enthusiastic, but not naïve: he envisaged the full range of potential effects of the internet on the world. In a 1999 interview, he said:

> Up until at least the mid-70s, we felt that we were still living in the guise of a single and absolute created society where there were known truths, and known lies, and there was no kind of duplicity or pluralism about the things that we believed in. That started to break down rapidly in the 70s, and that, I believe, has produced such a medium as the internet which absolutely establishes and shows us that we are living in total

fragmentation – I don't think we've even seen the tip of the iceberg; I think the potential of what the internet is going to do to society, both good and bad, is unimaginable. I think we are actually on the cusp of something exhilarating and terrifying.[8]

Between the two poles of exhilarating and terrifying lie the more everyday effects of the internet – benefits that we would not want to be without bring with them certain disadvantages or new problems to navigate. Educationalists have written about how children growing up in a digital world learn and think less sequentially and more cyclically, less conceptually and more visually, while both learning and expression take place through a mix of visual and verbal content – observations that, in themselves, are neither good nor bad, just different from the typical thought processes of earlier generations. But they also note that the ability of children to concentrate has declined dramatically, and their ability to read for protracted periods of time without a break or a distraction.

This increase in distracted behaviour, and an accompanying tendency to anxiety, has drawn significant attention, not only with reference to child development, but also to adult well-being. Andrew Sullivan, well known from *The Dish*, *The Daily Beast*, and *The Atlantic*, in a 2019 lecture at Yale University, noted that 2015 has been tagged as an important year in educational history. University culture has been changing, gradually and seemingly irrevocably, from an educational environment where students' ideas are challenged and stretched, and given a deeper and wider ground in which to flourish, to one in which having one's personal feelings and opinions challenged is regarded as an unsafe environment; a world of trigger warnings, safe spaces and retracted invitations. Sullivan pointed out that 2015, which seems to have been a watershed moment in this gradual change, was the first year when all undergraduate Freshers or Freshmen had grown up entirely in an online world. Around ten to fifteen years ago, Sullivan points out, you could certainly surf the net for hours if you wanted to, but it was still in a room on a desk, and the necessities of life – eating, sleeping, grocery shopping, laundry and travel – meant that even the keenest of bloggers and surfers had to disconnect. But not any more: now you can surf while you cook, while you eat, while you ride the metro; your phone is also your alarm clock so you go to sleep with it by your side, and wake up with it in the morning. Sixteen years after Bowie's prescient comments on an online world – both good and bad – Sullivan could see a correlation between the ubiquity of the personal device and the dramatic shifts in attitudes and expectations within Universities, of which are welcome but others deeply worrying. In a compelling account of his personal experience of this cultural shift, Sullivan described how his relationship to his own extensive online presence had morphed into one that felt less like life than like 'living-in-the-web', resulting, for a time, in a deterioration of physical and mental health. He writes:

> I'd begun to fear that this new way of living was actually becoming a way of not-living … I'd long treated my online life as a supplement to my real life … But then I began to realize, as my health and happiness deteriorated, that this was not a both-and kind of situation. It was either-or. Every hour I spent online was not spent in the physical world. Every minute I was engrossed in a virtual interaction I was not involved in a human encounter. Every second absorbed in some trivia was a second less for any form of reflection, or calm, or spirituality. 'Multitasking' was a mirage … (2016)

It would be easy to assume that Sullivan had reverted to an anti-internet view, but what his comments point towards is neither a re-dichotomization of online and offline, nor a claim that one is superior to the other. As he related further in his lecture, he neither gave up his internet presence, nor his belief in its usefulness – it is, as he points out, not digital technology *per se* that leads to distraction, but its ubiquity through the personal device so that, unless you deliberately choose otherwise, you are 'always on'.[9] What he describes, then, is not an antipathy to digital technology, but the experienced shared by many that, rather than constant availability enabling them to connect all the parts of their life into an integrated whole, that round-the clock distraction dilutes personal interaction both on- and offline. The expanded horizon promised by the internet can collapse, so that you seem to disappear inside it.

This particular problem is increasingly well-documented. Catherine Price, in her overview of the problem of distraction, quotes among her sources the renowned whistleblower Tristan Harris (2018). He asserts that the distracting or even 'addictive'[10] nature of the smartphone is no accident – it is designed precisely to be that way – and that manufacturers are motivated by commercial success, not benevolence, so attention to the consumer's quality of life or mental health may not rate highly in that process (Thompson 2019).

In the educational world, rising levels of anxiety have been observed, alongside difficulties with concentration and learning by heart, while nuanced debate has often given way to trading opinions. This tendency has been connected by some to the brevity of communication that social media has engendered, together with its tendency to polarize opinion and promote a sense of outrage. Angela Gorrell, in *Always On*, describes both the life-enhancing aspects of online connectivity, and also the potential for social media to contribute to a 'diminished humanness', noting that people feel free to express degrees of negativity towards others online that they never would if you were looking them in the face. Social media, she says, has a tendency to 'flatten' human relationships, and in turn the way users see and relate to and, therefore, experience the presence of God's love (2019, pp. 109–11). Online life delivers both the ability to connect with people across the world, and the potential to dehumanize those with whom we are connected. In the practice of faith this means that we need constant reminders to take our humanized reality with us into online space.

In relationship to church culture, a further element to consider is the privilege of access to the internet. In any environment where screens are ubiquitous, it is easy to forget that many people have limited or no internet access, and while for some this may be by choice, for many it is an economic issue. Not everyone has a personal device, or access to a home computer. While church culture has been pilloried for being behind the curve (and not without justification), it is equally problematic for church communities to imply that ownership of digital devices is a tool of access to community. To ignore this would be to lose touch with the gospel's priority for the poor; again this reinforces the point that debates over digital culture in church should not collapse into binary opposition; a more complex and imaginative approach is called for.

Missio Dei – Resistance to the Conflation of Gospel and Culture

From Bowie and Sullivan to Harris, Price and Gorrell, then, an array of critiques of the shadow side of digital technology are proffered, not by Luddite naysayers, but by enthusiastic and dedicated users who nevertheless signal that mixed with the benefits are inbuilt cultural and ethical problems that need to be faced. On the surface, it is not hard to grasp that a cultural movement may have both positive and negative tendencies, or different applications. Yet within the world of faith and church, it seems that many communities get completely hamstrung, and rather than finding creative ways to embrace the benefits while critiquing the pitfalls of digital culture, they end up in a flattened argument between those who are pro- or anti- digital culture. Returning to *missio Dei*, that part of our theological history stands as a reminder that when two cultures meet, it is vital to embrace and be critiqued by our situatedness in the world, while resisting the temptation to conflate the gospel with the culture in which we are embedded. Of course one can argue that those who resist cultural change are changed by it in any case (Dawn 1997). But if that argument insulates us from seeing difficulties with aspects of digital life, it merely re-dichotomizes the debate into a stand-off between online and offline. Simply to identify the 'digital age' flatly, without bringing any cultural critique to bear upon it, runs the risk once again of conflating culture with ideology, and forgetting that this is only one culture, one language, one mode of human expression, among many.

Critical Engagement of Digital Culture Within Worship Practice

For eight years I worked as the Dean of Marquand Chapel at Yale University, an ecumenical chapel encompassing more than 30 denominations, which – through its connection to the Institute of Sacred Music, Worship and the Arts – leans heavily towards engaging the arts in worship, in both experimental and established forms. I inherited Marquand Chapel with those features already in place, and wide open for development. But the chapel notably lacked digital engagement, to the extent that it seemed culturally slightly out of step. Gradually we introduced various modes of digital media, for creative expressions of worship, for increasing access, and for communicating about the chapel and our work. At each stage we considered how digital formats would enable authentic expressions of worship, but without engaging all things digital just because we could.

Example 1: Livestreaming Worship

As the chapel continued to flourish, pressure began to mount from various quarters to livestream our worship. There was lengthy discussion among colleagues as to whether we had an obligation as a teaching institution to offer more direct dissemination of our methods, as well as an ongoing connection for alumni. But I felt it was important to ask whether this was motivated by a desire to invite people to participate remotely, or merely to give them a fly-on-the wall view – effectively, to watch other people worshipping. It is fundamental to the idea of gathered worship that every person is a participant, rather than an audience. As digital technology has developed, this has occurred online in several different ways; worship can be entirely online, rather than an extension of a church with a physical location, and this is by no means a second-best replacement for 'real' church – in fact, in some ways it is an easier mode of connection than the hybrid model that connects 'live' and online concurrently.[11] In religious TV, radio broadcasts and online worship, both as a presenter and a producer, I have often been involved in creating an on-screen or on-air worship that enables the viewer to be a participant, and it is important to consider the different modes of engagement that are possible. If the entire congregation is on-air, or online, there is no 'live'[12] congregation. In TV and radio, this creates a certain level of intimacy between presenters and viewers or listeners. The studio or recording venue is staged in a particular way to create a sense of invitation. If a live congregation is recorded and broadcast, it takes some work to ensure that those in the room remain authentic in their expression of worship rather than acting to camera; similarly it is important for the act of worship to be deliberately inviting to the viewer or listener.

Despite technical differences between TV, radio and internet broadcasting, there are similarities in the aims and values of gathering remote congregations for worship. The easy availability of livestreaming technology leads some people simply to put a camera in the room to enable remote viewing, but this alone is not sufficient to gather a 'hybrid' congregation successfully. To create an environment for prayer or worship, leaders, preachers, pastors and musicians need to speak directly to online participants as well as those they can see physically. Livestreaming worship requires the tacit permission of every member of the live congregation, but not only because of the murky legal waters you can find yourself in if you livestream someone without their consent. The success of the venture depends in part on 'live' and dispersed members of the congregation being aware and welcoming of each other, to ensure that the experience is interactive, rather than voyeuristic.

While livestreamed and hybrid worship can work well, applying that to the particular setting of Marquand Chapel was a somewhat different proposition, for two reasons. The first was a set of questions around what exactly we would livestream, given that, not unlike practices typical of the Alt*Worship movement, our worship was often cyclical, not sequential, with different expressions of worship running concurrently, without a single visual focus. A typical service might see some painting their prayers on a wallboard while others would lie or sit on carpets in contemplation; music might come from solo or ensemble singers or musicians, while all manner of interactive prayer stations might be engaged around the room. When we gathered the whole group together, readings, songs and prayers might be spoken or sung from multiple points around the room, and not always with a microphone. Sometimes the whole congregation moved from one point in the Chapel to another, in the style of a pilgrimage. Our broadly ecumenical congregation would offer prayers that varied from predictable liturgical responsorial to multiple forms of extempore prayers. The degree of pedagogy, planning and community learning that went in to this form of worship meant that it was not chaotic, but simple livestreaming might have made it seem so – it would have taken a pretty sophisticated TV recording to convey the experience of the room on to a screen. For many of our services, then, it would have been difficult to make live-streaming work simply in terms of where to point a camera.

But livestreaming was problematic for a second reason. The forms of worship we had developed required high degrees of vulnerability both from worship leaders and congregation, even within a trusting community. Our pedagogical approach was to do as much imaginative work as possible to be as sure as we could that worship would 'work' for the congregation, but we also allowed for risk-taking, and as students planned and led worship, there was always the potential for new and untried forms of worship to fall flat. While it is safe enough to experiment (and sometimes to fail) within a trusted community, that courage would have been flattened by broadcasting. But the congregation were also making themselves vulnerable in worship, for while most people do not mind being caught on camera singing a hymn or listening to a sermon, our congregation would often engage creatively and physically in worship, and expressed discomfort at the idea of being watched onscreen by unidentified viewers. Even if we had the capacity to livestream or record those services in a way that invited participation rather than watching other people worship, the very fact of putting a camera in the room would have changed – and in these cases, limited – the experience for those in the room.

It is well documented that it is impossible to broadcast anything without changing it. Neil Postman noted that introducing any form of communications media into an existing situation never simply transmits what it observes, it changes that situation. The comparison is made with the introduction of a new species into a natural environment that may to be a potential site of flourishing for that species; its introduction, however, changes the environment into which it is placed, such that the outcome for both is entirely unpredictable (Postman 1970). In our situation, because our chapel services were renowned for their innovation and their success within a college community, people came from far and wide to experience it, and to learn from our practices. It was often put to us that if we livestreamed the services, others could see what we did. But we needed to weigh up how sharing our worship onscreen would change the very thing we set out to share, knowing that the ecology of the room would change. The idea that because something is good it must be livestreamed is therefore fundamentally flawed. On balance, we concluded that while some parts of our worship might livestream successfully, others would not.[13]

Example 2: Personal Devices in Worship

The years during which our discussions of livestreaming progressed saw a rapid increase in the use of personal devices in the worship space. Asked why they spent so much time recording worship on their phones or tablets, a few students said that they wanted to share it with others who are not there, but the more prevalent answer was they wanted to have a recording so that they could experience the worship again later. It was clear that individuals recording on their phone changed the ecology of the room just as much as a livestreaming. But in addition, we asked to what extent a person remains fully present in worship if they are mentally in online space, rather than attuned to what is happening in the room. If worshipers were recording in order to repeat the experience later, had they really entered into the experience in the moment? And if they were not really engaged in worship as they created their media, was that veering into watching others worship? As Sullivan put it, it is impossible to be engrossed in two interactions – a virtual and a live encounter – at the same time (2016). One member of our worship team described her experience of being in Chapel with her own phone turned to silent for the service: 'When people stand beside me recording the worship on their phones,' she said, 'it's not that I'm anxious about being recorded, it's more that I seem to be sitting among a roomful of people who are, in theory, worshipping together, but while their bodies are present, their minds are elsewhere.'

There is a paradox to consider here. While there is no denying that a hybrid online-offline congregation can connect people across physical distance with a good outcome, a potential and less desirable consequence is that people using personal devices are physically present in the room, but not actually 'present' to the situation, in the sense of being engaged in the live experience. Even though our online and offline lives flow into each other all the time, the belief that we can be in two places at once, paying equal attention in both dimensions, seems to be a fallacy.[14] This is one interpretation of what happens in worship when people attempt to share their live experiences as they happen.

In Marquand Chapel, then, our aim was to explore the benefits of digital culture in relationship to worship without adopting it uncritically. As we opened up regular community conversations, and surveyed opinion, comments around the use of personal devices in worship were illuminating. One semester, while seeking ways to reduce our carbon footprint, we set up an experiment in the reduction or elimination of paper. We invited worshipers to download songs and service sheets onto their personal devices, instead of printing. As a college chapel, this congregation had an average age of 27, and every member used screens all day long in the library or classroom, as well as in personal and social contexts. Yet a surprisingly high proportion were utterly disenchanted at the sight of a roomful of people reading from screens, and with the feeling that community worship, in the last half hour before lunch, was just like everything else they did in tying them to a screen. Many of our community expressed a desire for worship to be substantially different from what they did all day long, not the same.

Example 3: Unplugged

Another semester we invited people to a trial in which everyone who did not strictly need digital tech in order to participate[15] was invited to turn off their phone before entering chapel, to see whether it enabled them to focus on what happened in the room, engage with others in worship, and give themselves a break from screens. As a predominantly student-age community, we anticipated that there might be pushback on this, but were surprised to find a high level of enthusiasm for adopting this as a community agreement. Feedback from surveys indicated that for many people, personal devices had become an all-day-long habit they would prefer to break every now and then, but found it hard to do so alone, and more possible within a community agreement. To complete the circle, we agreed on certain elements of our worship that would be good to share more widely – a sermon, a song, or prayers that did not betray personal situations in the room – and agreed that other parts of worship were 'off limits' for recording. We also identified an area in the chapel that would never be caught on camera, so if there were those who felt inhibited by being recorded at worship, their privacy could be respected. We appointed one person to record and share those items, enabling others to turn off their devices and enter fully into the live experience.

In the music world, a trend for 'unplugged' music began in November 1989,[16] as musicians whose work usually depended on amplified sound were invited to perform entirely acoustic versions of their songs. Fans were able to hear songs in an entirely new way – suggestive, perhaps, of what the songs had sounded like when they were first written. There was a profound response to the freshness of this presentation of music; the brilliance of technology had opened up undreamed of musical possibilities over the previous decades, but there was suddenly a thirst for simplicity and a stripping back to the honesty of the unplugged sound. Something analogous seemed to happen as we opened up a digitally 'unplugged' space in our chapel; not that people wanted to exchange one reality for another, but that offering different modes of engagement seemed to bring a range of responses, from relief and rest, to wonder and illumination.

It is worth asking, then, in this digital age, whether among all the ways that church and theological communities are engaging with new media and the online world, one thread of that work might be to model ways for people to moderate the extent to which they are tied to their devices. 'Unplugged' rooms already exist in many retreat centres, and are being introduced in some schools. Those who have church or chapel buildings at their disposal have a prime opportunity to offer digital-free (or digitally moderated)[17] space for those who find it almost impossible to switch off their phone and leave it in their pocket, offering a secure place – something like a coat-check room – where people can tag their phone and give it in at the door. There is a place for creating an environment that positively makes a feature of not being 'on', that offers a place of rest for those who are screen-exhausted, and a creative or contemplative space where people can diversify their modes of engagement to include offline experience.

Conclusion

I would venture, then, that in navigating the vast horizon of the digital age, the Church could usefully draw on lessons learned from *missio Dei* – its recognition that no single culture corresponds exactly with the gospel, and that no one culture should, in the name of the gospel, impose its values on others, but that each should have the humility to see where God is at work in cultural forms, language and media other than their own. As the digital age continues to transform our own culture, it is important to bear in mind that alongside its many benefits comes the risk that we could unwittingly adopt a mindset of cultural superiority – the very mis-step that *missio Dei* set out to correct. The lasting lesson of the *missio Dei* discourse is to critique our own cultural bias, especially if it seems unquestioned, ubiquitous and irresistible. If our worship practices are to develop in a good and beneficial relationship to digital technology, we need neither to adopt every possibility uncritically, nor to be behind the curve. Our digital engagement needs to be imaginative, contextually appropriate and tailored to each specific setting. And, along with those life-enhancing possibilities, the equally radical move is to offer spaces where people can switch off when they need to.

Recognizing the gospel as counter-cultural should lead us away from the tendency to draw battle lines between those who embrace and those who are suspicious of digital culture, and allow for a more nuanced, critical embrace of its possibilities. Arguing for or against digital engagement in absolute terms can be a distraction from the more important aim of asking in each particular situation what enables or diminishes human flourishing. The glory of God, as Irenaeus put it, is 'a human being fully alive' – and if God is at work in our digital world, it will be just as much by offering resistance to the pressures of our culture, as it will to maximizing their glories.

Notes

1 This chapter is adapted from the keynote speech at the 2019 conference, at which I was asked to bring theological perspective of *missio Dei* to bear on the discussion of digital culture.

2 It has been extensively argued that this kind of dichotomization fails to understand the way in which – in digital cultures – online and online life are no longer neatly delineated. See, for instance, Hine, C., 2015, *Ethnography for the Internet: Embodied, Embedded, Everyday*, London, New York, Bloomsbury Academic.

3 I use 'church' in this chapter to refer to the whole body of people, not only to those authorized, ordained or employed institutionally.

4 Hartenstein used the phrase *missio Dei* as a distinct idea from *missio ecclesiae*, though not necessarily placing it within the Trinity. This was in the background when the International Missionary Council

met at Willingen in 1952, and though the phrase *missio Dei* was not used at the conference, the idea it encapsulates was explored extensively; when Hartenstein wrote up his account of the conference later, he used the phrase *missio Dei* to articulate this new way of thinking about mission.

5 This idea played out especially strongly in the Alt*Worship communities of the 1990s and 2000s, particularly in regard to the engagement of music and the arts in worship regardless of whether their origin was notionally 'sacred' or 'secular'.

6 The 'seeker sensitive' model, based on the idea that the church's worship is deliberately designed to reach non-believers, is usually attributed to Bill Hybels and dates back to the formation of Willow Creek Church in 1975; the development of the idea does arguably have a longer history, possibly tracing its roots back through the twentieth century to others who have combined entertainment with ministry, such as Robert Schuller, who began a church at a drive-in movie in 1955, and healer and evangelist-entertainer Aimee Semple McPherson (1890–1944).

7 C. Michael Hawn (2003, ch. 7) describes the function of individual worship hymns and songs in terms of sequential or cyclical form. Sequential describes a song that develops by unfolding a story or an idea that makes sense only by having a beginning, a middle and an end, and being sung in the right order. A cyclical song, on the other hand, is shorter and is repeated a number of times; rather than its duration unfolding a developing idea, its repetitions, especially when combined with musical variations, allow for both the idea and the feeling in the song to be intensified and absorbed more deeply. By comparison to ways of reading, if a sequential hymn is like exegesis, a cyclical song is more like *Lectio Divina*. Using the same idea to contrast forms of liturgy and worship, traditional forms tend to have a sequential movement from beginning to end, while Alt*Worship and its successors are more cyclical in nature, deliberately offering the worshipper the option to engage in all the movements of an act of worship, or only one or two, but more noticeably, the possibility of experiencing the elements of that worship in any order, rather than in a preordained sequence that is built in to a traditional liturgy.

8 David Bowie, interviewed by Jeremy Paxman on BBC Newsnight in 1999.

9 The iPhone was introduced in January 2007.

10 This phenomenon has often been described in terms of 'addiction', and there is some evidence that neurological responses to digital technology, and especially to smartphones, is similar to that of substance addiction. However in general I prefer to focus on the idea of 'distraction', because while addiction necessarily indicates a relationship to a toxic substance, the smartphone itself is not necessarily toxic – indeed,

it can be life-enhancing. For most people, then, the issue is not one of addiction, but of learning to choose, regulate and integrate multiple modes of communication into a life-enhancing whole.

11 One of the notable effects of the quarantines and lockdowns of the 2020 coronavirus pandemic has been that countless people who might otherwise not have experience this have discovered that engaging in worship online is not merely as a substitute for physically located church, but a different kind of engagement with a richness of its own – notably an experience that 'gathers' and connects people separated by distance or physical limitations.

12 I am using 'live' in this chapter to indicate those who are bodily in the room, and 'dispersed' to indicate those who participate remotely. I avoid using the word 'present', as it might suggest that those who engage remotely are not present; the actual experience of good online worship is that remote participants feel present, and should be acknowledged as such.

13 For many churches and ministers, the months of lockdown/ quarantine during the Covid-19 pandemic in 2020 was a moment of discovery; they were pleasantly surprised by the possibilities of creating online congregations who for whatever reason cannot meet in person. Some have noted that they had to learn how to create an online worship environment, and had not previously realized that it requires much more work than simply turning on a camera. Some churches and cathedrals have found that their online congregation is larger, and more far-flung, than their live one – and have stated their intent to continue online services and ministry.

14 One way of making that assessment is offered by Marshall McLuhan's Tetrad, which measures what is gained against what is lost. The losses come, according to the Tetrad, when the effect of a particular technology 'flips', and its negative opposite overwhelms its positive benefits (McLuhan, 2017, pp. 7–10, 24–7).

15 It is important to note that this was a community that positively welcomed and enabled those who used digital devices to assist with disabilities, learning styles, or other physical needs.

16 The first episode of 'Unplugged' was broadcast on MTV, 26 November 1989.

17 Creating digital-free spaces such as this need to offer freedom and relief for those who need to switch off, without excluding those (e.g. sight- or hearing-impaired community members) for whom a digital device is essential to access.

References

Arthur, E., 2010, 'Missio Dei', in Butare-Kiyovu, J. (ed.), *International Development from a Kingdom Perspective*, Pasadena: WCIU Press.

Bays, Daniel H., 2011, *A New History of Christianity in China*, Oxford: Wiley-Blackwell.

Cooke, A., 2004, *Letter from America*, New York: Knopf.

Conn, Peter J., 1996, *Pearl S. Buck: A Cultural Biography*, Cambridge: Cambridge University Press.

Dawn, M., 1997, 'You Have to Change to Stay The Same', in Cray, Dawn et al, *The Postevangelical Debate*, London: SPCK.

Englesviken, T., 2003, 'Missio Dei: The understanding and mis-understanding of a theological concept in European churches and missiology', *International Review of Mission*, Vol. 92, No. 367.

Gorrell, Angela, 2019, *Always on: Practicing Faith in a New Media Landscape*, Grand Rapids: Baker Academic.

Hartenstein, Karl, 1934, 'Wozu nötigt die Finanzlage der Mission', *Evangelisches Missions-Magazine*, vol. 79, pp. 217–29.

Hawn, C. M., 2003, *Gather into One*, Grand Rapids: Wm. B. Eerdmans Publishing Company.

McCulloch, G., 2020, *Because Internet: Understanding the New Rules of Language*, New York: Penguin Random House.

McLuhan, Marshall and Eric, 2017, *The Lost Tetrads of Marshall McLuhan*, New York, London: OR Books.

Postman, Neil, 1970, 'The reformed English curriculum', in Eurich, Alvin C. (ed), *High School 1980: The Shape of the Future in American Secondary Education*, New York: Pitman, pp. 160–8.

Price, C., 2018, *How To Break Up With Your Phone*, London: Trapeze.

Rowe, Noel, 2005, 'The Glory of God: Humanity Fully Alive – Poetry, Theology and Emptiness', *Australian EJournal of Theology*, August, No. 5.

Sullivan, A., 2019, 'Technology and the Soul', lecture delivered at the Yale Institute of Sacred Music, 9 April.

Sullivan, A., 2016, 'I used to be a human being', *New York Magazine*, September, http://nymag.com/intelligencer/2016/09/andrew-sullivan-my-distraction-sickness-and-yours.html, accessed 15 April 2019.

Thompson, N., 2019, 'Tristan Harris: Tech is "Downgrading Humans": It's Time to Fight Back', *Wired*, April, www.wired.com/story/tristan-harris-tech-is-downgrading-humans-time-to-fight-back/?utm_source=onsite-share&utm_medium=email&utm_campaign=onsite-share&utm_brand=wired, accessed 20 April 2019.

Torrance, J., 1996, *Worship, Community, and the Triune God of Grace*, Downers Grove, Illinois: InterVarsity Academic.

10

Back to the Roots or Growing New Branches: Preaching, Orality and Mission in a Digital Age

FRIDA MANNERFELT

Introduction

There is a strong connection between mission and preaching. Theologians might differ in their opinion of whether this is a good thing or not (Niyonsata 2018, pp. 458–71; Shelton 1987, pp. 67–73; Le Grys 1998, p. x), but there is almost always a notion of some sort of link. This is of course due to biblical roots. Although we may not know the *content* of actual sermons (Edwards 2004, p. 79), the New Testament is quite explicit about how preaching is part of the Church's mission: The apostles 'went everywhere preaching the word' (Acts 8.4, AV) and when people 'believed Philip preaching the things concerning the kingdom of God, and the name of Jesus Christ, they were baptized, both men and women' (Acts 8.12, AV). This notion of a connection is also at play in church practice. For example, scriptural passages about preaching are central in Bible study material about evangelism and mission (Kuck 2004, p. 33). In homiletical reflection, mission is sometimes used to define the act of preaching itself, as in biblical scholar Duane Litfin's book *Paul's Theology of Preaching*. Litfin argues that to Paul, preaching is the oral proclamation of the gospel to unbelievers. As Paul chose to take on the role of 'the herald', so should preachers of today be heralds (2015, pp. 339–49). Furthermore, this applies also to digitally mediated church practice, as many congregations share sermons or entire services online, in the hope that this will further mission (*Dagen* 2019, pp. 6–7).

An example of how this connection might be conceived theologically is found in World Council of Churches' definitions of church and mission. Its document *You Are the Light of the World: Statements on Mission* from 2005 states:

> The mission of the Church ensues from the nature of the Church as the body of Christ, sharing in the ministry of Christ as Mediator between God and his creation. At the heart of the Church's vocation in the world is the proclamation of the kingdom of God inaugurated in Jesus the Lord, crucified and risen. Through its internal life of eucharistic worship, thanksgiving, intercessory prayer, through planning for mission and evangelism, through a daily life-style of solidarity with the poor, through advocacy even to confrontation with the powers that oppress human beings, the churches are trying to fulfil this evangelistic vocation. (Matthey 2005, p. 8)

Likewise, the 2013 Faith and Order paper on *The Church: Towards a Common Vision* envisions the Church's mission as 'to be a community of witness, proclaiming the kingdom which Jesus had first proclaimed, inviting human beings from all nations to saving faith' (World Council of Churches 2013, p. 6). The churches are sent to continue the ministry of Christ, and since Jesus preached the kingdom of God in words and deeds, the church also preaches it. In short: although there is more to mission than preaching, preaching is a core component.

This means that if one seeks to understand how God's mission is to be carried out in a digital era, it is important to investigate what it could mean to preach in such a cultural context. Consequently, the aim of this single case study is to examine preaching that is shaped by and for a digital era. Which are its characteristics and how could these qualities be understood? To achieve this, I will analyse five sermons of a preacher who serves in a thoroughly digitalized setting, from a church tradition that has emerged hand in hand with digital technology: Swedish Hillsong Church pastor Andreas Nielsen. The sermons will be analysed using the theoretical concepts of orality, literacy and secondary orality. The most prominent representative of this approach is professor of English literature Walter J. Ong, who used it to describe how the means of communication affect the structure of human thought and communication. In the light of digitalization, this concept has been further developed by scholars like John Miles Foley and Lars Ole Sauerberg. They regard the digital era as a higher-level technological restoration/reinvention of an oral culture, and the era of literacy and printing press in Western society as an anomaly coming to an end; a 'Gutenberg parenthesis'. In the analysis, St Augustine's preaching will be used as an example to distinguish the general characteristics of preaching in an oral culture, and as a contrast to chisel out some of the features of secondary orality and the effects of digital technology on preaching. The article closes with a short discussion of what this might imply for mission in general and preaching in particular.

Orality and Literacy as a Theoretical Approach

In his seminal work *Orality and Literacy. The Technologizing of the Word* (1982 (2002)), Walter J. Ong claims that human thought and communication is shaped by the way it is mediated. In an *oral culture* you know what you can recall, which makes mnemonic patterns like formulas and proverbs important. Communication is characterized by being additive (and then ... and then ...), aggregative ('wise Odysseus' or 'fair Helena'), redundant (repetitive), agonistically toned, empathetic, close to experience, conservative and traditionalist. Since the aim is to remember, originality consists not in the introduction of new materials, but in fitting traditional material effectively into each unique situation and/or audience. As vocabulary is limited, bodily activity is important to convey meaning. This points to something fundamental in an oral culture: thinking and communication are deeply interpersonal and interdependent, and exist only in the present. As soon as a word is spoken, it is gone forever (pp. 33–67).

A *literate culture*, on the other hand, is characterized by the endurance of the word, and the solitude of reader and writer. You are alone when you compose a text, or as Ong puts it: 'the writer's audience is always fiction'. In a literate culture, things like analysis, reflexivity, distance, objectivity and subordination of thought are possible. Originality in content is appreciated, and since there is no immediate connection between writer and reader, a larger vocabulary is needed to provide accurate descriptions. That is also possible, since you are able to 'store' words in dictionaries. With print, these characteristics are further accentuated (pp. 78–107).

Over the years Ong's work has been used to shed light on various phenomena, including preaching and mission. Drawing upon Ong, historian Emmet McLaughlin (1991) makes some interesting observations. First, that there was a fluid border between preaching and liturgy in the early Middle Ages. In this primarily oral cultural setting, preaching had a strong resemblance to prayer: it was short, simple reproduction of traditional material in formulaic style, and the audience did not appreciate the performer stepping outside of the conservative, oral tradition. Second, this explains the widespread idea that regarding preaching, the early Middle Ages was a 'dark age'. McLaughlin argues that this historiography is a product of rising literacy and the transition from an oral to a literary culture. When you move into something new, you tend to have a negative view of the old. Third, it makes us aware of how prejudices affect definitions of preaching in our own time. In a highly literate and typographic culture, it is hard for us to understand and appreciate religion that is based on oral performance and ritual.

Fourth, that preaching as we often define it today is not oral (even if you might think it is) but an orality that *builds on* literacy. It is not true orality, but literacy with a high degree of oral residue. According to McLaughlin, preaching as we know it springs forth in the post-Constantinian context, when a large number of converts in the cities made it impossible to manage the long, rigorous person-to-person catechism. Instead bishops gave catechetical sermons in Lent. This kind of instructive, non-liturgical preaching was often oratorical, not oral, and fostered by the rising social level of both clergy and laity. However, this elite-preaching was not the kind of preaching that would take place in most local churches on a Sunday morning. McLaughlin concludes: 'For the ordinary believer of the Church's first millennium the Christian experience was a liturgical one – the Mass and the sacraments above all' (pp. 87–107).

Lastly, McLaughlin's approach sheds light on missionary preaching. He shows that already from the end of the first century, it vanished and was replaced by a recruitment practice that relied on orality. It was conducted as informal, interpersonal contacts, and the conversion process was characterized by the practice of *traditio*, 'giving over' prayers, the creed and Bible passages to be learned by heart. He also points to the fact that it was during the early Middle Ages that most of Europe was successfully converted to Christianity, and that those conversions were not normally prompted by the persuasiveness of the preached word. He writes: '[a]ll of our evidence for both the ancient and early medieval Churches argues for the primacy of the act'. It was acts, miraculous and/or political acts, that prompted a decision to act, to worship the proper god in a proper manner (pp. 106–7).

In our own time, the theories of Ong continue to be of relevance. His concept of a secondary orality following the era of literacy is widely used to shed light on new media technology. Ong argues that, for example, television seems to prompt this kind of orality, that has

> striking resemblance to the old in its participatory mystique, its fostering of communal sense, its concentration on the present moment, and even its use of formulas. But it is essentially a more deliberate and self-conscious orality, based permanently on the use of writing and print, which are essential for the manufacture and operation of the equipment and for its use as well. (pp. 133–5)

Scholars have continued the reflection in the light of digitalization. Here one might refer to professor of classical studies and English, John Miles Foley, and the Pathway Project. Foley argues that humankind's oldest and newest thought-technologies, oral tradition and the internet (OT and IT) are fundamentally alike. He is careful to point out that this does not mean absolute equivalence, just that they share a fundamental functionality (2012, pp. 17–19). He writes: 'In contrast to the fixed, spatial linearity of the conventional page and the book, the twin technologies of OT and IT *mime the way we think* – by navigating along pathways within an interactive network' (pp. 7–8).

In Denmark, professor of culture studies Ole Sauerberg coined the phrase 'Gutenberg Parenthesis' in the history of media, literature and culture in Western societies. Sauerberg argues that the era of the printing press – with a focus on the individual, the book as authoritative, literature as something solid, and the concept of copyright – is an anomaly coming to its end. The internet-based digital culture is a kind of higher-level technological restoration or reinvention of human cognition and communication before the era of printing: oral, liquid, interactive, iterative (Sauerberg 2009, pp. 64, 79–80). Sauerberg's colleague, Tom Pettitt, has further developed the concept, emphasizing especially the aspects of memory and performance in mediation (2012a, pp. 53–72). However, Pettitt is eager to point out that the hypothesis ought to be understood in a non-reductionistic way. In the article 'Bracketing the Gutenberg parenthesis' he discusses how the metaphor itself is misleading. 'There is no implication here, as sometimes in metaphorical applications, that a 'parenthesis' is something over and done with' (p. 96). Pettitt also take pains to point out that he is less certain than Ong and Foley that media technology changes the way humans think. There is a connection between media and cognition, but to Pettitt influence comes not only from media technology, but society as a whole, and that influence runs in both directions (pp. 97–8).

In the following section, these developed theories of secondary orality will be applied to preaching in a digital era.

However, first some qualifications need to be made. First, the secondary orality discourse contains at least two extensive 'hen-or-the-egg' conundrums. Is it media that affects individuals and societies or is it the other way around? Is it spoken words or signs that are the fundamental element of human thought? The purpose of this study is not to offer a solution to these questions. Thus, the purpose here is to hold up this theoretical approach as a lens and point to some interesting aspects of preaching and mission in a digital era. Second, the purpose of doing this is not to argue that we need to learn from the past, but to do something that I think is very important in the study of digitally mediated Christian practices: discuss this present time phenomenon against the backdrop of a longer time perspective (as do Berger 2018, pp. 7–8; Blair 2010, pp. 1–5; Halldorf 2014, pp.14–15). Third, it is important to be particular in the study of digital practices (Berger, pp. 104–5; Hutchings, p. 233). Thus, the insights presented here do not pertain to all preaching in the digital era. But they can say something about *these* sermons from *this* preacher in *this* setting with *this* use of technology, that might be useful for understanding preaching and mission in a digital era in a broader perspective.

Preaching at the Beginning and the End of 'the Gutenberg Parenthesis'

The preacher I have selected for this single case study is Andreas Nielsen, the lead pastor of Hillsong Sweden. He is chosen as a representative of a so-called mega-church that is rapidly growing in Sweden right now (Aronson 2016, p. 9). Historian Peter Horsfield argues that the rapid growth of this kind of charismatic and neo-pentecostal churches is due partly to the cultural patterns of digital, electronic media. He writes: '[h]ighly technological in their media use, they subordinate the stability, order and linearity of textual Christianity to the dynamics of oral culture' (2015, pp. 272–3). Founded in Sydney, Australia, in 1983, Hillsong church has spread to more than 19 countries throughout the world. Sociologist Gerardo Martí defines it as 'an ongoing elaboration of evangelicalism, much of which has recently merged with a softer form of Pentecostalism (often called Charismatic Christianity)' (2017, p. 377). However, in the Swedish context, Hillsong Church is an outspoken part of the Pentecostal movement.

Digital media are integral to everything the Church does, including liturgy and preaching. Extensive online media practices like videos, blogs, live streaming and continuous social media updates of the Church, pastors and other leaders uphold the network. Digital media also enable Hillsong to enact the global ambition it has always had, its mission of spreading the gospel and planting churches (Martí 2017, p. 378: Klaver 2015, p. 423). In one of the sermons Nielsen meta-reflects on this topic. To him, digital technology is 'the package' needed to make young people discover Jesus (Nielsen 2019a).

On any given Sunday, Nielsen preaches up to four sermons in services that gather around 4,000 people in Stockholm alone (*P3 dokumentär*). Sometimes these sermons are streamed to other Hillsong campuses in Sweden, such as the one in the country's second largest city, Gothenburg. The practice of streaming sermons is very common in Hillsong Church, and even when the preacher is present in the room, there is always a real-time cast on screens (Klaver 2015, p. 425). In Hillsong Sweden, some of these sermons are recorded and published on the church homepage as podcasts, available at Acast, Spotify and iTunes. Short, edited videos that contain the core message of the sermon are regularly posted in social media with reference to the podcast and a call to listen to it. These videos are shared by others in social media, as well as the podcasts themselves.

The sermon material considered here consists of five such sermon podcasts from January to March 2019, here referred to as Sermons A–E. The sermons range in length from 37 to 49 minutes, and all but one was streamed to other campuses in Sweden. During the sermons screens are used to show the preacher and to project pictures and some of the Bible verses that the preacher refers to.

To shed light on how orality is at play in Nielsen's preaching, and how a higher level technological secondary orality might differ from that, I will use the preaching of St Augustine. He is chosen not just because he is one of the few preachers from the early church that we have a fair number of records from, but because his preaching could be considered an example of preaching with an orality that builds on literacy, with high oral residue – just as Nielsen's would be expected to be. Furthermore, as John D. Schaeffer has shown, Augustine's *De Doctrina Christiana* could be read as his way of figuring out how to fusion orality and literacy (1996, pp. 1133–45). In short: a preacher from the left side of the Gutenberg parenthesis will be used in order to shed light on a preacher on the border of the other side of the parenthesis.

Performance

The reason why our knowledge about Augustine's preaching is so extensive is that skilled stenographers (which he probably employed himself) wrote down his words as he was preaching (Borgehammar 2019, p. 274). That he was aware of the possibility of a future, literate audience is evident. Augustine occasionally refers to the scribes, telling the audience that he hopes that his words would suffice until the sermon is transcribed (Schaeffer 1996, p. 1135). This awareness also come across in Nielsen's sermons, as he on two occasions mentions that this might become a podcast. Here we may note that neither Augustine nor Nielsen talks directly to the future audience, as, for example, preachers in video/tape recordings or tv/radio preachers sometimes do ('and to you who are listening at home ...') (Fahlgren 2006, pp. 218–36). The present situation and the people that are present in the room remain the preacher's priority.

This is especially evident in the interaction with the audience. Augustine's sermons are filled with references to congregational weeping, groaning, shouting, applauding (Schaeffer 1996, p. 1138). As he was preaching, he took account of the reactions and responses of the audience and commented on that, and the scribes faithfully wrote everything down, even comments made to wealthy ladies that decided to leave the Church since they did not like his preaching on the topic of vanity (Borgehammar 2019, p. 274).

In a similar manner, Nielsen continuously interacts with and comments on the audience that shouts, laughs, applauds, cheers, makes faces, comments and so on. This kind of interpersonal interaction that is characteristic of orality could also be said to be linked to the use of digital media. In their five-year study of the sermons by American evangelical megachurch pastor Craig Groechel, Clint Bryan and Mohammed Albakry argue that this kind of intense audience interaction style of sermon is characteristic of preaching in a setting affected by digital delivery systems. They argue that Groechel's intention in adapting content, language and delivery of his sermons to the 'unique discursive event of the downloadable message', is to connect relationally with his audience and lessen perceived barriers caused by spatial and temporal distance (Bryan and Albakry 2016, pp. 683–703). In Nielsen's preaching, this interaction with the audience recurrently relates to the presupposition that they are users of digital media. For example, they are told to google concepts, look out for podcasts, asked to share on social media, and invited to dance 'the floss dance' from the online computer game Fortnite. In this way, talk of digital media is used to create interaction in two ways. In the first instance, it is to make the audience laugh and feel included, and in the second it is an invitation to use digital technology to continue to interact with the sermon afterwards.

The impression of the sermons being created in the present moment in interaction with the audience is also supported by their length. Augustine's sermons could vary in length, since he could talk for over an hour if he was eager to put something across. Occasionally, he told his audience that he would return to the same topic in his next sermon. He never prepared his sermons in writing. He thought out beforehand what to say, but when he spoke, he extemporized (Borgehammar 2019, p. 275). Nielsen's sermons are also extemporized, and roughly thought out and structured in advance. This is evident in the Bible-quotations shown on screen, as well as the fact that in four out of five cases he mentions a list of points that he wanted to make. In Sermons C and E, he elaborates only on the first part of the list, and then rushes through the remaining points when the worship team starts playing softly in the background. In the two longest sermons, 45 and 49 minutes long, he gets carried away and begins to develop topics more thoroughly. He interrupts himself, promising that he will speak more about that in another sermon (Nielsen 2019c) or even 'a sermon later tonight' (Nielsen 2019e).

Content: Form and Bible Use

The markings of (secondary) orality are not just evident in the performance of the preachers, but also in content. As a master rhetorician in a thoroughly oral culture, Augustine's sermons are full of features characteristic of orality: narrative, various forms of dialogue, insistent repetition and antithesis. When preaching in church services, Augustine would choose brief Bible passages that supported the message he wished to bring across (Borgehammar 2019, p. 275). In his preaching, Augustine would use scripture and liturgy as a secular rhetor would draw on his *copia*, or fund of memorized material. This means that in support of his chosen theme he would bring one scriptural passage after another until the sermon became a "quilt of scriptural quotations and exegesis" (Schaeffer 1996, p. 1138). The preacher's own words merely served as stitches holding the pieces of scriptural fabric together. In *De Doctrina*, Augustine connects this ability to interpret scripture with scripture to having memorized it. Only a person who has internalized scripture to the extent that he knows it by heart can understand it properly (*De Doctrina*, pp. 51, 67, 71). In a key passage in book IV, Augustine writes:

> For a person who has to speak wisely on matters which he cannot treat eloquently close adherence to the words of

scripture is particularly necessary. The wisdom of what a person says is in direct proportion to his progress in learning the holy scriptures – and I am not speaking of intensive reading or memorization, but real understanding and careful investigation of their meaning. Some people read them but neglect them; by their reading they profit in knowledge, by their neglect they forfeit understanding. Those who remember the words less closely but penetrate to the heart of the scripture with the eyes of their own heart are much to be preferred, but better than either is the person who not only quotes scripture when he chooses but also understands it as he should. (*De Doctrina*, p. 205)

Just as a bard must remember a repertoire of oral formulas, or the orator memorize his *copia*, the speaker must internalize the words of Scripture so that he can recall them instantly and recite them. This (and prayer) promotes the understanding and the interpretation Augustine argues for in the first three books of *De Doctrina*. The result is expressed in the sermon as 'quilting' (Schaeffer 1996, p. 1138).

Oral features are abundant also in Nielsen's sermons. Repetitive, additive, aggregative, agonistic (hate/love are very frequently used, and he explicitly refers to 'heroes' and 'enemies'), antithetic, using slogans/proverbs ('we are building a church that will transform the nation'), formulas and narrative. However, there are also differences, mainly in the use of scripture. As in the case of Augustine, Nielsen usually starts his preaching with one or two Bible verses, as a 'springboard' into the topic of the sermon, but the way they proceed differs. Nielsen usually continues directly to the context and situation of the listeners and elaborates on how the listeners could transform that situation through applying the principle God wants them to learn from content of the Bible verse. The situation described is one of fear of change or pain, being cynical or delimited, feeling shy, lonely, anxious, and the listeners are recurrently invited to decide to change or commit to transformation. This applies to individuals as well as the community of the church. These descriptions are extensive and recurring. Thus, Nielsen's preaching could be characterized as therapeutic (Pembroke 2011, pp. 237–58).

Nielsen displays two different uses of Scripture, which may be categorized as either externalized or internalized. The externalized use is characterized by a literacy facilitated by the use of digital media. In a digital environment, knowledge is usually saved externally, also knowledge of the Bible (Phillips 2017, p. 73). Here, the Bible verses are selected beforehand, shown on screen and referred to by chapter and verse as they are read out aloud. They occur at the beginning of the sermon, and at the end of a longer argument to strengthen a point already made through reference to human experience, and/or as God's answer to how to handle the situation described.

The Bible texts that occur in this kind of usage are rarely from the Gospels, but rather from the Epistles or Old Testament. The passages that introduce the theme of the sermons are from Daniel 1.4, Psalms 121, Ephesians 3.20, James 3.1–10, Psalms 106.1–2. In four out of five sermons, the selected scripture passages shown on screen throughout the sermon are solely from the Epistles and OT. They usually appear as single verses or very short passages, read with reference only to the present context outlined by the preacher, and never with reference to their biblical context.

As theologian Peter M. Phillips has shown, this way of engaging with the Bible is enhanced in a digital media environment. In his study of Bible engagement within digital culture, Phillips finds that there has been a shift in the ordinary social performance of the Bible online. It is characterized by a change from propositional verses outlining core incarnational theology, like John 3.16, to verses with therapeutic content, like Jeremiah 29.11, Philippians 4.13 and Romans 12.2. The latter are anthropocentric (practice-oriented) in content, addressing psychological needs to deal with things like personal anxiety and security, picturing God as a benevolent bystander who encourages humans to transform their own minds and attitudes. The biblical texts are often fragmented and decontextualized, making the content of the text individualized and generalized, and thus applicable to any situation (Phillips 2019, pp. 42,

69–78, 111–13). Furthermore, the logic of digital media seems to increase therapeutic content. Phillips' study shows that it is therapeutic verses that bring about most interaction (liking, commenting, sharing). Phillips argues that this creates pressure on Bible sharers to share even more therapeutic verses. They have to 'play the social media game' and 'perform the Bible in a manner that is socially acceptable to the preconditions and preferences of social media' (2019, p. 80).

The internalized use of the Bible is displayed when Nielsen is drawing on memorized material. On these occasions, the verse or passage is introduced with the formula: 'The Bible says'. Here the Gospels are paraphrased or cited (however, there are only two occurrences of the formula 'Jesus said', both in Nielsen 2019c), but first and foremost narrated as *exempla* of the point made by the preacher. Like Augustine, he seems to be drawing on his biblical *copia* (to the extent that even a proverb by Euripides, 'tell me who your friends are ...' is attributed to the Bible, Nielsen 2019e) but while the church father is 'quilting', Nielsen usually quotes one passage at a time and separates his own words from Scripture by pointing out when he is drawing from Scriptural material. However, quilting occurs two times, in Nielsen 2019b and c.

Content: Reusing, Remixing and Passing on Tradition

One important feature of an oral culture is the practice of copying, reusing, remixing material without reference to its author. In Augustine's day it was common practice to give sermons that were not your own, and it was something that he encouraged as a way of spreading, but also controlling the content of the preached word (McLaughlin 1991, p. 100). Throughout the medieval era, preaching was characterized by such a cut-and-paste principle since the preacher's ability to reuse and remix gave authority (Claesson 2019, pp. 103–4). Scholars that study the Hillsong movement point to the fact that digital Hillsong material makes it easy to distribute words, videos and musical scores, allowing for an extensive and eclectic borrowing and duplication (Martí 2017, p. 380). This seems to apply also to sermon content. Several of Nielsen's choices of Scripture passages, topics and lists of points can be found on the Australian mother church website and on YouTube. The close connection is evident, also in the fact that Nielsen chooses to quote Scripture in English and the use of so-called Swenglish, a mix of Swedish and English words. Most notable is Nielsen 2019e, which – although it is not mentioned by Nielsen – is a compilation based on founder Brian Houston's 2018 book *There Is More: When the World Says You Can't, God Says You Can*.

Thus, digital media could be said to facilitate the reuse, remix and control features of an oral culture. This is also at play in the phenomenon I call 'co-preaching'. This occurs when you share a sermon on social media platforms. When someone does that, and especially when he or she frames the sermon with a (positive) comment, that person could be said to participate in the preaching event, reusing and remixing material.

Both communication style and the reuse/remix feature of orality is linked to the idea of passing on tradition. There is a certain content that is to be given over, and additional or new content is rarely included. This seems to be at play also in the content of these sermons, despite the large distance between Sweden and Australia. The technology of digital media makes this possible. Passing on of certain content via digital media could also be said to take place in the services as a whole. As argued by Ong and McLaughlin, in an oral culture liturgy is central. If you knew the fundamental prayers, hymns and the creed you knew everything you needed to know as a devout Christian. Preaching was not necessary, but when it did occur it was difficult to distinguish from liturgy, a handing down of tradition with as little innovation as possible (McLaughlin 1991, p. 115) In the Hillsong setting, the liturgy is highly structured and leaves little room for improvisation or surprises (Klaver 2015, p. 424). Each individual song is performed as close to the original recording as possible, with the same set of instruments, voices and tempo. Musical innovation, like the development of a specific Euro sound, has been shut down since the congregations preferred the original versions (Wagner 2014, pp. 59–73). Furthermore, as mentioned above, there was a fluidity between liturgy and sermon. This could also be said for Nielsen's preaching. This is especially evident in Nielsen 2019b on Psalm 121. The verse that Nielsen keeps repeating and develops most of the sermon on is 'I lift my eyes up to the mountain', which also happens to be a well-known Hillsong church song. But it is also at play in practice. In the end of all sermons, music starts playing softly in the background. The music enhances the message of the preacher as he reaches the climactic conclusion of the sermon and makes the transition from sermon to liturgy seamless. The sermon transitions into prayer, and as it does the music gets louder and more intense, until the preacher's prayer has ended when the singing begins anew. This fluid border between sermon and liturgy can however pose a bit of a problem for the preacher. On two occasions, Nielsen tells the worship team to wait or stop playing since he is not done yet with the sermon (Nielsen 2019c and e).

However, when it comes to both Bible use and reuse/remix, Nielsen 2019c differs from the rest of the sermons. It starts with a reference to the 2019 slogan of Hillsong vision conference: 'revival is in the air', but then there is a ten-verse uninterrupted reading. Nielsen comments that this is unusual and apologizes. Then he states that before he starts with his sermon, he wants to share some thoughts. He talks for about 15 minutes and mentions three times that he had prepared for this and thought about this, and 19 minutes into the sermon he states that 'now over to the sermon' and starts teaching from a list with seven points. This does not occur in the four other sermons. In the sermon-before-the sermon section the use of English words and concepts is remarkably lower, and similar material is not found online. This seem to be a sermon where Nielsen has contributed a larger amount of his own material. This is especially interesting, since this section in Nielsen 2019c contains more propositional and Gospel material than the four others combined, including the part where one of the 'quilting' occasions takes place. As mentioned earlier, this occurs in relation to an internalized usage of Scripture, pointing to a relation between memorization of Scripture passages and a different kind of content.

Authority

In an oral-based culture, there is a close connection between authority and the preacher as person. Authority is strongly charismatic in character, indicated by achievements of success in conversions, healings, powerful oral preaching, and the ability to induce ecstatic religious experience (Horsefield 2015, pp. 256–8). Such a connection between authority and person is characteristic of the digital era (Sligo 2018, pp. 328–42, Campbell 2010, pp. 251–76). In a close reading of Augustine's *De Doctrina Christiana*, Michael Glowasky points to how narrative was used to build up the speaker's authority in rhetorical speech. A speaker was judged on the basis of the composition of the speech, but also on his ability to show that he is a good person. The speaker's way of using *narratio* was considered the best way to build up such *ethos* (Glowasky 2018, pp. 179–80). In other words: being able to tell a story well pointed to both rhetorical skills and that you were a person who knew how the world works, i.e. a person worth trusting. In Nielsen's preaching, narratives are frequently used to build up ethos. That he is aware of this function of narrative is evident, as he makes a short meta-reflection on the power of stories in Nielsen 2019e, referring to how he often discusses this with one of his co-workers.

Nielsen tells extensive stories about his own everyday life as well as his life as a Christian. In this way he shows that he is someone who knows how the world works and what issues people struggle with in their lives. In Nielsen 2019d, this is further enhanced in a narrative about King David. According to Nielsen, King David was a person who used to burn for his calling, but one day he got bored and made a terrible mistake. When he turned to God and begged for forgiveness, God told him that he was a 'man of his heart'. He applies this to the listeners, but also to himself, as a leader who is burning for his vision to build a church where Christians can praise God, just like King David built a temple where the Christians (sic!) of that time could praise God.

The use of narrative is also a feature of therapeutic preaching. Scripture content is often presented as an elaborated narrative where the preacher's own experience and imagination are used to add material that can amplify the message the preacher wants to convey. There is, however, a risk involved in narrating: the material added might enhance the preacher's message at the expense of the biblical message (Pembroke 2011, pp. 237–58). This occasionally happens in the sermons considered here. For example, when Nielsen wants to underline how transformative it is to speak well of others, he tells two stories referring to 'the Bible'. One in the account of the adulterous woman in John 8. When Jesus talks to her, he chooses to find something that is right in her, and this turns her life around. This is also true of the woman at the well of Sychar in John 4. When Jesus focuses on what is right and positive, it transforms her life and she runs off into town, telling people that she has finally met some-one who could tell her who she really is (Nielsen 2019c). The biblical perspectives of forgiveness of sins (what is *not* right in humans) and the revelation of Jesus as God's Messiah (who *Christ* is) are lost in the narrative.

When turning to observe which authorities other than the Bible Nielsen is referring to, authority comes across as highly relational. For example, in every sermon there are mentions of 'Brian', referring to Brian Houston, National President of the Hillsong movement in Sydney. Brian is a role model in faith and ethics, Brian's vision guides the church, and Brian would kick Nielsen across the continent if he was unfaithful to his wife. This is constructed in a way that is strikingly similar to how the medieval preachers in the fourteenth- and fifteenth-century sermon material in Vadstena Monastery in Sweden refer to 'Birgitta', St Bridget of Sweden (Claesson 2019, p 103). It is clearly presupposed that everyone knows who 'Brian' is, and implied that Brian is an authority. It is noteworthy that there is never any mention of Houston's wife Bobbie, despite the fact that she shares the 'exceptional status as founder-leader' in Hillsong (Harrison 2017, p. 224). There is also always and exclusively reference to people within the church. Even when the preacher refers to research done by psychologists of religion, typically the reference is not to the researcher but to a person in the production team that learned this when he studied theology (Nielsen 2019e). In all five sermons there are people in the room mentioned by name, either as part of an anecdote or a joke, or in a moment of interaction as the preacher sees a reaction to what he says. The interpersonal and interdependent aspects are striking. Scholars working with secondary orality have emphasized the fact that in a digital era, these types of interpersonal communication as basis of authority are increasing, while the references to literal truth and facts are decreasing (Sligo 2018, pp. 328–42).

To sum up: turning the lens of secondary orality on a preacher in a context shaped by and for digital media points to some interesting features of preaching in a digital era. There is a strong focus on the present, instead of, for example, future listeners or past-time historical context of Scripture passages. It is highly interpersonal, both in performance and in how authority is expressed. Narrative is frequently employed as means to build authority and to convey and clarify the preacher's message. The remix and reuse of material is common, something that is linked to liturgy and the passing on of a tradition. All these features are facilitated or/and enhanced by digital technology and digital culture.

There are of course also many differences. In this article particularly Bible usage was mentioned, but commonly noticed is the influence of postmodernism, consumerism and late modern capitalism on the Hillsong movement (Klaver 2018, p. 431; Wagner 2014, pp. 59–73). However, since both digitally mediated preaching and the Hillsong movement are usually understood in the light of such differences, as something *new* and *alien* to Christian practice, the concept of secondary orality could add an important dimension to the understanding. Not least why the Hillsong church has been so successful in its mission to young people. As inhabitants of a secondary orality culture, their thinking is to some extent structured by that. This means that the Hillsong slogan 'welcome home' is not just a 'brand tagline' (Wagner 2014, p. 8), it is an adequate description of how someone brought up with new technology would feel in a church where message and practice are structured by the logic of digital media: at home. However, this message is enacted not just through the use of digital media. Nielsen 2019a talks about this in terms of being 'attractive' and mentions an example of how this was carried out in the church. A person who visited the annual Christmas show was amazed by the personal welcome he got and, according to Nielsen, all he wanted to talk about was how well he had been received before the show. Making people feel 'welcome home' is part of what makes the church attractive to others.

Conclusion

The concept of secondary orality suggests that, in some aspect, the characteristics of preaching in a digital era could be understood as returning to the roots and the conditions of preaching in early Christianity. This points to some areas of possible growth.

One might be the style and form of preaching. If you are to proclaim the kingdom of God in a cultural context at the end of the Gutenberg parenthesis, you would need to carefully consider how to do it. Perhaps a sermon with a high degree of literacy is not the best match for an orally inclined digital culture? Perhaps not even for the local church, if the congregation contains a larger portion of people immersed in digital technology?

Another area worth considering is content. In the oral culture of early Christianity, preaching was considered a giving over of traditional material, and thus hard to distinguish from liturgy. In a secondary orality cultural context, a more conscious incorporation of liturgical content and practices into the act of preaching might be a strategy worth exploring. This idea is supported in reflections from the 2018 World Council of Churches and Commission on World Mission and Evangelism conference in Arusha, Tanzania. Pondering the outcome of the conference, theologian Stephen Bevans suggests that 'prayer, contemplation, and practices of worship become more understood as essential, constitutive of mission' (Bevans 2018, p. 366).

As McLaughlin stated, in the oral culture of early Christianity, both preaching and mission were interpersonal and focused on acts. In her reflections on the Arusha conference, the professor of Theology and World Christianity, Kirsteen Kim, notes that this theme is gaining importance in the global discourse. This is not least evident in the sub theme of the conference: 'called to be transforming disciples'. In her opinion, it emphasizes that human participation in the *missio Dei* is about acts, a joining the work of the (relational) Trinity for the whole creation (2018, pp. 413–27). As, for example, Antonio Spadaro points out in his book *Friending God: Social Media, Spirituality and Community*, the preferences and preconditions of digital social media makes them well suited for this aspect of mission (2016, p. 34).

The concept of secondary orality thus indicates areas of possible growth for preaching and mission, but also areas where the garden might need to be pruned to make sure there is healthy growth. This pertains to the tendency of digital media to enhance features of orality. Especially intrapersonal features, like focus on the present situation, person-to-person interaction, personal authority, and the use of narrative, are amplified through digital media communication. Likewise, the act of passing on certain content and tradition (reuse/remix), is facilitated and enhanced by digital media. Although this might be an area of growth, there are also possible drawbacks. On digital social media platforms, algorithms tend to create 'bubbles' that confirm what an individual already knows and likes. In the same way, a strong focus on the interpersonal and extensive reuse/remix could cause preachers (and their congregations) to get caught up in a theological 'algorithm' where their understanding of God and Scripture is rarely questioned or nuanced. The fact that digital media also could be said to encourage an externalized use of the Bible further amplifies this tendency, putting the gospel at risk of being misrepresented.

As the concept of secondary orality sheds light on this risk, it also suggests a possible way to counter it: the internalization of scripture. As Augustine pointed out, memorizing larger portions of Scripture create a kind of safety net for interpretation, where each passage is understood in its biblical context. Internalized knowledge of a wider range of Scriptural material also facilitates the inclusion of propositional, theocentric content that could complement the therapeutic, anthropocentric. Nielsen 2019c could be said to be an example of how this could play out, with its increased amount of Gospel material and scriptural quilting. Stimulating the growth of this particular branch could further both mission and its core component preaching.

References

Aronson, Torbjörn, 2016, *Ett nytt karismatiskt landskap i Sverige*, Uppsala: Aeropagos i samarbete med Världen idag.

Augustine, *De Doctrina Christiana*, trans. R. P. H. Green, 1995, New York: Oxford University Press.

Berger, Teresa, 2018, *@Worship: Liturgical Practices in Digital Worlds*, London: Routledge.

Bevans, Stephen, 2018, 'Transforming Discipleship and the Future of Mission: Missiological Reflections after the Arusha World Mission Conference', *International Review of Mission*, Vol 107, No. 2, pp. 362–77.

Blair, Ann M, 2010, *Too Much to Know: Managing Scholarly Information before the Modern Age*, New Haven: Yale University Press.

Borgehammar, Stephan, 2019, 'Augustine – Preacher of Paradox and Promise in Early Fifth-century North Africa', in Cilliers, Johan and Hansen, Len (eds), *Preaching Promise Within the Paradoxes of Life*, Stellenbosch: African Sun Media.

Bryan, Clint and Albakry, Mohammed, 2016, '"To Be Real Honest, I'm Just Like You": Analyzing the Discourse of Personalization in Online Sermons', *Text & Talk*, Vol. 36, No. 6, pp. 683–703.

Campbell, Heidi, 2010, 'Religious Authority and the Blogosphere', *Journal of Computer-mediated Communication* Vol. 15, No. 2, pp. 251–76.

Claesson, Erik, 2019, 'Medeltida predikan', in Hagberg, Markus (ed.), *Den som hör er, han hör mig: perspektiv på kyrkans förkunnelse*, Skellefteå: Artos & Norma, pp. 91–110.

Cowan, Nelson R., 2017, 'Heaven and Earth Collide: Hillsong Music's

Evolving Theological Emphases', *Pneuma: The Journal of the Society for Pentecostal Studies*, Vol. 39, No 1, pp. 78–104.

Dagen, 2019, 'Webb-tv lockar till kyrkan', 23 July, pp. 6–7.

Edwards, O. C., 2004, *A History of Preaching: Volume 1*, Nashville: Abingdon Press.

Fahlgren, Sune, 2006, *Predikantskap och församling: Sex fallstudier av en ecklesial baspraktik inom svensk frikyrklighet fram till 1960-talet*, Uppsala: Uppsala Universitet.

Foley, John Miles, 2012, *Oral Tradition and the Internet: Pathways of the Mind*, Chicago: University of Illinois Press.

Glowasky, Michael, 2018, 'The Author is the Meaning: Narrative in Augustine's hermeneutics', *Scottish Journal of Theology*, Vol. 71, No. 2, pp 159–75.

Halldorf, Joel, 2014, 'De frälsande ordens form: Skriftlig materialitet och kyrklig identitet under 2000 år', in *Läsarna i distraktionernas tid: Bibel, kyrka och den digitala revolutionen*, Stockholm: Tro & Liv Skriftserie.

Harrison, Dreu, 2017, 'It Is (not) Alternative: On Hillsong's Visions as Sacrament and Spectacle', in Riches, Tanya and Wagner, Tom (eds), *The Hillsong Movement Examined: You Call me Out Upon the Waters*, London: Palgrave Macmillan, pp. 219–34.

Horsfield, Peter, 2015, *From Jesus to the Internet: A History of Christianity and Media*, West Sussex: Wiley Blackwell.

Houston, Brian, 2018, *There Is More: When the World Says You Can't, God Says You Can*, Glasgow: William Collins.

Hutchings, Tim, 2018, 'Ethnography, Representation, and Digital Media', in Ideström, Jonas and Stangeland Kaufman, Tone (eds), *What Really Matters: Scandinavian Perspectives on Ecclesiology and Ethnography*, Eugene, Oregon: Pickwick Publications, p. 227–36.

Hutchings, Tim, 2015, 'Real Virtual Community', *Word & World*, Vol. 35, No. 2, pp. 151–61.

Kim, Kirsteen, 2018, 'Theological Mission after the Arusha Conference on World Mission and Evangelism, 2018', *International Review of Mission*, Vol. 107, No. 2, pp 413–27.

Klaver, Miranda, 2015, 'Media Technology Creating "Sermonic Events": The Hillsong Megachurch Network', *Cross Currents*, Vol. 65, No 4, pp. 422–33.

Kuck, David W., 2004. 'Preaching on Acts for Mission Formation', *Currents in Theology and Mission*, Vol. 31, No. 1, pp. 32–9.

Le Grys, Alan, 1998, *Preaching to the Nations: The Origins of Mission in the Early Church*, London: SPCK.

Litfin, Duane, 2015, *Paul's Theology of Preaching: The Apostle's Challenge to the Art of Persuasion in Ancient Corinth*, Westmont, Illinois: InterVarsity Press Academic.

Martí, Gerardo, 2017, 'The Global Phenomenon of Hillsong Church:

An Initial Assessment', *Sociology of Religion: A Quarterly Review*, Vol. 78, No. 4, pp. 377–86.

Matthey, Jacques (ed.), 2005, *'You are the Light of the World': Statements on Mission by the World Council of Churches, 1980–2005*, Geneva: World Council of Churches.

McLaughlin, Emmet, 1991, 'The Word Eclipsed? Preaching in the Early Middle Ages', *Traditio: Studies in ancient and medieval history, thought and religion*, Vol. 46, pp. 77–122.

Mission and Evangelism: An Ecumenical Affirmation, in Matthey, Jaques (ed.), 2005, *You Are the Light of the World: Statements on Mission by the World Council of Churches, 1980–2005*, Geneva: World Council of Churches Publications.

Nielsen, Andreas, 2019a, 'En bättre version av dig' [podcast], produced by Hillsong Sweden, 7 January, https://hillsong.com/sv/sweden/podcast/2019/01/en-ba%cc%88ttre-version-av-dig/#.Xd54JOhKg2w, accessed 10 September 2020.

Nielsen, Andreas, 2019b, 'Show up in his presence' [podcast], produced by Hillsong Sweden, 27 January, https://hillsong.com/sv/sweden/podcast/2019/01/show-up-in-his-presence/#.Xd537OhKg2w, accessed 10 September 2020.

Nielsen, Andreas, 2019c, 'Vem får din röst' [podcast], produced by Hillsong Sweden, 11 March, https://hillsong.com/sv/sweden/podcast/2019/03/vem-far-din-rost/#.Xd53quhKg2w, accessed 10 September 2020.

Nielsen, Andreas, 2019d, 'Don't get used to it' [podcast], produced by Hillsong Sweden, 18 March, https://hillsong.com/sv/sweden/podcast/2019/03/dont-get-used-to-it-2/#.Xd52r-hKg2w, accessed 10 September 2020.

Nielsen, Andreas, 2019e, 'Bränn dina staket' [podcast], produced by Hillsong Sweden, 1 April, https://hillsong.com/sv/sweden/podcast/2019/04/bra%cc%88nn-dina-staket/#.Xd51KuhKg2w, accessed 10 September 2020.

Niyonsata, Francoise, 2018, 'Mission Is not Only about Preaching', *International Review of Mission*, Vol. 107, No. 2, pp. 458–71.

Ong, Walter J., 2002, *Orality and Literacy: The Technologizing of the Word*, London: Routledge.

P3 dokumentär, 2017, 'Hillsong – megakyrkan och succépastorn' [radio programme], Radio P3, 4 June.

Pembroke, Neil, 2011, 'Theocentric Therapeutic Preaching: A Sample Sermon with Commentary', *Practical Theology*, Vol. 5, No. 3, pp. 237–58.

Pettitt, Tom, 2012, 'Media dynamics and the lessons of history: The 'Gutenberg Parenthesis' as Restoration topos', in Hartley, J., Burgess, J. and Bruns, A. (eds), *A Companion to New Media Dynamics*, Malden, MA and Oxford: Wiley-Blackwell, pp. 53–72.

Pettitt, Tom, 2013, 'Bracketing the Gutenberg Parenthesis', *Explorations in Media Ecology*, Vol. 11, No. 2, pp. 95–114.

Phillips, Peter M., 2017, *Engaging the Word: Biblical Literacy and Christian Discipleship*, Abingdon: The Bible Reading Fellowship.

Phillips, Peter M., 2019, *The Bible, Social Media and Digital Culture*, New York/Abingdon: Routledge Focus.

Sauerberg, L. O., 2009, 'Preface: The Gutenberg Parenthesis – Print, book and cognition', *Orbis Litterarum*, Vol. 64, No. 2, pp. 79–80.

Schaeffer, John D., 1996, 'The Dialectic of Orality and Literacy: The Case of Book 4 of Augustine's *De Doctrina christiana*', *PMLA*, Vol. 111, No. 5, pp. 1133–45.

Shelton, Robert M., 1987, 'Mission as a Context for Preaching', *Austin Seminary Bulletin* (Faculty ed.), Vol. 103, No. 4, pp. 67–73.

Sligo, Frank, 2018, 'Truth value, Trump, and benign lies at the closing of the Gutenberg Parenthesis', *Communication Research and Practice*, Vol. 4, No. 4, pp. 328–41.

Spadaro, Antonio, 2016, *Friending God: Social Media, Spirituality and Community*, New York: The Crossroads Publishing Company.

Wagner, Tom, 2014, 'Branding, Music, and Religion: Standardization and Adaptation in the Experience of the "Hillsong Sound"', in Usunier, Jean-Claude and Farnham, Jörg Stoltz (eds), *Religion as Brands: New Perspectives on the Marketization of Religion and Spirituality*, Surrey, UK: Ashgate, pp. 59–73.

World Council of Churches, 2013, *The Church: Towards a Common Vision*, Faith and Order Paper No. 214, Geneva: World Council of Churches Publications.

PART 3

Public Theology and the Common Good

I I

Vulnerable Children and *Missio Dei* in a Digital Sphere

TIM J. DAVY

[The wicked] sits in ambush on Instagram;
  on the dark web he abuses the innocent.
His eyes stealthily watch for the helpless;
  he lurks in ambush like a lion in his thicket;
he lurks that he may ensnare the vulnerable;
  he blackmails the poor when he draws him into his
    network ...
Arise, LORD; O God, lift up your hand;
  forget not the afflicted.[1]

If digital culture is seen as a new environment in which God's mission is being worked out, what are the implications for the Church's participation in that mission? More specifically, what might the Church's mission to, for and with vulnerable children look like in this new sphere?

I begin this chapter by explaining what I mean by the terms, 'vulnerable children' (or 'children-at-risk') and '*missio Dei*', and how the two relate. I then explore how the emergence of the digital environment might change the conversation, or require new conversations; that is, how the Church's participation in the *missio Dei* might need to be adapted or contextualized to account for the digital sphere.

My main way of achieving this is to describe in selective detail some of the ways in which digital technology is being used to exploit vulnerable children and young people.

Clearly there is much that is positive about digital spaces, and many ways in which such technologies are being used to bring new connections and opportunities for people to witness the mission of the Church in action. However, Angela Gorrell is surely correct in her assessment of new media as a mixed offering with 'both glorious possibilities and profound brokenness'.[2] She expands:

> Glorious possibilities arise when new media is designed and used in view of Christian visions of the flourishing life. New media spaces and devices *can* be sites and instruments of God's unconditional love. However, in view of malformed visions of what the good life is, new media is developed and used for damaging purposes, which only deepens the conditions of the false life: malign circumstances, harmful practices, and destructive feelings. This is why new media is often a source of profound brokenness. (2019, p. 4, original emphasis)

Additionally Gorrell observes that 'new media extends suffering that occurs in physical spaces into digital spaces, and issues of suffering are increasingly integrated across people's online and in-person lives' (pp. 3–4). This simply cannot be ignored.

It is this darker side of the digital sphere that is of primary interest in the current chapter, the driving motivation for the conviction that the Church must face up to the realities and risks of the digital sphere; risks not just to ourselves, but to the most vulnerable in society. Without doing so I believe our missiology and mission practice will be deficient. We might also consider the ways in which the Church might be called to enter into places of 'risk' as part of our missional engagement.

Two caveats are worth setting out at this point. First, I am not advocating a posture of such risk-aversion that it prevents or discourages the Church from digital engagement. Such a simplistic and fear-based attitude would prevent our involvement from the many good opportunities open to us and, given the high uptake of digital among, for example, young people, we would struggle to connect with entire generations. But a positive engagement in the digital sphere must be informed by a deeper understanding of that context, in all its complexities.

The second caveat is that, given the selective nature of this chapter and its focus on some of the immense and difficult realities of the digital environment, it would be easy to feel overwhelmed. But the Church has been here before. While it is true that the Church (as well as society more broadly) needs to catch up, there are opportunities for the Church to speak and live the Kingdom of God into the digital sphere to, for and with vulnerable children. As such, the chapter should be read as just one aspect for consideration as the Church participates in God's mission in the digital sphere.

Definitions: Vulnerable Children and *Missio Dei*

Although this chapter is relatively short and with limited scope, it is important to give some attention to what I mean by the phrases 'vulnerable children' and '*missio Dei*'. Inherent in both is a degree of generality and ambiguity and, particularly for the latter, a history of contested understandings. We need, therefore, some degree of clarity, if only to set out my assumptions and give greater specificity to the language I am using. I begin with the term, 'vulnerable children'.

Vulnerable Children (also known as children-at-risk)

The Lausanne Movement's issue network focusing on children-at-risk offers the following definition, which they view as a helpful starting point:

> Children-at-risk are persons under 18 who experience an intense and/or chronic risk factor, or a combination of risk factors in personal, environmental and/or relational domains that prevent them from pursuing and fulfilling their God-given potential. (2014a)

The kinds of factors that might be included here, they suggest, are poverty, displacement, exploitation, neglect, violence, and so on. I use 'vulnerable children' in a wider sense to include children-at-risk.[3]

Missio Dei

Broadly, this Latin term meaning 'mission of God' can be understood 'as a reference to the Christian theological understanding of mission which seeks to ground Christian missionary theory and practice in the missionary activity of the Triune God' (Pachuau 2007, pp. 232–3).

To be sure, its meaning and historical development are contested, as is the very language of 'mission' itself.[4] Nevertheless, for the purposes of this chapter when I talk about *missio Dei* I am referring to a way of understanding the overarching purposes of God, articulated by the whole biblical story as it witnesses to the will of God to (in Paul's language) 'reconcile all things to himself' (Col. 1.20a) (Wright 2014, pp. 48–9). I understand this endeavour to be a holistic activity leaving no sphere untransformed: an articulation and demonstration of the Kingdom of God in all areas of life, including digital.

Importantly for this chapter, I also understand God's mission to be carried out not just on behalf of the weak but, crucially, carried out in the midst of and by means of weakness. So, with Richard Bauckham,

The gospel does not come to each person only in terms of some abstracted generality of human nature, but in the realities and differences of their social and economic [and, we might add, digital] situations. It engages with the injustices of the world on its way to the kingdom of God. This means that as well as the outward movement of the church's mission in geographical extension and numerical increase, there must also be this (in the Bible's imagery) downward movement of solidarity with the people at the bottom of the social scale of importance and wealth. It is to these – the poorest, those with no power or influence, the wretched, the neglected – to whom God has given priority in the kingdom, not only for their own sake, but also for all the rest of us who can enter the kingdom only alongside *them*. (2003, pp. 53–4, original emphasis)

This, I think, plays well into our theme. We must do our missiological thinking through a lens of weakness. Especially for those of us who live relatively safe and prosperous lives, we – the anomalous ones – must put in extra effort to learn from those who have a more typical and representative experience of life; that is, marked by poverty, marginalization, and/or significant levels of daily risk and vulnerability.

As Rosalee Velloso Ewell, Redcliffe's Principal and my co-teacher on Redcliffe's MA module on Vulnerable Children is fond of asking, 'Who is not in the room? Whose voices are not being heard?' So, when we talk about *missio Dei* in the digital sphere, we must be attentive to those who are marginalized, excluded, vulnerable, with little 'digital agency'.

Yet we should acknowledge that mission is not just done 'to' or 'for' people. As the language of the Lausanne Movement's working paper on children-at-risk indicates, mission is done among and 'with' them. Indeed, how might the church be taught and enriched by the very children and young people we are seeking to serve? (Lausanne Movement 2014b)

In an Old Testament focused essay, Christopher Seitz talks about mission in terms of '*getting at the something awry*' depicted in the results of human rebellion (1999, p. 3, original emphasis). 'Mission', he says, 'is God's address to humanity's forfeit' (p. 3). 'What Genesis 12 says about God using Abram and his descendants as a blessing, is said with an eye most explicitedly [sic] to the *innate human tendency to thwart and disrupt God's design for his people*, as this has been described in manifold ways in Genesis 1–11' (p. 5, my emphasis).

I think we can see the experience of vulnerable children in the digital sphere as being a heightened example of 'the innate human tendency to thwart and disrupt God's design for people'. It is to this experience I now turn.

Vulnerable Children and the Digital Sphere

The world is a risky, even dangerous place for those with little or no agency. This is true whether we are talking specifically about the digital environment or not. But what new or heightened risks does the digital sphere present for vulnerable children and young people?

A starting point could be to suggest that the digital sphere is not a 'neutral' or equal space. Reflecting on my own experience, as one who is able to take advantage of the opportunities to learn, to connect, to research, work and publish, the digital sphere often feels like a place of opportunity. Then again, I have agency. Yes, I am concerned about privacy data breaches. I am careful what personal details I post online. I have attended online safety workshops at my kids' schools. Fundamentally, I feel relatively in control of the risk. I have agency; but what about those who do not?[5]

Consider some of the opening paragraphs of a recently published UK Government White Paper on Online Harms (HM Government 2019). Here the Government identified a number of examples of the ways in which children and young people may be vulnerable in the online sphere, including the online activities of child sex offenders, and criminal gangs' use of digital platforms to glorify gang culture and violence, and sell weapons to young people (p. 5). Beyond such obvious illegal activity, the report also highlights mental health concerns, 'excessive screen time', online harassment, exposure to content relating to self-harm and suicide, and the issue of 'designed addiction' (pp. 5–6).

These risks or harms vary in severity and type. Some are designed risks – 'designed addiction' – and some have more to do with how tools have been used. The key message, however, is that children and young people are especially vulnerable to risks built into the digital sphere, and children who are already at risk have that risk compounded and heightened.

One example of this kind of situation is highlighted by the work of the charity Viva: Together for Children, whose 2018 Christmas appeal focused on the phenomenon of online sexual exploitation of children (Viva 2018, pp. 4–6). Taking the Philippines as a case study they noted that that area is described by UNICEF as 'the global epicentre of the live-stream sexual abuse trade', and name contributory factors such as 'rapid urbanization and technological advancements, coupled with rising social and economic inequality' (p. 4).

Viva also point out that the greatest demand for this live-streaming is from the West (p. 2). Digital technology has evidently been used to compound and innovate new methods and markets of abuse.

A second example of the darker side of the digital environment, and one that I will explore in more depth, is that of child criminal exploitation (CCE) in the UK, and the role that technology plays in this phenomenon. Of particular note is the popularized term 'County Lines', which refers to the practice of city-based drug gangs expanding their operations beyond their usual patch to reach towns and even rural areas. It has grown in public awareness in recent years and is now described as 'a systemic problem reported in almost every police force in the country' (Children's Society 2019, p. 4). Sophisticated use of ordinary digital technology has enabled criminal gangs to increase their reach, exploiting the vulnerable to achieve that expansion. Evangelina Moisi (2019) puts the issue in a particularly stark light:

> Evidently, technology and the cyber sphere are heavily embedded into the county lines world. It is through such technological methods that children become modern cyber slaves as, with their online and offline worlds becoming blurred, victims are under constant surveillance and lose their free will.

A recent report by the Children's Society highlighted some of the ways social media is used as a tool for CCE:

> Social media and digital technology are being used in a variety of ways in the context of the criminal exploitation through [the] county lines model. Examples shared by practitioners

included children being monitored through Snapchat or apps that allow geo tracking, the use of Airbnb to find [a] temporary base from which to deal drugs, and online banking for money laundering. (2019, p. 43)

A fuller account of some of the digital practices of criminal gangs is provided by a *Guardian* newspaper article, '"County lines" drug gangs tracking children via social media: Warnings on coercion and blackmailing over smartphones went unheeded, say experts, as child exploitation spirals' (Kelly 2019).

In this article, technology is described as 'the central organizing feature of the county lines business model' with digital technology making children 'easy pickings for drug gangs' whose technology use enables them to trap and control their victims. Some gang members become social media influencers and use their position on platforms like YouTube, Instagram and Snapchat to groom and recruit young people:

'When an older gang member – who is often like a local celebrity in their area – is taking the time to like or comment on your photos on Snapchat or Instagram then this is a huge deal to kids,' said Thomas. 'It's not hard to make them feel special and singled out. It's all very public.'

Such is the power of social media, the gangs' manipulative use of it has moved their effectiveness 'to another level'. Once recruited, children are coerced and controlled; for example, they are 'filmed by gangs being sexually abused, beaten and humiliated'. Additionally,

'Sometimes they deliberately put the videos online and then after a month you'll see the same child on Snapchat in a trap house [on] the other side of the country, trying to rebuild their dignity by showing that they are climbing up the gang hierarchy. We recently saw this scenario with a 12-year-old boy.'

These technologies are also used to track the young people's movements ('remote mothering'), using apps like Find My Friends, WhatsApp or Facetime. Such control makes it incredibly difficult for victims to escape or seek help:

> 'They have complete control of children through their phones,' said Sawyer. 'There is nowhere for them to hide ... This is often an invisible form of coercion and exploitation that is happening without any adults being able or willing to intervene,' said Sawyer. 'For these young people there is no difference between the online and offline worlds and we have to tackle this because we are facing a national crisis and this problem is only going to get worse.'

For those actively exploring how the Church engages in the digital sphere, such descriptions of the role of digital media and technology in the abuse of vulnerable children, either internationally or within our own borders, demands our attention.

My main concern in this chapter has been to highlight the need to reflect more deeply on the darker side of the digital sphere. As already stressed, this paints just part of the picture of the context of the digital sphere, yet it seems to be an area of digital engagement that society at large and the Church more specifically is struggling to comprehend or address.

Addressing Online Exploitation as Participation in the *Missio Dei*

In the brief, concluding section, I suggest some ways the Church might respond. Participating in the *missio Dei* involves an attentiveness to the context in which we find ourselves. If the Church is to participate fully in the *missio Dei* we must join with God in his work of restoration and reconciliation, addressing injustice online, offline and at the intersection between the two. But what could this look like?

Reflection

It is essential that we face up to the darker side of the web; it is not only a playground of imagination, creativity and opportunity. For many it is a deeply dangerous place. We should develop our understanding of the use of digital media to exploit the vulnerable. Critical in this is the task of hearing the voices of those who are most at risk of such exploitation. Such an increased attentiveness to the realities of the world, exhibited, for example, in Psalm 10 will naturally lead to lament. As I hinted at in the opening of the chapter, biblical texts give us a lens through which to notice harsh social realities, and a language to bring them to God. This is a deeply missional activity. Texts like Psalm 10 allow us – perhaps require us – to cry out to God on the behalf of others.[6]

Action

While it is easy to become overwhelmed by such harrowing stories of abuse in the digital sphere, missional engagement in the digital space means rejecting despair and embracing action. Supporting the work of church-based and other agencies tackling these complex problems will be essential for an engaged church.

Particularly inspiring is Viva's work with a local partner 'Philippine Children's Ministries Network' (PCMN) to tackle online sexual exploitation. Their aims are *'prevention* (raising awareness across society), *justice* (improving reporting through greater collaboration), and *restoration* (safe community reintegration of OSEC victims)' (Viva 2018, p. 5, original emphasis). It is also notable that they use youth advocates, young people who help raise awareness of the issues among children. This is particularly striking as the issue of 'agency' seems so critical to questions of vulnerability in the digital sphere. What would it mean for the Church to play a role in increasing the appropriate agency of children and young people in the digital sphere? Clearly a proactive attentiveness may be something that Church communities can model.

The Children's Society's prominent work on CCE is strategic and important, as is thirtyone:eight's focus on safeguarding.[7] Finally, the question needs to be asked why children and young people become so vulnerable in the first place. How can churches offer a sense of belonging and support to marginalized and vulnerable individuals and families? Supporting organizations such as Home for Good could be an important part of the Church's participation in this arena.

A final challenge to churches and to those of us thinking and engaging in missiological reflection on digital culture and technology: is the success of such exploitation indicative of our failure to demonstrate the flourishing vision of the Kingdom of God? Are our theological reflection and mission activities insufficiently informed by or connecting with the people that need them the most?

To borrow again from the language of Angela Gorrell, it is essential that those conversant in digital theology help the people of God understand and act on the 'profound brokenness' evident in the digital sphere, as well as the glorious possibilities. Such is our responsibility.

Notes

1 A reworking on parts of Psalm 10, based on the English Standard Version and my own translation.

2 I am indebted to Maggi Dawn who drew my attention to this phrase and Gorrell's volume in her plenary lecture at the 2019 CODEC symposium.

3 As used, for example, by the UK charity Home for Good. See Kandiah and Kandiah, *Home for Good*. See also the charity's website: www.homeforgood.org.uk.

4 See, for example, Flett 2010 and Stroope 2017.

5 While the focus of this chapter is on risk and harm, the related issue of digital inequality should also be acknowledged, especially coming to the fore during the Covid-19 pandemic. Children's ability to engage with the temporary shift of most education provision to home learning through online platforms has depended on reliable internet, access to appropriate devices, and sufficient IT skills. As such certain vulnerabilities will be compounded. For more on this see, for example, Holmes and Burgess 2010.

6 For more on how Psalm 10 might work in this way see Davy 2020b. See also Davy 2020a. I am indebted to Micah Network's Sheryl Haw who, in a devotions talk at Redcliffe College some years ago, pointed out the connection between psalms of complaint and the Church's obligation to lament on behalf of the suffering.

7 See https://thirtyoneeight.org/.

References

Bauckham, Richard, 2003, *Bible and Mission: Christian Witness in a Postmodern World*, Carlisle: Paternoster Press.

Children's Society, 2019, 'Counting Lives: Responding to Children who are Criminally Exploited'.

Davy, Tim J., 2020a, *The Book of Job and the Mission of God: A Missional Reading*, Eugene: Pickwick.

Davy, Tim J. 2020b, 'Connecting a Missional Reading of Psalm 10 with the Trafficking, Abuse, and Exploitation of Unaccompanied Asylum Seeking Children in Europe', in Miles, Glenn and Crawford, Crista (eds), *Traffick Jam with the Bread of Life: Theological Reflections on Sexual Exploitation and Human Trafficking*, Oxford: Regnum.

Flett, John, 2010, *The Witness of God: The Trinity, Missio Dei, Karl Barth and the Nature of Christian Community*, Grand Rapids: Eerdmans.

Gorrell, Angela, 2019, *Always On: Practicing Faith in a New Media Landscape*, Grand Rapids: Baker Academic.

HM Government, 2019, 'Online Harms White Paper', https://assets.publishing.service.gov.uk/government/uploads/system/uploads/attachment_data/file/793360/Online_Harms_White_Paper.pdf, accessed 10 September 2020.

Holmes, Hannah and Burgess, Gemma, 2020, '"Pay the Wi-fi or Feed the Children": Coronavirus has intensified the UK's digital divide', www.cam.ac.uk/stories/digitaldivide, accessed 10 September 2020.

Kandiah, Krish with Kandiah, Miriam, 2019, *Home for Good: Making a Difference for Vulnerable Children*, 2nd edn, London: Hodder & Stoughton.

Kelly, Annie, 2019, '"County lines" drug gangs tracking children via social media: Warnings on coercion and blackmailing over smartphones went unheeded, say experts, as child exploitation spirals', *Guardian* 5 February, www.theguardian.com/global-development/2019/feb/05/county-lines-drug-gangs-blackmailing-tracking-children-social-media, accessed 10 September 2020.

Lausanne Movement, 2014a, 'Who are Children-at-Risk: A Missional

Definition', www.lausanne.org/content/statement/children-at-risk-missional-definition.

Lausanne Movement, 2014b, 'Mission with Children at Risk', Lausanne Occasional Paper 66, www.lausanne.org/content/lop/mission-children-risk-lop-66, accessed 10 September 2020.

Moisi, Evangelina, 2019, '"County Lines": The Modern Cyber Slaves of Britain's Drug-Trafficking Networks', RUSU, www.rusi.org/commentary/'county-lines'-modern-cyber-slaves-britain's-drug-trafficking-networks, accessed 10 September 2020.

Pachuau, Lalsangkima, 2007, '*Missio Dei*', in Corrie, J. (ed.), *Dictionary of Mission Theology: Evangelical Foundations*, Nottingham: Inter-Varsity Press, pp. 232–4.

Seitz, Christopher R., 1999, 'Blessing for All Nations: Mission in the Hebrew Bible', Currents in World Christianity Position Paper, 106, Cambridge Centre for Christianity Worldwide.

Stroope, Michael, 2017, *Transcending Mission: The Eclipse of A Modern Tradition*, London: Apollos.

Viva: Together for Children, 2018, 'Light and Life for Filipino Children', *Life* magazine, No. 10, pp. 4–6, https://issuu.com/viva/docs/life-issue-10-uk-hires, accessed 10 September 2020.

Wright, Christopher J. H., 2014, *The Mission of God and the Task of the Church: Integral Mission and the Great Commission*, Singapore: International Fellowship of Evangelical Students.

12

Public Faith, Shame and China's Social Credit System

ALEXANDER CHOW

In September 2018, Beijing Zion Church was shut down by local government officials after refusing to install CCTV on their premises. Zion's senior pastor Ezra Jin has previously been a major advocate for the Chinese missionary movement, Back to Jerusalem, and with others has argued for unregistered churches to actively engage in Chinese civil society. While religious control has been tightening in China since 2014, recent events must also be connected to the first phase of China's Social Credit System – a means of assessing the trustworthiness of a person based on various criteria, ranging from financial credibility to behaviour on social media and broader society. This chapter argues that the rise of digital technologies like social media and CCTV complicate questions of religion and the public-private divide, both in Chinese and Western societies, and further suggests that these technological changes raise new questions to understandings of Christian mission in the digital age.

On Sunday afternoon, 9 September 2018, local police stormed the Beijing Zion Church (Beijing Xi'an jiaohui),[1] ordering worshippers to leave the premises, confiscating promotional materials, and banning church gatherings as illegal. By the next day, government authorities sealed off the church's rented facilities in Longbaochen Commercial Building (Longbaochen xiezilou). When Zion's senior pastor Ezra Jin (Jin Mingri) enquired about the return of church property, authorities slapped the church with a bill of 1.2 million yuan (approximately £140,000) in back rent and removal costs (Yiu and Law 2018).

The events surrounding the closure of Beijing Zion Church have been covered by international news media outlets (Yiu and Law 2018; Shepherd 2018; World Watch Monitor 2018). Most of these reports have noted that the church began to face trouble after February 2018, when the new Religious Affairs Regulations came into effect (State Council 2017). The new regulations increased pressures on religious groups, especially those like Zion, which were not registered with the main state-sanctioned Protestant organization, the Three-Self Patriotic Movement (TSPM). They also point out that Beijing authorities in April 2018 asked the church to install 24-hour closed-circuit television (CCTV) cameras in the building, with facial recognition technology. According to the Chinese state-run news outlet *Global Times*, this was for 'safety reasons' (Yin 2018). However, Jin explained, 'They wanted to put cameras in the sanctuary where we worship. The church decided this was not appropriate ... Our services are a sacred time' (Shepherd 2018).

Overall, these media outlets have tended to focus on the complexities related to Christian faith and practice in mainland China, often revolving around questions of freedom of religion and church–state relations.[2] Instead, this chapter attempts to situate the events around the closure of Beijing Zion Church within a broader discussion about digital surveillance in mainland China, especially related to the Social Credit System (*shehui xinyong tixi*). While many societies have mechanisms for assessing consumer credit risk, since 2014 the nationwide Social Credit System has taken this further by providing a single government system which assesses the economic and social reputation of every business and every person. Companies with bad social credit may have difficulties acquiring new loans and be charged higher taxes. For individuals, those with a low score may have similar financial restrictions; further repercussions include being publicly shamed on billboards or social media platforms, being denied from moving into a particular region or from sending one's children to certain schools, or being banned from travel on high-speed rail or airlines. A key tool for China's Social Credit System is through CCTV cameras (Chin 2018), such as the kind that were to be installed within the premises of Beijing Zion Church.

The Chinese Communist Party has long employed paper-based methods for the 'social management' of its citizens, such as the *dang'an* (personal dossier) and *hukou* (household registration) systems. While social management draws from Leninist roots, there is the added cultural emphasis in China whereby social control is legitimized as a means to achieve harmonious relationships in society (Hoffman 2017, p. 21; Liang, Das, Kostyuk and Hussain 2018, pp. 1055–7). In recent years, tensions have increased in Tibet and Xinjiang – two of China's autonomous regions with populations made up of primarily ethno-religious minorities, Tibetan Buddhists and Uighur Muslims respectively. Access to YouTube, Facebook and Twitter were all blocked in 2009, following their use to post videos and images of police beatings in Tibet and of riots in Xinjiang (Harwit 2014). This redirected Chinese social media usage to alternative technologies developed by Chinese internet firms – such as Youku, Renren, Weibo and WeChat (Weixin) – all of which are subject to the Chinese government's censors. In 2014, conflicts occurred in various Chinese cities, including suicide bombers and knife-wielding assailants. Chinese authorities quickly denounced these as 'terrorist attacks' and blamed Xinjiang-based militants. This resulted in greater restrictions in Xinjiang, with CCTV cameras and security checkpoints in train stations, hotels, shops and petrol stations, all equipped with facial recognition technologies (Chin and Bürge 2017). Xinjiang became a test site for measures which have become increasingly ubiquitous throughout the country.

The Social Credit System moves social management into the digital age by drawing on big data analysis of a multitude of data-gathering sources (Creemers 2016; Liang, Das, Kostyuk and Hussain 2018). However, as already suggested, this has further ramifications for religious groups. Following the 2017 update to Religious Affairs Regulations, the Ministry of Civil Affairs put out a notice that included requirements for religious organizations and their representatives to provide their social credit identifiers when registering religious activities (2019, art. 4 and 6). In effect, these actions add an extra layer of control over religious groups, given that many are seen as wellsprings of 'foreign infiltration' – whether that be from Islamic extremism, the Dalai Lama (in the case of Tibetan Buddhism), or the West (in the case of Christianity).

Western liberal sensibilities may be quick to attack such surveillance as infringing on individual rights to privacy. However, as we will see, there is rarely a clear-cut boundary between the 'public' and the 'private', especially when we speak of the digital age. Furthermore, Western ideals of a 'public sphere' (coined by Jürgen Habermas in hopes to restore a voice for the bourgeoisie) or a 'public square' (coined by Richard John Neuhaus reflecting American notions of democracy and freedom of religion) (Adams 2013, pp. 281–9) have never been fully realized in China (Chow 2018, pp. 4–7). This is not to say there is no such thing as public speech, but that all public discourse in mainland China is 'directed' through the mediating activities of state-sponsored propaganda and censorship (Cheek 2015, pp. 272–80). This chapter shows that, while urban Christianity in China has been growing in its self-understanding of mission and its use of technology for those purposes, the Chinese government has likewise been utilizing technological advances to manage its directed public space. This chapter also uses China's Social Credit System as a case study for broader theological reflections related to the Christian response to surveillance.

The Growth of Urban Christianity

Ezra Jin, the senior pastor of Zion Church, is a Korean ethnic minority born in Heilongjiang in Northeast China.[3] Jin turned to Christianity in the aftermath of the devastating Tiananmen Square incident of 4 June 1989. At the time as a student in the prestigious Peking University, Jin began visiting a local TSPM-registered church and converted to Christianity several months later. After graduating, he worked for a few years for a foreign company in Beijing, but in 1992 resigned from his job and pursued theological studies at the state-sanctioned Yanjing Seminary and worked for the TSPM-registered Gangwashi Church in Beijing, before going to Fuller Theological Seminary in California in 2002 to pursue a DMin degree. Upon returning to China in 2007, Jin decided to start a new church outside the TSPM system, Beijing Zion Church. This is important because, in China, Protestant and Catholic churches are often divided between those registered with the state through a religious body such as the TSPM (Protestant) or the Catholic Patriotic Association or unregistered 'house churches' (*jiating jiaohui*; mainly Protestant) or 'underground churches' (*dixia jiaohui*; mainly Catholic). The registered groups are often critiqued for allying themselves to the state, whereas the unregistered groups tend to maintain a clandestine existence. For Protestant groups, there is also some debate as to whether there is a kind of 'third church' (*disan jiaohui*) or 'third way' (*disan daolu*) or 'emerging church' (*xinxing jiaohui*) that mediates between registered and unregistered churches which are public and open, yet not compromised with the state (Chow 2018, pp. 108–9). Hence, Ezra Jin explains, 'having served in the TSPM for more than ten years I knew that it was not pleasing to God. So when I returned, I decided to serve in the house church' (Jin 2014a, p. 2). Yet, despite its unregistered and legally ambiguous status, the Church would grow, develop Korean and Mandarin language services, and, by the time it was banned in 2018, boasted over 1,500 weekly parishioners.

Ezra Jin's story of becoming a Christian is one that is quite common in his generation among those shaped by the Tiananmen Square incident. A number of significant leaders and supporters of the 1989 democracy movement – such as Zhang Boli, Xiong Yan, Ren Bumei and Yuan Zhiming – were forced into exile and subsequently converted to Christianity. The last of these names, Yuan Zhiming, was one of the writers of *River Elegy* (*He Shang*), the much-watched Chinese television series that aired in 1988, portraying the decline of Chinese culture and China's need for democracy and human rights; *River*

Elegy has been seen as a catalyst for many who were involved in the 1989 democracy movement. After becoming a Christian in exile in 1992, Yuan again used the power of film to produce videos such as *China's Confession (Shen Zhou)* and *The Cross (Shizijia)* – now portraying China's need for Christianity. Yuan explains:

> *River Elegy*'s conclusion was that the solution for China was democracy and human rights. But it was only when I got to the West that I realized that the root of this was Christianity. It was the Bible. It creates something more important than rights given by a constitution or a government. It creates God-given rights – endowed by our creator. This made rights something permanent and not dependent on a leader ...
>
> People said, '*River Elegy* was so popular, why don't you try to use broadcast media for God too?' So that was the origins of the series [*The Cross*]. (Johnson 2012)[4]

From the perspective of many onlookers, Deng Xiaoping's tanks crushed the hopes of Tiananmen Square protestors on 4 June 1989. However, for Yuan and a number of other exiled dissidents, they found greater hope in a transcendent source of change in China and the world.

This shift in understanding also occurred for many of this generation who stayed in China and became Christians. Prior to the 1990s, Chinese Christians were regarded as among the so-called 'four manys' (*si duo*) – many old, many women, many illiterate and many ill – that is, 'rice Christians' who were seen as legitimizing the Marxist rhetoric that religion is the opiate of the masses. This view was not only promoted by the Chinese Communist Party, but also by certain Christians associated with the TSPM (Bao 1989, p. 3). Many who were involved or supported the 1989 demonstrations were students in middle school or university. Those who found existential resolve in Christianity would become part of a growing cohort of young and well-educated professionals and intellectuals bringing shape to urban Christianity in China in the 1990s and first decades of the twenty-first century (Sun 2007; Yang 2005).[5]

Changing Understandings of Mission

In many ways, Beijing Zion Church is representative of a number of large urban unregistered churches in China. Tracing its history from conception until its closure in 2018 offers us glimpses into the changes in the understanding of mission for Chinese Christians, especially when compared to the older generation of unregistered churches.

We can see this in Ezra Jin's attempts to offer a stronger biblical and theological basis for mission as found in the name for his church: Zion. The name is not merely a reference to Jerusalem, but also to an important Chinese understanding of mission known as the 'Back to Jerusalem Movement' (Hattaway, Yun, Xu and Wang 2003; Chan 2013) – the subject of Jin's 2011 DMin dissertation at Fuller Theological Seminary, written in Korean and later published in English (Jin 2016). The movement is said to have begun in the 1940s when a number of Chinese Christian evangelistic bands organized work in the Western parts of China. As it has continued to develop, especially in the 1980s until the early 2000s, many of those involved have argued that the gospel began in Jerusalem and has travelled through Europe, North America and Asia, and now is the time for Chinese Christians to bring it back to Jerusalem.

Jin's doctoral dissertation was critical of some of the promoters of the Back to Jerusalem Movement. In particular, he made a distinction between the movement as it has developed within China and individuals and organizations promoting the vision from outside China (2016, pp. 20–2). Part of the concern is a difference in focus, as the missionaries within China saw mission work as done by the Chinese church and, as such, were to be financially supported from within, as opposed to needing organizations in Europe and the United States to fund their work. Furthermore, Jin was concerned that the various individuals and organizations promoting the Back to Jerusalem Movement from outside China had questionable biblical understandings and tended to argue for a dispensational view of Zionism. In contrast, his dissertation, supervised by the New

Testament scholar Seyoon Kim, attempted to offer a stronger biblical basis for the movement within China. Jin argued that Zion was not the literal geographic location of Jerusalem but a symbolic term pointing to Christ's eschatological reign. In his view, a more appropriate biblical theology of mission must encompass the bringing of all nations back to God. This is why the title of his work takes 'Back to Jerusalem' and appends to it the phrase 'with all nations' (pp. 157–63).

Ezra Jin's understanding of mission continued to change in 2010 when he, along with some 200 other Chinese church leaders, were invited to join the Lausanne Conference in Cape Town. However, most of these church leaders were stopped by Chinese authorities from passing the Chinese border to attend the conference. Later in 2013, Chinese church leaders were again invited to attend a subsequent meeting held in Seoul at the Asian Church Leaders Forum. It was at this latter meeting that a vision of 'Mission China 2030' was promoted, urging the Chinese church to send 20,000 missionaries out from China by 2030 (Jin 2013; Jin 2016, pp. 161–2). For Jin and other Chinese church leaders, the growth of urban Christianity is accompanied by a growing sense of mission to include evangelism within and beyond China, and the Chinese church's role in the global church's understanding of global mission.

A further understanding of mission can be found in an increasingly strong sense of the church's need to be involved in Chinese civil society. Jin attributes his understanding of this to the writings of Li Fan, a social commentator in Beijing, who argued that the Chinese church is the largest group of NGOs in Chinese civil society (2014b). For other urban church leaders, the main turning point was the disastrous May 2008 earthquake in Sichuan province. We can see this demonstrated through the online and print periodical *Almond Flowers* (*Xinghua*) produced by the Beijing Shouwang Church (Shouwang jiaohui), another unregistered urban church. At the beginning of that year, *Almond Flowers* produced articles related to matters often discussed among unregistered urban churches, such as the question of church registration and Christian understandings of marriage and family. However, after the

2008 earthquake, the Autumn issue had the theme of 'Social Concern' (*Shehui guanhuai*) which spoke about the need for Christians to offer financial and social aid, underscoring the Chinese church's existence as an NGO serving Chinese civil society. This was followed by the Winter special issue on the 'Cultural Mandate' (*Wenhua shiming*), drawing from Dutch Neo-Calvinism to legitimate social engagement. One author concluded, 'God's word or biblical truth must enter into a culture and, expressing itself in every domain of this culture, become God's common grace in human society. This is the church's cultural mandate' (Sun 2008, p. 31, *translation mine*).

Hence, while the church has been developing within urban centres of China, strengthening in both intellectual and economic bases, it has also been experiencing changing understandings of mission. First, as opposed to the early-twentieth-century development of evangelistic bands focusing on bringing the gospel to other Chinese in Asia, the vision of Mission China 2030 is much more encompassing seeing the Chinese church as part of the global mission of the church worldwide. Second, as opposed to the historic house church movement from the Cultural Revolution (1966–76) until the 1990s which tended to underscore a separatist understanding of the church with society, drawing on Christian fundamentalism, mission for the unregistered urban churches includes a stronger sense of a public faith which engages social concerns.[6] Third, these churches have less of a concern maintaining a clandestine existence but, instead, argue for a more open profile. As we will discuss further, this has also included negotiating Christian public presence in the restrictive digital space that is managed by the mainland Chinese government.

Negotiating the Digital Age in China

Much of what has been discussed so far has focused on the shifting nature of Christianity in urban China since the 1990s. While the intellectual history has been largely shaped by the events following 4 June 1989, China has also advanced economically, through its so-called 'socialist market economy', and technologically, especially through the advent of the internet in the country since 1994. By 2017, China boasted of having over 700 million internet users with 95% accessing it through mobile phones. As a country with among the most internet users in the world, it is also one of the most restrictive systems in the world due to its so-called 'Great Firewall of China' (Barme and Sang 1997), which blocks access to foreign websites such as Facebook, Twitter and Wikipedia, as well as acting as a surveillance and censorship tool for content produced within the country. Some netizens in China attempt to circumvent such restrictions or *fanqiang* – literally, to climb over the wall – by using VPN technologies; but these are often blocked and access can be intermittent and vary depending on region. For urban Christians wishing to produce an open and digital profile, this becomes a much more complicated space to negotiate.

In the case of Zion Church, the choice of digital platforms is fairly focused on its mission, as described on its website, to build the 'Kingdom of God in the family, in society and in the whole earth, until the nations return to the discipleship community of Zion' (Zion Church 2018, *translation mine*). In many ways, its approach is similar to large evangelical churches in the West in their use of technology in promoting its sermons and various programmes. However, its website was hosted in the United States so, while it can be blocked by the Great Firewall of China, the church's content could not be easily deleted by Chinese censors. This also meant the ability to update or read the website requires working VPN access. It perhaps indicates why the site was not updated after it was banned and is no longer available. Zion also ran a series of social media accounts. It used a WeChat social media account for about five years, which was closed abruptly by officials in June 2018; a series of alternative WeChat accounts would also be closed in June and August 2018. Furthermore, as the church produced video recordings of its church services, it published them on the Chinese video hosting site Youku, which was also shut down (SCI China Correspondent 2018). The irony of this last point about videos is that, while Jin was happy for services to be video recorded for the church's social media accounts, he was not willing for CCTV cameras to be put in the sanctuary because, as he explained, 'Our services are a sacred time.'

While some churches follow Zion's pattern of using technology to facilitate a mission to build the Kingdom of God, others have used the internet as a discursive space for theological and social commentary. In many ways, this is an extension of China's history of print culture dating to the development of woodblock printing in the Tang dynasty (618–907), when Chinese intellectuals instrumentalized the technology to spread their ideas in the Chinese public space.[7] When Protestant missionaries introduced moveable-type to China in the late-eighteenth century (Reed 2011), Chinese Christian intellectuals would likewise follow suit and introduce Christian periodicals in the early-twentieth century, such as the Protestant *Truth and Life* (*Zhenli yu Shengming*) (Ling 1980, pp. 62–5, 71; Barwick 2011, pp. 69–70) and the *Catholic Review* (*Shengjiao zazhi*) (Starr 2016, pp. 100–27; Lai and Li 2017, pp. 166–86), and in the late-twentieth century, such as the *Christian Culture Review* (*Jidujiao wenhua pinglun*) (Fällman 2008, pp. 23–5).

With the advent of the internet, Chinese Christians would begin to cross from print culture into digital culture. The online digital format allows content to be more easily copy-and-pasted and distributed through multiple digital platforms. One of these periodicals, *The Banquet* (*Aiyan*), was produced by the Beijing pastor Cai Zhuohua from 2002 until 2008 and operated a hybrid model of both print and digital editions; but due to the complexities of producing and distributing paper copies through the postal system, it was constantly encouraging its readers to move to the online format (Wielander 2013, pp. 89–91). Another periodical that offered print and digital editions, and mentioned earlier in this chapter, is Shouwang's *Almond Flowers*, which was produced from 2007 until it ended with three final issues in 2013 – two years after the church was evicted from its property and its pastors and elders arrested. Despite these setbacks, since 2011, Shouwang continues to produce an online-only periodical *@Shouwang* (previously known as *Shouwang Online Journal* [*Shouwang wangluo qikan*]). As periodicals, *The Banquet, Almond Flowers* and @ *Shouwang* collected writings from a variety of figures and promoted a range of topics, from Christian theology and practice within contemporary China, to legal commentary produced by Christian lawyers and legal scholars. They were also hosted on servers based outside mainland China. Like Zion, while they could be blocked by the Great Firewall of China, their content could not be easily deleted by Chinese censors. However, it also suggests that there is a limited ability for other Chinese netizens to access the content, given that they would need the technological means to 'climb over the wall'.

A different approach to technology may be seen in a figure such as Wang Yi. Formerly a law professor at Chengdu University and human rights lawyer, Wang was recognized as one of China's 50 most influential public intellectuals in the politically liberal leaning periodical, *Southern People's Weekly* (2004). After defending a number of house churches, Wang converted to Christianity and became the senior pastor of the Early Rain Reformed Church (*Qiuyu zhi fu guizheng jiaohui*), which was later renamed the Early Rain Covenant Church (*Qiuyu shengyue jiaohui*).

As a pastor, Wang Yi was active using a variety of blogging and microblogging technologies to promote his theological and political commentary. While he utilized blogging platforms hosted both inside and outside China, he also became increasingly vocal on the Chinese social media platforms Weibo and WeChat (Vala and Huang 2017, pp. 176–81). In contrast to the regular issues of periodicals such as *The Banquet* and *Almond Flowers*, the public intellectual Wang Yi utilized technologies that enabled him to communicate his ideas much more idiosyncratically, responding to recent events more quickly. As he was regularly using Chinese blogging and microblogging platforms, this garnered a much larger readership; but it could also more easily be taken down, as was the case after he was arrested and his church closed by government authorities in December 2018. In a surprising turn of events, 48 hours after his arrest, members of the church circulated a public letter that

Wang Yi had penned in anticipation of his arrest entitled 'My Declaration of Faithful Disobedience', which was widely publicized in Chinese and English, both within and outside China (Wang 2018). Members of the church continue to post updates on Wang Yi and the church through platforms hosted outside China, such as Facebook and Github.[8]

In each of these examples, we see different uses of technology to support different understandings of mission. For a church like Zion, the digital presence facilitates a mission of building the Kingdom of God. For others, their digital engagement is an extension of their civic engagement, sustaining the church's relationship with the state and the society. These realities became much more complicated when the latest Religious Affairs Regulations came into effect in February 2018, which now require internet religious activities to have prior permission from relevant government bodies (State Council 2017, art. 47, 48 and 68). Of course, as all of these churches were unregistered, none of them could appropriately request permission for their online religious activities.

The changes in the Religious Affairs Regulations reflect a larger national narrative as found within the latest Cybersecurity Law (National People's Congress 2016, art. 1) which underscores a policy of so-called 'Cyberspace Sovereignty' (*wangluo kongjian zhuquan*). This upholds a view that for the state to be truly sovereign, it needs not only to protect itself from outside forces, but also to manage the development of inside forces. It is the latter point that brings us back to China's Social Credit System, which is a means of putting checks and balances on those who are within China's borders.[9] It is the management of individuals not merely through imprisonment of those 'guilty' of breaking specific laws, but also through highlighting the 'shame' of those with bad behaviour[10] – through billboards and social media – and preventing them from access to exclusive benefits for socially trustworthy citizens.

Conclusion

China's entrance into the digital age has offered new vistas for innovation – whether this be for urban Christians developing their understanding of mission or the Chinese state's evolution of social management. Yet, this is not simply a matter for Christians *out there* in a one-party state such as socialist China. Internet surveillance, CCTV and other technologies are ubiquitous in Western liberal democracies as well. While some may be afraid of Big Brother watching in an Orwellian state, many will also unwittingly give up their privacy to multinational corporations such as Google or Facebook for the convenience of targeted search results, newsfeeds and advertisements – in the name of consumerism or, as Shoshana Zuboff (2019) puts it, 'surveillance capitalism'. How do or should Christians in China and elsewhere respond to such tensions?

In this chapter, we may interpret the various Chinese Christian aspirations of mission as a growing understanding and participation in the *missio Dei*. What then is the relationship between mission and social credit? We all have social credit, whether we are within the borders of China or not, and while Christ is the central figure of Christianity, it is the church that represents this central figure on earth for others to encounter. Christian lives are imperfect mirrors of God's mission in this world. The social credit of Christians imperfectly reflects the social credit of God.

Related to this is the question of what constitutes public theology. It is a concept which has arisen to underscore the publicness of Christianity in the face of secularism's attempts to privatize all forms of religiosity. It is said that religious faith and practice is about personal choice at home and has no bearing on matters of public concern, and that the pulpit is no place to discuss politics. Charles Taylor makes a distinction between the 'modern, bounded self' and the 'porous self' of an earlier enchanted world. The former emphasizes the autonomy of individuals who see themselves 'as invulnerable, as master of the meaning of things', whereas the porous self is vulnerable 'to spirits, demons, cosmic forces' (Taylor 2007, p. 38).

The bounded self is characteristic of many Western societies, whereby individual morality is related but separate from matters of public concern. Contrastingly, across two millennia of Chinese history, Confucianism has upheld an integrated relationship between the private and the public, whereby the individual has a porous relationship with the other. Hence, the Chinese ideal of 'inward sageliness, outward kingliness' (*neisheng waiwang*) asserts that individual moral transformation is a prerequisite for enacting change in the society and the world around them. This is perhaps also suggested in Luke 6.45 when Jesus states, 'for it is out of the abundance of the heart that the mouth speaks'. In other words, the public is an outworking of the private. Digital technologies increasingly blur the line between public and private (Lyon 2001, pp. 20–3), and in many ways are returning our societies to have more porous selves in enchanted and digitized worlds.

While we often consider technologies such as the internet as limitless, offering a digital space that transcends the physical space, the Chinese legal system seeks to build a fence or, better, a wall (or a Great Firewall) along its physical borders. A wall, of course, is meant to keep dangers out and to protect treasures that are within. This is why Eric Stoddart (2016) argues that surveillance technologies should not only be understood in terms of control, but also from the perspective of care – as a faithful parent or teacher or friend may watch over the well-being of others. It would be naive to see the Chinese government as simply a power-hungry authoritarian state; it also exists to care for its citizens and to bring about unity and stability for a diverse and sometimes contentious society.

Theologically, Stoddart reminds us that 'a Christian response to surveillance must involve a deeply practical appreciation of the contingency of this, God's world' (2016, p. 6). Governments and multinational corporations may use surveillance for a mixture of benevolent and malevolent purposes, but their abilities to control this world is finite. Furthermore, it is God who has bestowed upon them the authority that they have (Rom. 13). Christians are called to acknowledge the One who truly transcends the physical – and the digital – space. Cyberspace sovereignty is but a pale imitation of Divine sovereignty, the ultimate source of authority in China and throughout the cosmos.

Notes

1 Chinese terms in this chapter will be offered using pinyin romanization of the Mandarin language, as is the convention for scholarly work related to mainland China.

2 Much of this is shaped by the priorities of Western liberal democracies. For instance, while much of the Anglophone literature discusses 'freedom of religion' (*zongjiao ziyou*), the Chinese constitution only guarantees 'freedom of religious belief' (*zongjiao xinyang ziyou*). This is an important distinction as it suggests that, while religious belief (and non-belief) may have legal standing, various religious practices can be deemed illegal.

3 Biographical information of Ezra Jin comes from a number of sources, though much of this information is based on a pamphlet he edited (Jin 2014a) and an interview conducted by Yu Jie (Yu and Wang 2010, pp. 49–77).

4 In 2015, Yuan Zhiming was accused of raping fellow democracy activist Chai Ling in 1990, before either of them became Christians. Yuan subsequently resigned from the organization which produced the Christian videos, China Soul for Christ Foundation (Morgan 2015).

5 There are of course other factors than the Tiananmen Square incident that has brought shape to urban Christianity. Another major factor has been the growth of the socialist market economy since the 1990s, which has led to the rise of 'boss Christians' (*laoban Jidutu*) amongst entrepreneurs within coastal regions such as Wenzhou (Cao 2011). However, the focus of the discussion in this chapter is mainly amongst those sometimes described as 'intellectual elite Christians' (*zhishi jingying Jidutu*) (Chow 2018, pp. 92–114).

6 In many respects, this echoes the developments that have come out of the Lausanne 1974 conference where church leaders of Africa, Asia, and Latin America argued that evangelical mission needed to affirm both evangelism and social responsibility, in what was variably termed 'integral mission' or 'holistic mission' (Stanley 2013, pp. 151–79; Samuel and Hauser 1989; Kirkpatrick 2019).

7 In these respects, there are many parallels between Christianity in Europe and Confucianism in China, given that both were used to offer a philosophical basis for the state at the time and chose to promote their ideas through print culture. For a discussion on the relationship

between Chinese Christianity and Chinese digital culture more fully in another article (Chow *forthcoming*; Cheek 2015, pp. 35–9).

8 www.facebook.com/earlyraincovenantchurch and https://github.com/chengduqiuyu/-/issues.

9 A further question may be raised about whether such aspirations of China's sovereignty is limited by the physical borders of mainland China, or may extend beyond. This is perhaps one of the concerns in 2014 and 2019 of Beijing's reach into Hong Kong.

10 The idea that different contexts can be understood as either a 'guilt culture' or a 'shame culture' was first raised by the anthropologist Ruth Benedict (1946). While it may be useful to state that certain cultures are more disposed to focusing on 'guilt' or 'shame', we should also be careful not to distil all cultures down to one position or the another. Andy Crouch (2015) shows how the technological age has highlighted the challenges of honour and shame within Western societies, in his article on the practice of 'doxing' another person's private information for online bullying on social media. Recent missiological literature engages 'shame' in terms of how one experiences sin and the need to reconceptualize soteriological categories with the notion of 'honour', for evangelistic and pastoral purposes (Wu 2012; Georges and Baker 2016). Care needs to be taken when diagnosing the experiences of 'guilt' or 'shame'. It may be true that these experiences can come from personal or original sin. It may also be true that a person or an institution may be manipulating, harassing, or abusing another.

References

Adams, Nicholas, 2013, 'Interreligious Engagement in the Public Sphere', in Cheetham, David, Pratt, Douglas and Thomas, David (eds), *Understanding Interreligious Relations*, Oxford: Oxford University Press, 2013, pp. 281–305.

Bao Zhimin, 1989, 'Facing Reality and Responding to Challenges: On Ten Years of Chinese Church Reconstruction', trans. Francesca Rhys, *Chinese Theological Review*, Vol. 5, No. 3, pp. 1–6.

Barme, Geremie R. and Sang Ye, 1997, 'The Great Firewall of China', *Wired* (1 June), available at www.wired.com/1997/06/china-3, archived at https://perma.cc/VF4G-6NJP, accessed 10 September 2020.

Barwick, John, 2011, 'Liu Tingfang: Christian Minister and Activist Intellectual', in Hamrin, Carol Lee with Bieler, Stacey (eds), *Salt and Light 3: More Lives of Faith That Shaped Modern China*, Eugene, OR: Pickwick Publishers, pp. 59–80.

Benedict, Ruth, 1946, *The Chrysanthemum and the Sword: Patterns of Japanese Culture*, Boston: Houghton Mifflin.

Cao Nanlai, 2011, *Constructing China's Jerusalem: Christians, Power, and Place in Contemporary Wenzhou*, Stanford: Stanford University Press.

Chan, Kim-kwong, 2013, 'The Back to Jerusalem Movement: Mission Movement of the Christian Community in Mainland China', in Ma, Wonsuk and Ross, Kenneth R. (eds), *Mission Spirituality and Authentic Discipleship*, Oxford: Regnum, pp. 172–92.

Cheek, Timothy, 2015, *The Intellectual in Modern Chinese History*, Cambridge: Cambridge University Press.

Chin, Josh and Bürge, Clément, 2017, 'Twelve Days in Xinjiang: How China's Surveillance State Overwhelms Daily Life', *Wall Street Journal*, 20 December, www.wsj.com/articles/twelve-days-in-xinjiang-how-chinas-surveillance-state-overwhelms-daily-life-1513700355, accessed 10 September 2020.

Chin, Josh, 2018, 'Chinese Police Add Facial-Recognition Glasses to Surveillance Arsenal', *Wall Street Journal*, 7 February, www.wsj.com/articles/chinese-police-go-robocop-with-facial-recognition-glasses-1518004353, accessed 10 September 2020.

Chow, Alexander, 2018, *Chinese Public Theology: Generational Shifts and Confucian Imagination in Chinese Christianity*, Oxford: Oxford University Press.

Chow, Alexander, forthcoming, 'Public Theology Behind the Great Firewall of China', in Hutchings, Tim and Clivaz, Claire (eds), *Christianity and the Digital Humanities*, Berlin: De Gruyter.

Creemers, Rogier, 2017, 'Cyber China: Upgrading Propaganda, Public Opinion Work and Social Management for the Twenty-First Century', *Journal of Contemporary China*, Vol. 26, No. 103, pp. 85–100.

Crouch, Andy, 2015 'The Return of Shame', *Christianity Today*, Vol. 59, No. 2, pp. 32–40.

Fällman, Fredrik, 2008, *Salvation and Modernity: Intellectuals and Faith in Contemporary China*, Lanham, MD: University Press of America.

Georges, Jayson and Baker, Mark D., 2016, *Ministering in Honor-Shame Cultures: Biblical Foundations and Practical Essentials*, Downers Grove, IL: IVP Academic.

Harwit, Eric, 2014, 'The Rise and Influence of *Weibo* (Microblogs) in China', *Asian Survey*, Vol. 54, No. 6, pp. 1059–87.

Hattaway, Paul, Brother Yun, Xu, Peter Yongze and Wang, Enoch, 2003, *Back to Jerusalem: Called to Complete the Great Commission*, Carlisle: Piquant.

Hoffman, Samantha, 2017, 'Managing the State: Social Credit, Surveillance and the CCP's Plan for China', *China Brief*, Vol. 17, No. 11, pp. 21–7, https://jamestown.org/program/managing-the-state-social-credit-surveillance-and-the-ccps-plan-for-china/, accessed 10 September 2020.

Jin, Ezra, 2013, 'A Landmark Encounter: The Significance of the ACLF for the church in China', *Lausanne Global Analysis*, Vol. 2, No. 5, www.lausanne.org/content/lga/2013-11/a-landmark-encounter-the-significance-of-the-aclf-for-the-church-in-china, archived at https://perma.cc/BZ8F-HBZZ, accessed 10 September 2020.

Jin, Ezra (ed.), 2014a, *Emerging Urban Churches in China*, CCRC.

Jin, Ezra, 2014b, 'For Our Faith and for Our Society', unpublished lecture, 'Religious Freedom and Chinese Society: A Symposium of Case Analysis', Center on Religion and Chinese Society, Purdue University, West Lafayette, IN, 5–7 May.

Jin, Ezra, 2016, *Back to Jerusalem with All Nations: A Biblical Foundation*, Oxford: Regnum.

Johnson, Ian, 2014, 'Jesus vs. Mao? An Interview With Yuan Zhiming', *New York Review of Books*, 4 September, www.nybooks.com/daily/2012/09/04/jesus-vs-mao-interview-yuan-zhiming, archived at https://perma.cc/HEP8-BD37, accessed 10 September 2020.

Kirkpatrick, David C., 2019, *A Gospel for the Poor: Global Social Christianity and the Latin American Evangelical Left*, Philadelphia: University of Pennsylvania Press.

Lai, Pan-chiu and Li Lili, 2017, 'Chinese Catholic Responses to Sino-Japanese War: A Study of Xu Zongze's Public Theology of War and Peace', in Z. Huang, Paulos (ed.), *Yearbook of Chinese Theology*, Leiden: Brill, pp. 166–86.

Liang Fan, Das, Vishnupriya, Kostyuk, Nadiya and Hussain, Muzammi M., 2018, 'Constructing a Data-Driven Society: China's Social Credit System as a State Surveillance Infrastructure', *Policy and Internet*, Vol. 10, No. 4, pp. 415–53.

Ling, Samuel D., 1980, 'The Other May Fourth Movement: The Chinese "Christian Renaissance", 1919–1937', PhD dissertation, Philadelphia, PA: Temple University.

Lyon, David, 2001, *Surveillance Society: Monitoring Everyday Life*, Buckingham: Open University Press.

Ministry of Civil Affairs, 2019, 'Guanyu zongjiao huodong changsuo banli faren dengji shixiang de tongzhi' (Notice concerning procedures for the registration of sites for religious activities), *Religious Affairs Bureau, Ministry of Civil Affairs*, 5 January,www.gov.cn/gongbao/content/2019/content_5395498.htm, accessed 10 September 2020.

Morgan, Timothy C., 2015, 'Prominent Chinese Christian Convert Accuses Another of Rape', *Christianity Today*, 27 February, www.christianitytoday.com/news/2015/february/convert-chai-ling-accuses-yuan-zhiming-rape-china-soul-aga.html, accessed 10 September 2020.

National People's Congress, 2016, 'Cybersecurity Law 2016', *Standing Committee of the National People's Congress*, 7 November, www.gov.cn/xinwen/2016-11/07/content_5129723.htm, English translation at www.chinalawtranslate.com/en/2016-cybersecurity-law/, accessed 10 September 2020.

Reed, Christopher A., 2011, *Gutenberg in Shanghai: Chinese Print Capitalism, 1876–1937*, Vancouver: UBC Press.

Samuel, Vinay and Hauser, Albrecht (eds), 1989, *Proclaiming Christ in Christ's Way: Studies in Integral Evangelism*, Oxford: Regnum.

SCI China Correspondent, 2018, 'Who Wants to Evict Zion Church Beijing?' *St Charles Institute*, 1 September, www.stcharlesinstitute. org/voices/2018/9/1/who-wants-to-evict-zion-church-beijing, archived at https://perma.cc/3GYT-RPYJ, accessed 10 September 2020.

Shepherd, Christian, 2018, 'For a "house church" in Beijing, CCTV cameras and eviction', *Reuters*, 30 August, www.reuters.com/article/ us-china-religion/for-a-house-church-in-beijing-cctv-cameras-and-eviction-idUSKCN1LF0EF, archived at https://perma.cc/R9J2-5LU3, accessed 10 September 2020.

Southern People's Weekly, 2004, 'Yingxiang Zhongguo gonggong zhishifenzi 50 ren' (The Influence of China's 50 Public Intellectuals), *Nanfang renwu zhoukan [Southern People's Weekly]*, 9 September, http://business.sohu.com/s2004/zhishifenzi50.shtml, archived at https://perma.cc/TN3N-KXGZ, accessed 10 September 2020.

Stanley, Brian, 2013, *The Global Diffusion of Evangelicalism: The Age of Billy Graham and John Stott*, Downers Grove, IL: IVP Academic.

Starr, Chloë F., 2016, *Chinese Theology: Text and Context*, New Haven, CT: Yale University Press.

State Council, 2017, 'Religious Affairs Regulations 2017', *State Council of the People's Republic of China*, 26 August, www.gov.cn/zhengce/ content/2017-09/07/content_5223282.htm, English translation at www.chinalawtranslate.com/en/religious-affairs-regulations-2017/, accessed 10 September 2020.

Stoddart, Eric, 2016, *Theological Perspectives on a Surveillance Society: Watching and Being Watched*, Abingdon: Routledge.

Sun Mingyi, 2007, 'Renshi Zhongguo chengshi jiating jiaohui' (Understanding the Urban House Church in China), *Jumu (Behold)*, 26 May, p. 12–17.

Sun Mingyi, 2008, 'Zhongguo jiaohui chengsheng guan ji wenhua shiming lianxiang' [The Relationship Between Sanctification and the Cultural Mandate in the Chinese Church], *Xinghua [Almond Flowers]*, Winter, pp. 25–31.

Taylor, Charles, 2007, *A Secular Age*, Cambridge, MA: Belknap Press.

Vala, Carsten and Huang, Jianbo, 2017, 'Three High-Profile Protestant Microbloggers in Contemporary China: Expanding Public Discourse or Burrowing into Religious Niches on Weibo?', in Travagnin, Stefania (ed.), *Religion and Media in China: Insights and Case Studies from the Mainland, Taiwan and Hong Kong*, New York: Routledge, pp. 167–86.

Wang Yi, 2018, 'My Declaration of Faithful Disobedience', trans. China Partnership, 4 October, www.chinapartnership.org/blog/2018/12/

my-declaration-of-faithful-disobedience, archived at https://perma.cc/AFN8-J5AA, accessed 10 September.

Wielander, Gerda, 2013, *Christian Values in Communist China*, Abingdon: Routledge.

World Watch Monitor, 2018, 'China Bans Zion, Beijing's Biggest House Church', *Christianity Today*, 10 September, www.christianitytoday.com/news/2018/september/china-bans-zion-beijing-house-church-surveillance-ezra-jin.html, accessed 10 September 2020.

Wu, Jackson, 2012, *Saving God's Face: A Chinese Contextualization of Salvation through Honor and Shame*, Pasadena, CA: William Carey International University Press.

Yang Fenggang, 2005, 'Lost in the Market, Saved at McDonald's: Conversion to Christianity in Urban China', *Journal for the Scientific Study of Religion*, Vol. 44, No. 4, pp. 435–7.

Yin Han, 2018, 'Beijing closes Christian house church for conducting illegal activities', *Global Times*, 11 September, www.globaltimes.cn/content/1119249.shtml, archived at https://perma.cc/PE6J-6MJP, accessed 10 September 2020.

Yiu Pak and Law, Elizabeth, 2018, 'Beijing charges shuttered church $170,000 after eviction', *AFP*, 26 September, https://news.yahoo.com/beijing-charges-shuttered-church-170-000-eviction-105823937.html, archived at https://perma.cc/JH6P-42VH, accessed 10 September 2020.

Yu Jie and Wang Yi, 2010, *Yi sheng yi shi de yangwang* (The expectation for whole life), Taipei: Christian Arts Press.

Zion Church, 'Zion Church', 2018, archived on 7 November at https://web.archive.org/web/20181107214305/http://www.zionbeijing.com/, accessed 10 September 2020.

Zuboff, Shoshana, 2019, *The Age of Surveillance Capitalism: The Fight for a Human Future at the New Frontier of Power*, London: Profile Books.

Conclusion

13

Conclusion: *Missio Dei* in a Digital Age

PETER M. PHILLIPS

This volume does not claim to be the final authority on *missio Dei* in a digital age – in fact, it is probably more like an opening shot – an invitation to a wider conversation about how *missio Dei* might be explored in the wider context of digital culture and the increasing impact of digital technology and the effects of mediatization. The problem is that digitalization and its implications are far too extensive to be dealt with adequately in this book. Digital is changing everything from the media technology we use to communicate, to our shift to data-driven research, to our (often unhelpful) focus on self-therapy and self-image, to the ability of rogue states and rogue individuals to disrupt global events, elections and news cycles, to the wide-spread dissemination of glocal culture. In a world where K-Pop and TikTok users can be accused of disrupting one of Trump's pre-election rallies, we are clearly in exciting/disturbing new territory.

But this is about epistemology and philosophy as much as it is about media. Digital changes everything, and the omnipresence of digital, its pervasive presence through most global cultures, means that it is affecting everyone at the same time. Moreover, the speed of change is phenomenal. Luciano Floridi has been right to point to this as the Fourth Industrial Revolution if only in terms of the massive multi-layered impact such a paradigm shift is causing (2014). The fact that everything is changing so rapidly around digitalization, digital technology and its many applications, and its impact on global cultures, implies that the sort of reflection offered in the various chapters in this book needs to be sustained.

In the many forms that *missio Dei* has taken in the last couple of centuries, culminating especially in the work of David Bosch (1991) and the Lausanne Movement, *missio Dei* is meant to be unrelentingly about God's initiative in salvation/in mission (Whitworth 2012, 2013). Bosch defines *missio Dei* as:

> God's self-revelation as the One who loves the world, God's involvement in and with the world, the nature and activity of God, which embraces both the church and the world, and in which the church is privileged to participate. (1991, p. 10)

As Andrew Kirk noted: 'All true theology ... has as its object the study of the ways of a God who is by nature missionary' (1997, p. 50). Before Kirk, Rowan Williams had noted:

> If we want to speak adequately of mission, we have to speak of the Trinity, of God's life as communion. To engage in mission is to be touched by the life of the Trinity, to be engaged in what the wisdom of God purposes, the polyphony of diverse created voices, human and non-human, reflecting back to God his own generous outpouring. (1994, p. 257)

Missio Dei is much more about God's activity than it is about human activity – although even Bosch cannot stay with God and has to shift into the Church's activity. So, in books by Chris Wright (2006, 2010) and a keynote lecture by N. T. Wright (2010), this means that the Bible is God's story rather than our story, a story written in five acts, a missional reading of that story, a kind of salvation history from God's perspective. I note that very often, however, *missio Dei* becomes instrumentalized or contextualized – it becomes about our part in the outworking of mission – more about *missio Ecclesiae* than true *missio Dei*. See Chris Wright's later book on the mission of God's people (2010) and N. T. Wright's lecture on the *missio Dei* (2019) in which he affirms that for the early Church mission meant the great renewal of the heavens and the earth but talks much more about the historical activity of mission through the Church. But in the end, *missio Dei* has to start and end with what God is up to and not just be about what culture is doing or what the Church is doing in any specific manifestation of culture. As Chris Wright says:

> Fundamentally, our mission (if it is biblically informed and validated) means our committed participation as God's people, at God's invitation and command, in God's own mission within the history of God's world for the redemption of God's creation. (2006, p. 9)

In a way, when we put the initial symposium together, we could have reflected more on whether our title pushed reflection on God's activity as a missionary God into a subordinated mode. Having a symposium on *Missio Dei in the Digital Age* aimed at learning from practitioners and academics, organized by an academic centre exploring digital culture, resulted in an exploration of how things worked in practice and how digital culture influences us or how things work out in the digital. The conversation pivoted onto the second part of the title, *digital culture*, and less onto the first, *missio Dei*. It is part of the all-embracing nature of digital – it is a selfish culture/technology that wants to have all the focus on itself. But also, digital theology is a new thing and we need to resist the urge to focus more on the novelty factor of digitalization and less on the staid factor of theology. As such, digitalization takes central stage and minimizes the focus on God's activity which is much less easy to comprehend within a digital setting simply because some of the conversations highlighting that activity are only now being given a vocabulary within our conversations about practice.

Having said that, I recently asked five digital practitioners to explore the missional activity of God during Covid-19, thinking that they would all focus on digitalization. In fact, they mentioned digital but focused much more on hybridity and on all the manifold ways in which they and God have ministered in offline ways, or sought to create analogue alternatives to access digital resources (phone sermons, paper service sheets, blackboards at the end of the garden gate, rosaries). So, it is not set that a theological exploration of digital will always focus on the latter. Indeed, here in this collection we need to note the focus on the non-digital and active role that writers have played in noting the limitations of digital and the positives of physical engagement.

At the same time, this is part of making those kinds of conversation understandable to those conversing. So, at the very outset of the volume, in the Introduction, we explored the concepts of 'Water Buffalo' and 'iPhone' theology. The interesting aspect of both of these concepts is that they conceptualize theology through something else, often a common aspect of a specific culture. So, we could easily flip *missio Dei* into a discussion of how theology might be explored in the vernacular of a particular culture. We've been doing this throughout history but especially since Vincent Donovan's *Christianity Rediscovered* (1996) and Lamin Sanneh's work on translating the Gospel for different cultures (1989). Indeed, this then brings in all the commonplace discussions represented in this book of how digital reflection on *missio Dei* invokes communication theory, cultural theory, mediatization theory and all the practices associated with all of these subject area.

It is important to question why this happens. Some of it we have talked about in the Introduction – the drift towards digital theology as a kind of context theology. As Donovan did a kind of embedded ethnography of Masai culture's appropriation of Christian rites and practices, so here we explore digital culture's appropriation of Christian themes. In both instances, the culture can take over the Christian elements to such an extent that we can end up losing the Christian for the indigenous. In my own background in Johannine studies, there is an active conversation about whether John's Gospel *actively opposes* a Gnostic interpretation of the Jesus event or *forges* the very context for such an interpretation or *is writing up* such an interpretation. Where does the culture or theology start or end?

Katherine Schmidt's Chapter 2 argues persuasively that

digital technology should be seen not as a communication tool but rather as a culture in its own right – including technology, symbols, languages and history. Schmidt's thinking reminds me of discussions about essential similarities between Marshall McLuhan's figure/ground/medium and Bruno Latour's Actor Network Theory (Stalder 1998). In both, the medium or ground is the essence of the culture rather than the messages which are conveyed from one actor to another. Culture is the network created by our communication. So, when McLuhan said that the medium was the message, he was making a cultural rather than a communicative point. So also, in perhaps a less straightforward way, Latour's discussion of ANT depends upon a form of culture in which the actors communicate. This culture determines the forms of interaction within the Actor-Network model.

My problem with this collapse of technology into culture, and a subsequent theological collapse into contextual theology (or Rei Crizaldo's local theology in Chapter 4, which seems to be more like a form of theological ethnography) is that we end up potentially conflating everything to do with contemporary society into media studies. But neo-liberal politics/economics, globalization, information technology, postmodernism and all of that bundle of things which characterize contemporary global culture, *both* pre-date digitalization *and* may post-date it. Digitalization is the phenomenon of the present, but it is unlikely that come the development of biological computing or quantum computing, neo-liberalism is going to collapse. I am not convinced that digital technology is a culture *per se* despite my own use of the term. It is a global culture, part of globalization, but at the same time does not fully capture what culture is. Having said that, the chapters in this book (especially those by Baker, Crizaldo, Dawn, the Dranes, Hollinghurst and Schmidt) are surely right in arguing that we now live in a digital world. This is the context which we need to interpret; this is locus in which we do our theology. But at the same time, they are all correct in thinking that digital does not fully sum up what it means to be human in this time and place. Digital culture seems to be an imprecise culture, a shell of a culture, a misshapen culture which needs a more radical re-assessment than did Donovan's engagement with the Masai.

These are all helpful things to discuss.

And in this volume, we are opening up the questions rather than finding concluding answers. For at the moment there seems fewer answers than there are questions. We seem to have jumped almost willingly into a hermeneutical whirlpool centred around mediatization and culture. So much of our thinking around digital culture becomes mapped onto, immersed in, bedevilled by, an unending conversation of digital culture, technology, symbolism. Our minds become obsessed with it. Digital becomes not only the medium we are discussing, but as Katherine Schmidt points out, it becomes the essence of the culture in which we are communicating. But if digital culture is the medium through which we are to discuss *missio Dei*, it is massively problematic if all we do is discuss digitality and are conceptually unable to escape its gravitational pull. The medium is now both the message and cage in which the message is imprisoned. The medium has become both the exclusive content and the exclusive mode of the message. This is mediatization theory run riot, especially when the message was meant to be about *missio Dei* all the time.

See how we have fallen, again, into the lure of the digital, blinded by its light. Let's take a look into the rather intense theological argumentation of Jean-Luc Marion who proposes a possible way out ...[1]

Digitalization, Marion argues, offers a plurality of images which wall up our eyes so that we can see nothing else (1991). Marion opens his argument arguing that we now live in the era of the image, the world of the image. I have queried this elsewhere (Phillips 2019, pp. 30–1) since I think that humanity has always been engaged in a visual culture – we think, socialize and create visually. But certainly things feel more self-consciously visual in contemporary society, there seem to be more images in public space. Indeed, Delpech-Ramey looks at Andy Warhol's celebration of wrappers and, picking up from Giorgio Agamben, argues that this art form creates images with halos, images with individuated presence (2007, pp. 89, 93). But these images become distorted in their presentation of commercial detritus as art, their halos tarnished because upon analysis they cannot represent the original. The plurality of images creates a world of images disconnected from their original referents, which therefore makes everything invisible (Marion1991, pp. 48–9).

Indeed, this means that such images, without reference to anything but themselves, are simply idols. This proposal becomes a reflection on contemporary culture where the metaphysical principle is 'to be is to be perceived' – a startlingly appropriate definition of much of selfie/TikTok digital culture which valorizes 'self-as-image [*un moi-comme-image*]' (Marion 1991, p. 51), and which reduces that which cannot be seen to the status of unimaginable or 'unimaginable' (p. 54). In these terms, we see our problem with digitalization and digital culture. It is an idol which is always self-referential, always drawing us into self-absorption and self-pleasure. It is an idol which can never move beyond itself to reveal the invisible, to reveal love, to reveal the divine. We try to talk of *missio Dei* in digital culture but our eyes/thoughts/desires are drawn to the idol of the digital (the perceived reality = 'to be is to be perceived') rather than to the invisible work of the divine.

Only by washing our eyes in the pool of Siloam, the pool of the Sent One, like the man born blind in John 9, will we be granted a view of the invisible, argues Marion (1991, p. 64). So, in contradiction to the plurality of idols which wall up our eyes with their self-referential images, proposes we cast our attention towards the divine, our gaze upon God as icon, 'the invisible par excellence' (p. 56), and upon Jesus as the 'icon of the invisible God' (Col. 1.15). Fixing our gaze upon the invisible God, argues Marion (and the Bible), always leads to a crossing of gazes, for as we look at God, we find that we are the object of God's own gaze of love. We gaze upon the icon and become aware 'of seeing another gaze that sustains mine, confronts it, and eventually overwhelms it' (p. 57). But Christ as icon overflows with meaning by always pointing back to the Father. Our gaze does not remain on him but on the one who sent him. He is the 'visible image of the invisible *as invisible*'.

By allowing the gaze of the invisible to fall upon us, the icon becomes a place of 'transpiercing', of communion and of the overflow of meaning. While an image as idol remains impassive to our gaze, an icon allows us to be seen/to feel ourselves seen. An icon therefore becomes a place of veneration, where 'it is necessary ... to cross the visible image and be exposed to the invisible counter-gaze of the prototype' (p. 59).[2] However, the icon does not draw attention to itself but by the paradoxically kenotic process of being written takes up a translucency or disfiguration or effacement in order to invite the counter-gaze. The icon, like Christ, does not cling to glory, but empties itself of presence, and is pierced for our transgressions. As the icon becomes disfigured, like Christ, it becomes transparent to the divine gaze. As Paul made clear to the Galatians, we portray Christ crucified because in him at that moment we see the grace of the invisible God most clearly (Gal. 3.1–5).

I repeat: the only way out, when we are blinded by the idolatrous images of digitality, is to focus on God. To move from the culture to the divine: to move from digitality to *missio Dei*, and in turn from the practicalities of mission to the reality of God. The only way out is to focus on God.

For me, in listening to the papers we have brought together in this volume, this is their corporate and individual genius. At times, each of them shifts their eyes to the divine and realizes that God sees them. There are moments here of communion, of transpiercing gazes, of the meeting of eyes across eternity. Those moments are found especially in Jonny Baker's exploration of missional imagination; in Maggi Dawn's wariness of digital culture as the ground of worship and devotion; in Rei Crizaldo's exploration of the amplified, amputated and simulated body of Christ; in Frida Mannerfelt's exploration of biblical quilting; in Steve Hollinghurst's exploration of meeting the 'digital Jesus'; in the Dranes' exploration of ASMR; in Katherine Schmidt's distancing of seeing digital as just a toolkit. It is seen in every moment when each author lifts their eyes up from the blinding wall of digitalization and realizes themselves or their subject matter to be the object of God's gaze. At such moments, we escape the selfishness of digitality and are exploring *missio Dei*. At such moments, we share communion with the missional God.

Marion, of course, is not for everyone, and the discussion of icons as places of divine presence would have many a digital puritan running for the hills. Indeed, even the discussion of images in general as being self-serving, self-referential idols is itself a rather manufactured thing when set against the truisms that a picture paints a thousand words, that beauty is in the eye of the beholder, that we are never closer to God than when we behold the beauty of his creation.

But maybe this construct does enough work for us if it reminds us that if we are to properly observe what is happening in digital culture, then we often need to pull ourselves away from its clutches and its terms of reference. If we are to properly observe *missio Dei* in the digital age, we need to focus more on God than on the digital. Just as Sarah Pink urges us in *Digital Ethnography* (2015), not to focus on digital devices because this will fetishize them, so perhaps in our ongoing reflections on *missio Dei* in the digital age, we need to pay more attention to our missional God. He is the prototype, the first gaze, the beginning of all things, and the end.

Notes

1 The following reflection is drawn from three sources: Marion 2004, especially chs 3 and 4, pp. 46–88; Williams 2012; Delpech-Ramey 2007.

2 Here, referring back to Plato's theory of 'forms' or 'ideas', 'prototype' refers to the subject of the icon, the image of the divine or holy which it seeks to re-present to the viewer. Without this re-presentation, the icon would simply be a screen and therefore an idol. In classical Orthodox theology, the icon is a window into heaven, a portal to the divine. It is not venerated of itself, but it is the nature of the divine thus present in the icon which is venerated (Williams 2012).

References

Bosch, David, 1991, *Transforming Mission*, Maryknoll, NY: Orbis Books.

Delpech-Ramey, Joshua, 2007, 'The Idol as Icon: Andy Warhol's Material Faith', *Journal of Theoretical Humanities*, Vol. 12, No. 1, pp. 87–96.

Donovan, Vincent, 1996, *Christianity Rediscovered*, Maryknoll, NY: Orbis.

Floridi, Luciano, 2014, *The Fourth Revolution*, Oxford: Oxford University Press.

Kirk, Andrew, 1997, *The Mission as Theology and Theology as Mission*, New York and London: Continuum.

Marion, Jean-Luc, 2004, *The Crossing of the Visible*, trans. J. A. Smith, San Francisco: Stanford University Press.

Phillips, Peter, 2019, 'The Power of Visual Culture and the Fragility of the Text', in Hamidović, David, Clivaz, Claire, Bowen Savant, Sarah (eds), *Ancient Manuscripts in Digital Culture: Visual Culture, Data Mining and Communication*, Leiden: Brill, pp. 30–49.

Pink, Sarah, Horst, Heather, Postill, John, Hjorth, Larissa, Lewis, Tanja and Tacchi, Jo, 2015, *Digital Ethnography: Principles and Practice*, London, Sage Publications.

Sanneh, Lamin, 1989, *Translating the Message: The Missionary Impact on Culture*, Maryknoll, NY: Orbis.

Stalder, Felix, 1998, 'From Figure/Ground to Actor-Networks: McLuhan to Latour', unpublished paper presented at Many Dimensions Conference, Toronto, http://felix.openflows.com/html/mcluhan_latour.html, accessed 10 September 2020.

Whitworth, David, 2012, *Missio Dei and the Means of Grace*, PhD thesis, www.research.manchester.ac.uk/portal/files/54522330/FULL_TEXT.PDF, accessed 10 September 2020.

Whitworth, David, 2019, *Missio Dei and the Means of Grace*, Eugene, OR: Pickwick Publications.

Williams, Rowan, 1994, *Open to Judgement: Sermons and Addresses*, London: Darton, Longman and Todd.

Williams, Rowan, 2012, 'Idols, Images and Icons', Cadbury Lecture Series, online lecture, www.birmingham.ac.uk/schools/ptr/departments/theologyandreligion/news/2012/williams-lecture.aspx, accessed 10 September 2020.

Wright, Christopher, 2006, *The Mission of God: Unlocking the Bible's Grand Narrative*, Nottingham: InterVarsity Press.

Wright, Christopher, 2010, *The Mission of God's People: A Biblical Theology of the Church's Mission*, Grand Rapids, MI: Zondervan.

Wright, N.T., 2019, *The Early Christians and the Mission of God: The Michael Green Memorial Lecture*, recorded lecture, https://ntwrightpage.com/2020/03/30/the-early-christians-and-the-mission-of-god-the-michael-green-memorial-lecture/, accessed 10 September 2020.

Index